PRIVATE LIVES   BLITHE SPIRIT   HAY FEVER

NOEL COWARD

NOEL COWARD

PRIVATE LIVES
BLITHE SPIRIT
HAY FEVER

INTRODUCTION BY EDWARD ALBEE

Grove Press
New York

Grove Press
841 Broadway
New York, NY 10003

LIBRARY OF CONGRESS CATALOGING-IN-PUBLICATION DATA

Coward, Noel Pierce, Sir, 1899-1973
  Three plays.

  Reprint of the 1965 ed. published by Dell Pub. Co., which was issued in series:
A Delta book.
  CONTENTS: Blithe spirit.—Hay fever.—Private lives.
I. Title.
[PR6005.085A19 1979] 822'.9'12 79-52122
ISBN 0-8021-5108-6

Manufactured in the United States of America

First Evergreen Edition 1979

INTRODUCTION

Notes for Noel about Coward

Quite a few years ago—just before the Second World War, or maybe not—a poll was taken to find out who was the most famous person in the world. I have no idea how this was gone about, if it was, and with what degree of thoroughness, but the results were published—unless I dreamed it all, though I don't think I did—and the most famous person in the world was found to be Charlie Chaplin. I remember being surprised, having thought that it would have been Christ, perhaps, or Hitler. But then I thought about it, and realized that in spite of their considerable impact on what we choose to call our civilization, both Christ and Hitler (and I don't enjoy having the two of them in the same sentence any more than you do) had, in a worldwide context, a relatively localized influence. I realized that if the poll were on the level there would have been millions of people, in Asia and Africa, for example, whose brush with either the Christ or the Antichrist would have been minimal, and that these millions of people might much more likely have seen the funny man with the cane and the big shoes.

I doubt that Noel Coward made the top twenty on the world-wide list, but I would be surprised if his name did not figure high—at least in the European and North American tables. I have met people, to take a case or two, who could not place E. M. Forster, or Arnold Schönberg, or Brancusi, but I have never met anyone who said, "Who is Noel Coward?" Indeed, if you have written a number of famous plays, composed a clutch of songs which have become embedded in the standard repertory, written and directed well-known films, and acted, to acclaim, for years and years, who in hell is *not* going to know who you are?

Consider my astonishment, then, over the following telephone exchange between the publishers of this present collection and myself.

"Mr. Albee, we wonder if you'd like to do the introduction to a collection of Noel Coward's plays we're planning."

(Brief pause on my side, not caused by my wondering if I'd like to, but only if I had the time, since I was working on a play of my own.)

"Mr. Albee?"

"Oh! Yes, I'd love to. How did you know I like his plays so much? Let's see now, I'll just have to read them over again . . . you know, to . . ."

"Well, we'll try to find you copies."

"What do you mean *find*?"

"Find. They're all out of print."

"You're kidding."

No, they were not kidding. Through some kind of negligence, Noel Coward's plays had been allowed to fall out of print in the United States. Happily, three of them are back again, in this collection.

Read them again, and if for some reason—like you're so young you've learned to read only this year, or you've been locked up without books since the twenties—you've never read them, try it. You're in for quite a treat.

Wait. "Treat" is not the word I'm after, though it is valid. "Experience" is better. You're in for quite an experience. I don't know if you will become slave to all three printed here (I am still very much subject to two of them), but you will, without question, be reminded of the three qualities possessed by all plays of any matter—literary excellence (by which I mean rhythm and sound), dramatic sure-footedness and pertinence.

Mr. Coward writes dialogue as well as any man going; it is seemingly effortless, surprising in the most wonderfully surprising places, and "true"—very, very true. He is, as well, a dramatic mountain goat; his plays are better made than most—but not in the sense of the superimposed paste job of form, but from within: order more than form. And Mr. Coward's subjects—

the ways we kid ourselves that we do and do not exist with each other and with ourselves—have not, unless my mind has been turned inward too long, gone out of date.

Notwithstanding it all, Noel Coward can be a bore. He bores his admirers every time ge gets within earshot of a reporter by announcing how old-fashioned a writer he is, how the theatre has left him behind, how he does not understand the—to use an expression vague and confusing enough to have become meaningless and therefore dangerous—"avant garde" playwrights of today, feels no sympathy with them.

It is difficult to imagine him wringing his hands and seeking reassurance when he says these things, and it is equally difficult to think that there is a smug tone to the voice, so I don't really know what Mr. Coward's problem is. Whatever it may be, let me remind him that the theatre goes in many directions simultaneously, and that plays like *The Adding Machine* or Georg Kaiser's *Gas*—both terribly "avant garde" for their day—are as musty now as anything by Scribe, while Gogol, say, has the laugh on everybody. Let me add that both Samuel Beckett and Harold Pinter—to grab an "avant garde" father-and-son combo out of the hat (also, hopefully, to choose two playwrights Mr. Coward is out of sorts about)—have, as their subjects, his own preoccupations, have, as well, a precisely honed sense of form and sound. Let me remind Mr. Coward further that what becomes old-fashioned has within it, from the start, the dry rot to permit the disintegration, that the fungus of public fashion, on the other hand, is superficial. To finish this point up, let me shoot out a question: What is the difference between a passacaglia written in a tone-row system and one composed tonally—save method, the stylistic point of departure?

But let me stop being churlish. A man I know and like and whose opinion I respect, a man involved with the theatre, a man who has produced the work of such playwrights as Beckett, Ionesco, Pinter, Arrabal and Ugo Betti, said to me not long ago that he greatly admired Noel Coward's plays, that he thought Coward a better playwright than Bernard Shaw and that Coward's plays would be on the boards long after most of the men writing today had been forgotten.

Now, I don't much like to make public judgments about other playwrights, for when I do I hear myself saying harsh things about Ibsen, for example, or boring people with my joy at seeing Brecht done correctly twice in my life. That is why I have put down what my producer friend said. I will only nod and say that this book contains some very fine playwriting, and that Noel Coward should relax about his work; it stands a very good chance of being with us for a long, long time.

—*Edward Albee*

September, 1964

BLITHE SPIRIT

An Improbable Farce In Three Acts

Produced by H. M. Tennent in association with John C. Wilson at the Picadilly Theatre, London, July 2, 1941. Directed by the author.

Original British Cast

RUTH CONDOMINE	Fay Compton
CHARLES CONDOMINE	Cecil Parker
ELVIRA	Kay Hammond
DR. BRADMAN	Martin Lewis
MRS. BRADMAN	Moya Nugent
MADAME ARCATI	Margaret Rutherford
EDITH	Ruth Reeves

Produced and directed by John C. Wilson at the Morosco Theater, New York, November 5, 1941.

Original American Cast

RUTH CONDOMINE	Peggy Wood
CHARLES CONDOMINE	Clifton Webb
ELVIRA	Leonora Corbett
DR. BRADMAN	Philip Tonge
MRS. BRADMAN	Phyllis Joyce
MADAME ARCATI	Mildred Natwick
EDITH	Jacqueline Clarke

Editorial Note

This is the complete text for BLITHE SPIRIT as Mr. Coward wrote it. The playgoer, having seen a performance and turning now to the book, may discover that in the acting version some lines, and in certain cases short scenes, are missing.

The explanation is simple: those lines were eliminated on the stage because the play ran far beyond the usual time allotted to a Broadway production and because the necessity of bringing the curtain down at a reasonable and convenient hour seemed essential to the producer.

CHARACTERS

EDITH (a maid)
RUTH
CHARLES
DR. BRADMAN
MRS. BRADMAN
MADAME ARCATI
ELVIRA

The action of the play takes place in the living room of Charles Condomine's house in Kent.

ACT I   *Scene 1.*   Before dinner on a summer evening.

        Scene 2.   After dinner.

ACT II   *Scene 1.*   The next morning.

        Scene 2.   Late the following afternoon.

        Scene 3.   Early evening. A few days later.

ACT III *Scene 1.*   After dinner. A few days later.

        Scene 2.   Several hours later.

ACT ONE

SCENE I

The scene is the living room of the Condomines' house in Kent.
The room is light, attractive and comfortably furnished.
The arrangement of it may be left to the discretion of the pro-
ducer.
On the right there are French windows opening on to the gar-
den. On the left there is an open fireplace. At the back, on the
left, there are double doors leading into the dining room. Up
left, on an angle, there are double doors leading to the hall, the
stairs, and the servants' quarters.
When the curtain rises it is about eight o'clock on a summer
evening. There is a wood fire burning because it is an English
summer evening.
EDITH *comes to table with tray of drinks.*
RUTH *comes in. She is a smart-looking woman in the middle*
thirties. She is dressed for dinner but not elaborately.

RUTH: That's right, Edith.

EDITH: Yes'm.

RUTH: Now you'd better fetch me the ice bucket.

EDITH: Yes'm.

RUTH: Did you manage to get the ice out of those little tin trays?

EDITH: Yes'm—I 'ad a bit of a struggle though—but it's all right.

RUTH: And you filled the little trays up again with water?

EDITH: Yes'm.

RUTH: Very good, Edith—you're making giant strides.

EDITH: Yes'm.

RUTH: Madame Arcati, Mrs. Bradman and I will have our

coffee in here after dinner and Mr. Condomine and Dr. Bradman will have theirs in the dining room—is that quite clear?

EDITH: Yes'm.

RUTH: And when you're serving dinner, Edith, try to remember to do it calmly and methodically.

EDITH: Yes'm.

RUTH: As you are not in the Navy it is unnecessary to do everything at the double.

EDITH: Very good, 'M.

RUTH: Now go and get the ice.

EDITH [*straining at the leash*]:   Yes'm.

[*She starts off at full speed.*

RUTH: *Not* at a run, Edith.

EDITH [*slowing down*]:   Yes'm.

[EDITH *goes.* CHARLES *comes in. He is a nice-looking man of about forty wearing a loose-fitting velvet smoking jacket.*

CHARLES: No sign of the advancing hordes?

RUTH: Not yet.

CHARLES [*going to the cocktail tray*]:   No ice.

RUTH: It's coming. I've been trying to discourage Edith from being quite so fleet of foot. You mustn't mind if everything is a little slow motion tonight.

CHARLES: I shall welcome it. The last few days have been extremely agitating. What do you suppose induced Agnes to leave us and go and get married?

RUTH: The reason was becoming increasingly obvious, dear.

CHARLES: Yes, but in these days nobody thinks anything of that sort of thing—she could have popped into the cottage hospital, had it, and popped out again.

RUTH: Her social life would have been seriously undermined.

CHARLES: We must keep Edith in the house more.

[EDITH *comes in slowly with the ice bucket.*

RUTH: That's right, Edith—put it down on the table.

EDITH: Yes'm.

[*She does so.*

CHARLES: I left my cigarette case on my dressing table, Edith— would you get it for me?

EDITH: Yes, sir.

[*She runs out of the room.*

CHARLES: There now!

RUTH: You took her by surprise.

CHARLES [*at the cocktail table*]: A dry Martini I think, don't you?

RUTH: Yes, darling—I expect Madame Arcati will want something sweeter.

CHARLES: We'll have this one for ourselves anyhow.

RUTH [*taking a cigarette and sitting down*]: Oh dear!

CHARLES: What's the matter?

RUTH: I have a feeling that this evening's going to be awful.

CHARLES: It'll probably be funny, but not awful.

RUTH: You must promise not to catch my eye—if I giggle—and I'm very likely to—it will ruin everything.

CHARLES: You mustn't—you must be dead serious and if possible a little intense. We can't hurt the old girl's feelings however funny she is.

RUTH: But why the Bradmans, darling? He's as skeptical as we are—he'll probably say the most dreadful things.

CHARLES: I've warned him. There must be more than three people and we couldn't have the Vicar and his wife because (a) they're dreary, and (b) they probably wouldn't have approved at all. It had to be the Bradmans. [EDITH *rushes into the room with* CHARLES' *cigarette case. Taking it*] Thank you, Edith. Steady does it.

EDITH [*breathlessly*]: Yes, sir.

[EDITH, *with an obvious effort, goes out slowly.*

CHARLES: We might make her walk about with a book on her head like they do in deportment lessons. [CHARLES *gives* RUTH *cocktail*] Here, try this.

RUTH [*sipping it*]: Lovely—dry as a bone.

CHARLES [*raising his glass to her*]: To *The Unseen!*

RUTH: I must say that's a wonderful title.

CHARLES: If this evening's a success I shall start on the first draft tomorrow.

RUTH: How extraordinary it is.

CHARLES: What?

RUTH: Oh, I don't know—being in right at the beginning of something—it gives one an odd feeling.

CHARLES: Do you remember how I got the idea for "The Light Goes Out"?

RUTH: Suddenly seeing that haggard, raddled woman in the hotel at Biarritz—of course I remember—we sat up half the night talking about it—

CHARLES: She certainly came in very handy—I wonder who she was.

RUTH: And if she ever knew, I mean ever recognized, that description of herself—poor thing . . . here's to her, anyhow . . . [*She finishes her drink*

CHARLES [*takes her glass and goes to drinks table*]: Have another.

RUTH: Darling—it's most awfully strong.

CHARLES [*pouring it*]: Never mind.

RUTH: Used Elvira to be a help to you—when you were thinking something out, I mean?

CHARLES [*pouring out another cocktail for himself*]: Every now and then—when she concentrated—but she didn't concentrate very often.

RUTH: I do wish I'd known her.

CHARLES: I wonder if you'd have liked her.

RUTH: I'm sure I should—as you talk of her she sounds enchanting—yes, I'm sure I should have liked her because you know I have never for an instant felt in the least jealous of her—that's a good sign.

CHARLES: Poor Elvira.

RUTH: Does it still hurt—when you think of her?

CHARLES: No, not really—sometimes I almost wish it did— I feel rather guilty—

RUTH: I wonder if I died before you'd grown tired of me if you'd forget me so soon?

CHARLES: What a horrible thing to say . . .

RUTH: No—I think it's interesting.

CHARLES: Well to begin with I *haven't* forgotten Elvira—I *remember* her very distinctly indeed—I remember how fascinating she was, and how maddening—[*sits*] I remember how badly she played all games and how cross she got when she didn't win—I remember her gay charm when she had achieved her own way over something and her extreme acidity when she didn't—I remember her physical attractiveness, which was tremendous—and her spiritual integrity which was nil . . .

RUTH: You can't remember something that was nil.

CHARLES: I remember how morally untidy she was . . .

RUTH: Was she more physically attractive than I am?

CHARLES: That was a very tiresome question, dear, and fully deserves the wrong answer.

RUTH: You really are very sweet.

CHARLES: Thank you.

RUTH: And a little naïve, too.

CHARLES: Why?

RUTH: Because you imagine that I mind about Elvira being more physically attractive than I am.

CHARLES: I should have thought any woman would mind—if it were true. Or perhaps I'm old-fashioned in my views of female psychology. . . .

RUTH: Not exactly old-fashioned, darling, just a bit didactic.

CHARLES: How do you mean?

RUTH: It's didactic to attribute to one type the defects of another type—for instance, because you know perfectly well that Elvira would mind terribly if you found another woman more attractive physically than she was, it doesn't necessarily follow that I should. Elvira was a more physical person than I—I'm certain of that—it's all a question of degree.

CHARLES [*smiling*]:   I love you, my love.

RUTH: I know you do—but not the wildest stretch of imagination could describe it as the first fine careless rapture.

CHARLES: Would you like it to be?

RUTH: Good God, no!

CHARLES: Wasn't that a shade too vehement?

RUTH: We're neither of us adolescent, Charles, we've neither of us led exactly prim lives, have we? And we've both been married before—careless rapture at this stage would be incongruous and embarrassing.

CHARLES: I hope I haven't been in any way a disappointment, dear.

RUTH: Don't be so idiotic.

CHARLES: After all your first husband was a great deal older than you, wasn't he? I shouldn't like to think that you'd missed out all along the line.

RUTH: There are moments, Charles, when you go too far.

CHARLES: Sorry, darling.

RUTH: As far as waspish female psychology goes, there's a strong vein of it in you.

CHARLES: I've heard that said about Julius Caesar.

RUTH: Julius Caesar is neither here nor there.

CHARLES: He may be for all we know—we'll ask Madame Arcati.

RUTH: You're awfully irritating when you're determined to be witty at all costs—almost supercilious.

CHARLES: That's exactly what Elvira used to say.

RUTH: I'm not at all surprised—I never imagined—physically triumphant as she was—that she was entirely lacking in perception.

CHARLES: Darling Ruth!

RUTH: There you go again . . .

CHARLES [*kissing her lightly*]: As I think I mentioned before— I love you, my love.

RUTH: Poor Elvira.

CHARLES: Didn't that light, comradely kiss mollify you at all?

RUTH: You're very annoying, you know you are—when I said "Poor Elvira" it came from the heart—you must have bewildered her so horribly.

CHARLES: Don't I ever bewilder you at all?

RUTH: Never for an instant—I know every trick.

CHARLES: Well, all I can say is that we'd better get a divorce immediately . . .

RUTH: Put my glass down, there's a darling.

CHARLES [*taking it*]: She certainly had a great talent for living —it was a pity that she died so young.

RUTH: Poor Elvira.

CHARLES: That remark is getting monotonous.

RUTH: Poor Charles, then.

CHARLES: That's better.

RUTH: And later on, poor Ruth, I expect.

CHARLES: You have no faith, Ruth. I really do think you should try to have a little faith.

RUTH: I shall strain every nerve.

CHARLES: Life without faith is an arid business.

RUTH: How beautifully you put things, dear.

CHARLES: I *aim* to please.

RUTH: If I died, I wonder how long it would be before you married again?

CHARLES: You won't die—you're not the dying sort.

RUTH: Neither was Elvira.

CHARLES: Oh yes, she was, now that I look back on it—she had a certain ethereal, not quite of this world quality—nobody could call you even remotely ethereal.

RUTH: Nonsense—she was of the earth earthy.

CHARLES: Well, she is now, anyhow.

RUTH: You know that's the kind of observation that shocks people.

CHARLES: It's discouraging to think how many people are shocked by honesty and how few by deceit.

RUTH: Write that down, you might forget it.

CHARLES: You underrate me.

RUTH: Anyhow it was a question of bad taste more than honesty.

CHARLES: I was devoted to Elvira. We were married for five years. She died. I missed her very much. That was seven years ago. I have now, with your help, my love, risen above the whole thing.

RUTH: Admirable. But if tragedy should darken our lives, I still say—with prophetic foreboding—poor Ruth!

[*Bell.*

CHARLES: That's probably the Bradmans.

RUTH: It might be Madame Arcati.

CHARLES: No, she'll come on her bicycle—she always goes everywhere on her bicycle.

RUTH: It really is very spirited of the old girl.

CHARLES: Shall I go, or shall we let Edith have her fling?

RUTH: Wait a minute and see what happens.

[*There is a slight pause.*

CHARLES: Perhaps she didn't hear.

RUTH: She's probably on one knee in a pre-sprinting position waiting for cook to open the kitchen door.

[*There is the sound of a door banging and* EDITH *is seen scampering across the hall.*

CHARLES: Steady, Edith.

EDITH [*dropping to a walk*]:   Yes, sir.

[MRS. BRADMAN *comes to* RUTH—*shakes hands.* DR. BRADMAN *shakes hands with* CHARLES. DR. BRADMAN *is a pleasant-looking middle-aged man.* MRS. BRADMAN *is fair and rather faded.*

EDITH: Dr. and Mrs. Bradman.

DR. BRADMAN: We're not late, are we? I only got back from the hospital about half an hour ago.

CHARLES: Of course not—Madame Arcati isn't here yet.

MRS. BRADMAN: That must have been her we passed coming down the hill—I said I thought it was.

RUTH: Then she won't be long. I'm so glad you were able to come.

MRS. BRADMAN: We've been looking forward to it—I feel really quite excited . . .

DR. BRADMAN [*shaking hands with* RUTH]:   I guarantee that Violet will be good—I made her promise.

MRS. BRADMAN: There wasn't any need—I'm absolutely thrilled. I've only seen Madame Arcati two or three times in the village—I mean I've never seen her do anything at all peculiar, if you know what I mean.

CHARLES: Dry martini?

DR. BRADMAN: By all means.

CHARLES: She certainly is a strange woman. It was only a chance remark of the Vicar's about seeing her up on the Knoll on Midsummer Eve dressed in sort of Indian robes that made me realize that she was psychic at all. Then I began to make inquiries—apparently she's been a professional in London for years.

MRS. BRADMAN: It is funny, isn't it? I mean anybody doing it as a profession.

DR. BRADMAN: I believe it's very lucrative.

MRS. BRADMAN: Do you believe in it, Mrs. Condomine—do you think there's anything really genuine about it at all?

RUTH: I'm afraid not—but I do think it's interesting how easily people allow themselves to be deceived . . .

MRS. BRADMAN: But she must believe in herself, mustn't she—or is the whole business a fake?

CHARLES: I suspect the worst. A real professional charlatan. That's what I am hoping for anyhow—the character I am planning for my book must be a complete impostor, that's one of the most important factors of the whole story.

DR. BRADMAN: What exactly are you hoping you get from her?

CHARLES [handing DR. and MRS. BRADMAN cocktails]: Jargon, principally—a few of the tricks of the trade—it's many years since I went to a séance. I want to refresh my memory.

DR. BRADMAN: Then it's not entirely new to you?

CHARLES: Oh, no—when I was a little boy an aunt of mine used to come and stay with us—she imagined that she was a medium and used to go off into the most elaborate trances after dinner. My mother was fascinated by it.

MRS. BRADMAN: Was she convinced?

CHARLES [get's cocktail for himself]: Good heavens, no—she just naturally disliked my aunt and loved making a fool of her.

DR. BRADMAN [laughing]: I gather that there were never any tangible results?

CHARLES: Oh sometimes she didn't do so badly. On one occasion when we were all sitting round in the pitch dark with my mother groping her way through Chaminade at the piano, my aunt suddenly gave a shrill scream and said that she saw a small black dog by my chair, then someone switched on the lights and sure enough there was.

MRS. BRADMAN: But how extraordinary.

CHARLES: It was obviously a stray that had come in from the street. But I must say I took off my hat to Auntie for producing it, or rather for utilizing—even Mother was a bit shaken.

MRS. BRADMAN: What happened to it?

CHARLES: It lived with us for years.

RUTH: I sincerely hope Madame Arcati won't produce any livestock—we have so very little room in this house.

MRS. BRADMAN: Do you think she tells fortunes? I love having my fortune told.

CHARLES: I expect so—

RUTH: I was told once on the pier at Southsea that I was surrounded by lilies and a golden seven—it worried me for days. [ALL *laugh*.

CHARLES: We really must all be serious, you know, and pretend that we believe implicitly, otherwise she won't play.

RUTH: Also, she might really mind—it would be cruel to upset her.

DR. BRADMAN: I shall be as good as gold.

RUTH: Have you ever attended her, Doctor—professionally, I mean?

DR. BRADMAN: Yes—she had influenza in January—she's only been here just over a year, you know. I must say she was singularly unpsychic then—I always understood that she was an authoress.

CHARLES: Oh yes, we originally met as colleagues at one of Mrs. Wilmot's Sunday evenings in Sandgate . . .

MRS. BRADMAN: What sort of books does she write?

CHARLES: Two sorts. Rather whimsical children's stories about enchanted woods filled with highly conversational flora and fauna, and enthusiastic biographies of minor royalties. Very sentimental, reverent and extremely funny.

[*There is the sound of the front doorbell.*

RUTH: Here she is.

DR. BRADMAN: She knows, doesn't she, about tonight? You're not going to spring it on her.

CHARLES: Of course—it was all arranged last week—I told her how profoundly interested I was in anything to do with the occult, and she blossomed like a rose.

RUTH: I really feel quite nervous—as though I were going to make a speech.

[EDITH *is seen sedately going towards the door.*

CHARLES: You go and meet her, darling.

[EDITH *has opened the door, and* MADAME ARCATI'S *voice, very high and clear, is heard.*

MADAME ARCATI: I've leant my bike up against that little bush, it will be *perfectly* all right if no one touches it.

EDITH: Madame Arcati.

RUTH: How nice of you to have come all this way.

[RUTH *and* CHARLES *greet her simultaneously.* MADAME ARCATI *enters. She is a striking woman, dressed not too extravagantly but with a decided bias towards the barbaric. She might be any age between forty-five and sixty-five.* RUTH *ushers her in.*

CHARLES [*advancing*]:   My dear Madame Arcati!

MADAME ARCATI: I'm afraid I'm rather late, but I had a sudden presentiment that I was going to have a puncture so I went back to fetch my pump, and then of course I didn't have a puncture at all.

[MADAME ARCATI *takes off cloak and hands it to* RUTH.

CHARLES: Perhaps you will on the way home.

MADAME ARCATI: Doctor Bradman—the man with the gentle hands!

DR. BRADMAN: I'm delighted to see you looking so well. This is my wife.

MADAME ARCATI: We are old friends— [*Shakes hands with* MRS. BRADMAN] We meet coming out of shops.

CHARLES: Would you like a cocktail?

MADAME ARCATI [*peeling off some rather strange-looking gloves*]:   If it's a dry martini, yes—if it's a concoction, no. Experience has taught me to be very wary of concoctions.

CHARLES: It is a dry martini.

MADAME ARCATI: How delicious. It was wonderful cycling through the woods this evening—I was deafened with bird-song.

RUTH: It's been lovely all day.

MADAME ARCATI: But the evening's the time—mark my words. [*She takes the cocktail* CHARLES *gives her. To others*] Thank you. Cheers! Cheers!

RUTH: Don't you find it very tiring bicycling everywhere?

MADAME ARCATI: On the contrary—it stimulates me—I was

getting far too sedentary in London, that horrid little flat with the dim lights—they had to be dim, you know, the clients expect it.

MRS. BRADMAN: I must say I find bicycling very exhausting.

MADAME ARCATI: Steady rhythm—that's what counts. Once you get the knack of it you need never look back—on you get and away you go.

MRS. BRADMAN: But the hills, Madame Arcati—pushing up those awful hills—

MADAME ARCATI: Just knack again—down with your head, up with your heart, and you're over the top like a flash and skimming down the the other side like a dragonfly. This is the best dry martini I've had for years.

CHARLES: Will you have another?

MADAME ARCATI [holding out her glass]:   Certainly. [CHARLES takes her glass and refills it at drinks table] You're a very clever man. Anybody can write books, but it takes an artist to make a dry martini that's dry enough.

RUTH: Are you writing anything nowadays, Madame Arcati?

MADAME ARCATI: Every morning regular as clockwork, seven till one.

CHARLES [gives MADAME ARCATI cocktail]:   Is it a novel or a memoir?

MADAME ARCATI: It's a children's book—I have to finish it by the end of October to catch the Christmas sales. It's mostly about very small animals, the hero is a moss beetle. [MRS. BRADMAN laughs nervously] I had to give up my memoir of Princess Palliatini because she died in April—I talked to her about it the other day and she implored me to go on with it, but I really hadn't the heart.

MRS. BRADMAN [incredulously]:   You talked to her about it the other day?

MADAME ARCATI: Yes, through my control, of course. She sounded very irritable.

MRS. BRADMAN: It's funny to think of people in the spirit world being irritable, isn't it? I mean, one can hardly imagine it, can one?

CHARLES: We have no reliable guarantee that the after life will be any less exasperating than this one, have we?

MRS. BRADMAN [laughing]: Oh, Mr. Condomine, how can you!

RUTH: I expect it's dreadfully ignorant of me not to know— but who was Princess Palliatini?

MADAME ARCATI: She was originally a Jewess from Odessa of quite remarkable beauty. It was an accepted fact that people used to stand on the seats of railway stations to watch her whizz by.

CHARLES: She was a keen traveler?

MADAME ARCATI: In her younger days, yes—later on she married a Mr. Clarke in the Consular Service and settled down for a while . . .

RUTH: How did she become Princess Palliatini?

MADAME ARCATI: That was years later. Mr. Clarke passed over and left her penniless with two strapping girls—

RUTH: How unpleasant.

MADAME ARCATI: And so there was nothing for it but to obey the beckoning finger of adventure and take to the road again —so off she went, bag and baggage, to Vladivostok.

CHARLES: What an extraordinary place to go!

MADAME ARCATI: She had cousins there. Some years later she met old Palliatini who was returning from a secret mission in Japan. He was immediately staggered by her beauty and very shortly afterwards married her. From then on her life became really interesting.

DR. BRADMAN: I should hardly have described it as dull before.

RUTH: What happened to the girls?

MADAME ARCATI: She neither saw them nor spoke to them for twenty-three years.

MRS. BRADMAN: How extraordinary.

MADAME ARCATI: Not at all. She was always very erratic emotionally.

[The double doors of the dining room open and EDITH comes in.

EDITH [nervously]: Dinner is served, Mum.

RUTH: Thank you, Edith. Shall we?

[EDITH retires backwards into the dining room.

MADAME ARCATI: No red meat, I hope?

RUTH: There's meat, but I don't think it will be very red—would you rather have an egg or something?

MADAME ARCATI [*she and* RUTH *rise*]: No, thank you—it's just that I make it a rule never to eat red meat before I work—it sometimes has an odd effect . . .

CHARLES: What sort of effect?

MADAME ARCATI: Oh, nothing of the least importance—if it isn't very red it won't matter much—anyhow, we'll risk it.

[MRS. BRADMAN *rises.* MADAME ARCATI *goes out first with* RUTH *followed by* MRS. BRADMAN, DR. BRADMAN *and* CHARLES.

RUTH: Come along, then—Mrs. Bradman—Madame Arcati—you're on Charles's right . . .

[THEY *all move into the dining room as the lights fade on the scene.*

SCENE II

[*When the lights go up again, dinner is over, and* RUTH, MRS. BRADMAN *and* MADAME ARCATI *are sitting having their coffee.*

MADAME ARCATI: . . . on her mother's side she went right back to the Borgias which I think accounted for a lot one way and another—even as a child she was given to the most violent destructive tempers—very inbred, you know.

MRS. BRADMAN: Yes, she must have been.

MADAME ARCATI: My control was quite scared the other day when we were talking—I could hear it in her voice—after all, she's only a child . . .

RUTH: Do you always have a child as a control?

MADAME ARCATI: Yes, they're generally the best—some mediums prefer Indians, of course, but personally I've always found them unreliable.

RUTH: In what way unreliable?

MADAME ARCATI: Well, for one thing they're frightfully lazy and also, when faced with any sort of difficulty, they're rather apt to go off into their own tribal language which is naturally unintelligible—that generally spoils everything and wastes a great deal of time. No, children are undoubtedly more satisfactory, particularly when they get to know you and understand your ways. Daphne has worked for me for years.

MRS. BRADMAN: And she still goes on being a child—I mean, she doesn't show signs of growing any older?

MADAME ARCATI [*patiently*]: Time values on the "Other Side" are utterly different from ours.

MRS. BRADMAN: Do you feel funny when you go off into a trance?

MADAME ARCATI: In what way funny?

RUTH [*hastily*]: Mrs. Bradman doesn't mean funny in its comic implication, I think she meant odd or strange—

MADAME ARCATI: The word was an unfortunate choice.

MRS. BRADMAN: I'm sure I'm very sorry.

MADAME ARCATI: It doesn't matter in the least—please don't apologize.

RUTH: When did you first discover that you had these extra-ordinary powers?

MADAME ARCATI: When I was quite tiny. My mother was a medium before me, you know, and so I had every opportunity of starting on the ground floor as you might say. I had my first trance when I was four years old and my first protoplasmic manifestation when I was five and a half—what an exciting day that was, I shall never forget it—of course the manifestation itself was quite small and of very short duration, but, for a child of my tender years, it was most gratifying.

MRS. BRADMAN: Your mother must have been so pleased.

MADAME ARCATI [*modestly*]: She was.

MRS. BRADMAN: Can you foretell the future?

MADAME ARCATI: Certainly not. I disapprove of fortune-tellers most strongly.

MRS. BRADMAN [*disappointed*]: Oh, really—why?

MADAME ARCATI: Too much guesswork and fake mixed up with it—even when the gift is genuine—and it only very occasionally is—you can't count on it.

RUTH: Why not?

MADAME ARCATI: Time again—time is the reef upon which all
our frail mystic ships are wrecked.

RUTH: You mean because it has never yet been proved that the
past and the present and the future are not one and the same
thing.

MADAME ARCATI: I long ago came to the conclusion that
nothing has ever been definitely proved about anything.

RUTH: How very wise.

[EDITH *comes in with a tray of drinks. This she brings over to
the table by* RUTH. RUTH *moves a coffee cup and a vase to
make room for it.*

RUTH: Edith, we don't want to be disturbed for the next hour
or so for any reason whatsoever—is that clear?

EDITH: Yes'm.

RUTH: And if anyone should telephone, just say we are out
and take a message.

MRS. BRADMAN: Unless it's an urgent call for George.

RUTH: Unless it's an urgent call for Dr. Bradman.

EDITH: Yes'm.

[EDITH *goes out swiftly.*

RUTH: There's not likely to be one, is there?

MRS. BRADMAN: No, I don't think so.

MADAME ARCATI: Once I am off it won't matter, but an interruption during the preliminary stages might be disastrous.

MRS. BRADMAN: I wish the men would hurry up—I'm terribly
excited.

MADAME ARCATI: Please don't be—it makes everything very
much more difficult.

[CHARLES *and* DR. BRADMAN *come out of the dining room. They
are smoking cigars.*

CHARLES [*cheerfully*]:   Well, Madame Arcati—the time is drawing near.

MADAME ARCATI: Who knows? It may be receding!

CHARLES: How very true.

DR. BRADMAN: I hope you feel in the mood, Madam Arcati.

MADAME ARCATI: It isn't a question of mood—it's a question
of concentration.

RUTH: You must forgive us being impatient. We can perfectly easily wait though, if you're not quite ready to start . . .

MADAME ARCATI: Nonsense, my dear, I'm absolutely ready— [*she rises*] Heigho, heigho, to work we go!

CHARLES: Is there anything you'd like us to do?

MADAME ARCATI: Do?

CHARLES: Yes—hold hands or anything?

MADAME ARCATI: All that will come later—[*She goes to the window*] First a few deep, deep breaths of fresh air—[*Over her shoulder*] You may talk if you wish, it will not disturb me in the least.

[*She flings open the windows wide and inhales deeply and a trifle noisily.*

RUTH [*with a quizzical glance at* CHARLES]: Oh, dear!

CHARLES [*putting his finger to his lips warningly*]: An excellent dinner, darling—I congratulate you.

RUTH: The mousse wasn't quite right.

CHARLES: It looked a bit hysterical but it tasted delicious.

MADAME ARCATI: That cuckoo is very angry.

CHARLES: I beg your pardon?

MADAME ARCATI: I said that cuckoo is very angry . . . listen . . .

[*They all listen obediently.*

CHARLES: How can you tell?

MADAME ARCATI: Timbre . . . No moon—that's as well, I think —there's mist rising from the marshes—[*A thought strikes her*] There's no need for me to light my bicycle lamp, is there? I mean, nobody is likely to fall over it?

RUTH: No, we're not expecting anybody else.

MADAME ARCATI: Good-night, you foolish bird. You have a table?

CHARLES: Yes. We thought that one would do.

MADAME ARCATI [*closing the window. She comes over to the table and touches it lightly with her finger*]: I think the one that has the drinks on it would be better.

DR. BRADMAN [*lifting off the tray*]: Change over.

CHARLES [*to* RUTH]: You told Edith we didn't want to be disturbed?

RUTH: Yes, darling.

MADAME ARCATI [*walking about the room—twisting and untwisting her hands*]:   This is a moment I always hate.

RUTH: Are you nervous?

MADAME ARCATI: Yes. When I was a girl I always used to be sick.

DR. BRADMAN: How fortunate that you grew out of it.

RUTH [*hurriedly*]:   Children are always much more prone to be sick than grown-ups, though, aren't they? I know I could never travel in a train with any degree of safety until I was fourteen.

MADAME ARCATI [*still walking*]:   Little Tommy Tucker sings for his supper, what shall he have but brown bread and butter? I despise that because it doesn't rhyme at all—but Daphne loves it.

DR. BRADMAN: Who's Daphne?

RUTH: Daphne is Madame Arcati's control—she's a little girl.

DR. BRADMAN: Oh, I see—yes, of course.

CHARLES: How old is she?

MADAME ARCATI: Rising seven when she died.

MRS. BRADMAN: And when was that?

MADAME ARCATI: February the sixth, 1884.

MRS. BRADMAN: Poor little thing.

DR. BRADMAN: She must be a bit long in the tooth by now, I should think.

MADAME ARCATI: You should think, Dr. Bradman, but I fear you don't—at least, not profoundly enough.

MRS. BRADMAN: Do be quiet, George—you'll put Madame Arcati off.

MADAME ARCATI [CHARLES *brings piano chair down to table*]:   Don't worry, my dear—I am quite used to skeptics—they generally turn out to be the most vulnerable and receptive in the long run.

RUTH: You'd better take that warning to heart, Dr. Bradman.

DR. BRADMAN: Please forgive me, Madame Arcati—I assure you I am most deeply interested.

MADAME ARCATI: It is of no consequence—will you all sit round the table please and place your hands downwards on it?

[RUTH, MRS. BRADMAN *and* DR. BRADMAN *are seated at table.*
CHARLES: What about the lights?
MADAME ARCATI: All in good time, Mr. Condomine. [*The four of them sit down at each side of a small square table.* MADAME ARCATI *surveys them critically, her head on one side. She is whistling a little tune*] The fingers should be touching . . . that's right . . . I presume that that is the gramophone, Mr. Condomine?
CHARLES: Yes—would you like me to start it? It's an electric one.
MADAME ARCATI: Please stay where you are—I can manage— [*She goes over to the gramophone and looks over the records*] Now let me see—what have we here—Brahms—oh dear me, no—Rachmaninoff—too florid—where is the dance music?
RUTH: They're the loose ones on the left.
MADAME ARCATI: I see.
[*She stoops down and produces a pile of dance records—these she sorts rapidly on the piano.*
CHARLES: I'm afraid they're none of them very new.
MADAME ARCATI: Daphne is really more attached to Irving Berlin than anybody else—she likes a tune she can hum—ah, here's one—"Always"—
CHARLES [*half jumping up again*]:   "Always"!
RUTH: Do sit down, Charles—what is the matter?
CHARLES [*subsiding*]:   Nothing—nothing at all.
MADAME ARCATI: The light switch is by the door?
RUTH: Yes, all except the small one on the desk, and the gramophone.
MADAME ARCATI: Very well—I understand.
RUTH: Charles, do keep still.
MRS. BRADMAN: Fingers touching, George—remember what Madame Arcati said.
MADAME ARCATI: Now there are one or two things I should like to explain, so will you all listen attentively?
RUTH: Of course.
MADAME ARCATI: Presently, when the music begins, I am going to switch out the lights. I may then either walk about the room for a little or lie down flat—in due course I shall

draw up this dear little stool and join you at the table—I
shall place myself between you and your wife, Mr. Condomine, and rest my hands lightly upon yours—I must ask
you not to address me or move or do anything in the least
distracting—is that quite, quite clear?

CHARLES: Perfectly.

MADAME ARCATI: Of course I cannot guarantee that anything
will happen at all—Daphne may be unavailable—she had a
head cold very recently, and was rather under the weather,
poor child. On the other hand, a great many things might
occur—one of you might have an emanation, for instance,
or we might contract a poltergeist which would be extremely
destructive and noisy . . .

RUTH [*anxiously*]: In what way destructive?

MADAME ARCATI: They throw things, you know.

RUTH: No—I didn't know.

MADAME ARCATI: But we must cross that bridge when we come
to it, mustn't we?

CHARLES: Certainly—by all means.

MADAME ARCATI: Fortunately an Elemental at this time of the
year is most unlikely . . .

RUTH: What do Elementals do?

MADAME ARCATI: Oh, my dear, one can never tell—they're
dreadfully unpredictable—usually they take the form of a very
cold wind . . .

MRS. BRADMAN: I don't think I shall like that—

MADAME ARCATI: Occasionally reaching almost hurricane ve-
locity—

RUTH: You don't think it would be a good idea to take the
more breakable ornaments off the mantelpiece before we
start?

MADAME ARCATI [*indulgently*]: That really is not necessary,
Mrs. Condomine—I assure you I have my own methods of
dealing with Elementals.

RUTH: I'm so glad.

MADAME ARCATI: Now then—are you ready to empty your
minds?

DR. BRADMAN: Do you mean we're to try to think of nothing?

MADAME ARCATI: Absolutely nothing, Dr. Bradman. Concentrate on a space or a nondescript colour that's really the best way . . .

DR. BRADMAN: I'll do my damnedest.

MADAME ARCATI: Good work!—I will now start the music.

[*She goes to the gramophone, puts on the record of "Always," and begins to walk about the room; occasionally she moves into an abortive little dance step, and once, on passing a mirror on the mantelpiece, she surveys herself critically for a moment and adjusts her hair. Then, with sudden speed, she runs across the the room and switches off the lights.*]

MRS. BRADMAN: Oh dear!

MADAME ARCATI: Quiet—please . . . [*Presently in the gloom* MADAME ARCATI, *after wandering about a little, draws up a stool and sits at the table between* CHARLES *and* RUTH. *The gramophone record comes to an end. There is dead silence*] Is there anyone there? . . . [*A long pause*] Is there anyone there? [*Another long pause*] One rap for yes—two raps for no —now then—is there anyone there? . . . [*After a shorter pause the table gives a little bump*]

MRS. BRADMAN [*involuntarily*]:   Oh!

MADAME ARCATI: Shhhh! . . . Is that you, Daphne? [*The table gives a louder bump*] Is your cold better, dear? [*The table gives two loud bumps very quickly*] Oh, I'm so sorry—are you doing anything for it? [*The table bumps several times*] I'm afraid she's rather fretful . . . [*There is a silence*] Is there anyone there who wishes to speak to anyone here? [*After a pause the table gives one bump*] Ah! Now we're getting somewhere. No, Daphne, don't do that, dear, you're hurting me . . . Daphne, dear, please . . . Oh, oh, oh! . . . be good, there's a dear child . . . You say there is someone there who wishes to speak to someone here? [*One bump*] Is it I? [*Two bumps*] Is it Dr. Bradman? [*Two bumps*] Is it Mrs. Bradman? [*Two bumps*] Is it Mrs. Condomine? [*Several very loud bumps, which continue until* MADAME ARCATI *shouts it down*] Stop it! Behave yourself! Is it Mr. Condomine? [*There is a dead silence for a moment, and then a very loud single bump*] There's someone who wishes to speak to you, Mr. Condomine . . .

CHARLES: Tell them to leave a message.

[*The table bangs about loudly.*

MADAME ARCATI: I really must ask you not to be flippant, Mr. Condomine . . .

RUTH: Charles, how can you be so idiotic? You'll spoil everything.

CHARLES: I'm sorry—it slipped out.

MADAME ARCATI: Do you know anybody who has passed over recently?

CHARLES: Not recently, except my cousin in the Civil Service, and he wouldn't be likely to want to communicate with me —we haven't spoken for years.

MADAME ARCATI [*mystically*]:   Are you Mr. Condomine's cousin in the Civil Service? [*The table bumps violently several times*] I'm afraid we've drawn a blank . . . Can't you think of anyone else? Rack your brains . . .

RUTH [*helpfully*]:   It might be old Mrs. Plummet, you know— she died on Whit Monday . . .

CHARLES: I can't imagine why old Mrs. Plummet should wish to talk to me—we had very little in common.

RUTH: It's worth trying, anyhow.

MADAME ARCATI: Are you old Mrs. Plummet?

[*The table remains still.*

RUTH: She was very deaf—perhaps you'd better shout—

MADAME ARCATI [*shouting*]:   Are you old Mrs. Plummet? [*Nothing happens*] There's nobody there at all.

MRS. BRADMAN: How disappointing—just as we were getting on so nicely.

DR. BRADMAN: Violet, be quiet.

MADAME ARCATI [*rising*]:   Well, I'm afraid there's nothing for it but for me to go into a trance. I had hoped to avoid it because it's so exhausting—however, what must be must be. Excuse me a moment while I start the gramophone again.

CHARLES [*in a strained voice*]:   Not "Always"—don't play "Always"—

RUTH: Why ever not, Charles? Don't be absurd.

MADAME ARCATI [*gently*]:   I'm afraid I must—it would be unwise to change horses in midstream if you know what I
mean . . .
[*She restarts the gramophone.*
CHARLES: Have it your own way.
[MADAME ARCATI *comes slowly back toward the table and sits
down again. After a few moments she begins to moan—then
in the darkness a child's voice is heard reciting rather breath-
ily "Little Tommy Tucker."*
DR. BRADMAN: That would be Daphne—she ought to have had
her adenoids out.
MRS. BRADMAN: George—please—
[MADAME ARCATI *suddenly gives a loud scream and falls off the
stool on to the floor.*
CHARLES: Good God!
RUTH: Keep still, Charles . . .
[CHARLES *subsides. Everyone sits in silence for a moment, then
the table starts bouncing about.*
MRS. BRADMAN: It's trying to get away . . . I can't hold it . . .
RUTH: Press down hard.
[*The table falls over with a crash.*
RUTH: There now!
MRS. BRADMAN: Ought we to pick it up or leave it where it is?
DR. BRADMAN: How the hell do I know?
MRS BRADMAN: There's no need to snap at me.
[*A perfectly strange and very charming voice says, "Leave it
where it is!"*
CHARLES: Who said that?
RUTH: Who said what?
CHARLES: Somebody said, "Leave it where it is."
RUTH: Nonsense, dear.
CHARLES: I heard it distinctly.
RUTH: Well, nobody else did—did they?
MRS. BRADMAN: I never heard a sound.
CHARLES: It was you, Ruth—you're playing tricks.
RUTH: I'm not doing anything of the sort. I haven't uttered.
[*There is another pause, and then the voice says, "Good eve-
ning, Charles."*

CHARLES [*very agitated*]: Ventriloquism—that's what it is—
ventriloquism . . .

RUTH [*irritably*]: What is the matter with you?

CHARLES: You must have heard *that*—one of you must have
heard *that!*

RUTH: Heard *what?*

CHARLES: You mean to sit there solemnly and tell me that
none of you heard anything at all?

DR. BRADMAN: I certainly didn't.

MRS. BRADMAN: Neither did I—I wish I had. I should love to
hear something.

RUTH: It's you who are playing the tricks, Charles—you're
acting to try to frighten us . . .

CHARLES [*breathlessly*]: I'm not—I swear I'm not.

[*The voice speaks again. It says, "It's difficult to think of what
to say after seven years, but I suppose good evening is as good
as anything else."*

CHARLES [*intensely*]: Who are you? [*The voice says, "Elvira,
of course—don't be so silly"*] I can't bear this for another
minute . . . [*He rises violently*] Get up, everybody—the enter-
tainment's over . . .

RUTH: Oh, Charles, how tiresome you are—just as we were
beginning to enjoy ourselves. What on earth is the matter
with you?

CHARLES: Nothing's the matter with me—I'm just sick of the
whole business, that's all.

DR. BRADMAN: Did you hear anything that we didn't hear
really?

CHARLES [*with a forced laugh*]: Of course not—I was only pretending . . .

RUTH: I knew you were . . .

MRS. BRADMAN: Oh dear . . . look at Madame Arcati!

[*MADAME ARCATI is lying on the floor with her feet up on the
stool from which she fell. She is obviously quite unconscious.*

RUTH: What are we to do with her?

CHARLES: Bring her round—bring her round as soon as possible.

DR. BRADMAN [*going over and kneeling down beside her*]: I think we'd better leave her alone.

RUTH: But she might stay like that for hours.

DR. BRADMAN [*after feeling her pulse and examining her eye*]: She's out all right.

CHARLES [*almost hysterically*]: Bring her round! It's dangerous to leave her like that . . .

RUTH: Really, Charles, you are behaving most peculiarly.

CHARLES [*going to* MADAME ARCATI *and shaking her violently*]: Wake up, Madame Arcati—wake up—it's time to go home!

DR. BRADMAN: Here—go easy, old man . . .

CHARLES: Get some brandy—give her some brandy—lift her into the chair—help me, Bradman . . . [RUTH *pours out some brandy while* CHARLES *and* DR. BRADMAN *lift* MADAME ARCATI *laboriously into an armchair. Leaning over her*]: Wake up, Madame Arcati—Little Tommy Tucker, Madame Arcati!

RUTH: Here's the brandy.

[MADAME ARCATI *gives a slight moan and a shiver.*

CHARLES [*forcing some brandy between her lips*]: Wake up!— [MADAME ARCATI *gives a prolonged shiver and chokes slightly over the brandy.*

MRS. BRADMAN: She's coming round.

RUTH: Be careful, Charles—you're spilling it all down her dress.

MADAME ARCATI [*opening her eyes*]: Well, that's that.

RUTH [*solicitously*]: Are you all right?

MADAME ARCATI: Certainly I am—never felt better in my life.

CHARLES: Would you like some more brandy?

MADAME ARCATI: So that's the funny taste in my mouth—well, really! Fancy allowing them to give me brandy! Doctor Bradman, you ought to have known better—brandy on top of trance might have been catastrophic. Take it away, please—I probably shan't sleep a wink tonight as it is.

CHARLES: I know I shan't.

RUTH: Why on earth not?

CHARLES: The whole experience has unhinged me.

MADAME ARCATI: Well, what happened—was it satisfactory?

RUTH: Nothing much happened, Madame Arcati, after you went off.

MADAME ARCATI: Something happened all right. I can feel it. [*She rises and sniffs*] No poltergeist, at any rate—that's a good thing. Any apparitions?

DR. BRADMAN: Not a thing.

MADAME ARCATI: No protoplasm?

RUTH: I'm not quite sure what it is, but I don't think so.

MADAME ARCATI: Very curious. I feel as though something tremendous had taken place.

RUTH: Charles pretended he heard a voice, in order to frighten us.

CHARLES: It was only a joke.

MADAME ARCATI: A very poor one, if I may say so—[*She walks about a little more*] Nevertheless, I am prepared to swear that there is someone else psychic in this room apart from myself.

RUTH: I don't see how there can be really, Madame Arcati.

MADAME ARCATI: I do hope I haven't gone and released something—however, we are bound to find out within a day or two—if any manifestation should occur or you hear any unexpected noises—you might let me know at once.

RUTH: Of course we will—we'll telephone immediately.

MADAME ARCATI: I think I really must be on my way now.

RUTH: Wouldn't you like anything before you go?

MADAME ARCATI: No, thank you—I have some Ovaltine all ready in a saucepan at home—it only needs hotting up.

DR. BRADMAN: Wouldn't you like to leave your bicycle here and let us drive you?

MRS. BRADMAN: I honestly do think you should, Madame Arcati, after that trance and everything—you can't be feeling quite yourself.

MADAME ARCATI: Nonsense, my dear, I'm as fit as a fiddle—always feel capital after a trance—rejuvenates me. Good night, Mrs. Condomine.

RUTH: It was awfully sweet of you to take so much trouble.

MADAME ARCATI: I'm sorry so little occurred—it's that cold of Daphne's, I expect—you know what children are when they have anything wrong with them. We must try again some other evening.

RUTH: That would be lovely.

MADAME ARCATI: Good night, Mrs. Bradman—

MRS. BRADMAN: It was thrilling, it really was—I felt the table absolutely shaking under my hands.

MADAME ARCATI: Good night, Doctor.

DR. BRADMAN: Congratulations, Madame Arcati.

MADAME ARCATI: I am fully aware of the irony in your voice, Doctor Bradman. As a matter of fact you'd be an admirable subject for telepathic hypnosis—a great chum of mine is an expert—I should like her to look you over.

DR. BRADMAN: I'm sure I should charmed.

MADAME ARCATI: Good night, everyone—next time we must really put our backs into it!

[*With a comprehensive smile and a wave of the hand, she goes out followed by* CHARLES. RUTH *sinks down into a chair, laughing helplessly.*

RUTH: Oh dear! . . . Oh dear! . . .

MRS. BRADMAN [*beginning to laugh too*]:   Be careful, Mrs. Condomine—she might hear you.

RUTH: I can't help it—I really can't—I've been holding this in for ages.

MRS. BRADMAN: She certainly put you in your place, George, and serves you right.

RUTH: She's raving mad, of course—mad as a hatter.

MRS. BRADMAN: But do you really think she *believes*?

DR. BRADMAN: Of course not—the whole thing's a put-up job —I must say, though, she shoots a more original line than they generally do.

RUTH: I should think that she's probably half convinced herself by now.

DR. BRADMAN: Possibly—the trance was genuine enough—but that, of course, is easily accounted for.

RUTH: Hysteria?

DR. BRADMAN: Yes—a form of hysteria, I should imagine.

MRS. BRADMAN: I do hope Mr. Condomine got all the atmosphere he wanted for his book.

RUTH: He might have got a great deal more if he hadn't spoiled everything by showing off . . . I'm really very cross with him. [*At this moment* ELVIRA *comes in through the closed French windows. She is charmingly dressed in a sort of negligee. Everything about her is grey: hair, skin, dress, hands, so we must accept the fact that she is not quite of this world.*
She passes between DR. *and* MRS. BRADMAN *and* RUTH *while they are talking. None of them sees her. She goes upstage and sits soundlessly on a chair. She regards them with interest, a slight smile on her face*] I suddenly felt a draught— there must be a window open.

DR. BRADMAN [*looking*].   No—they're shut.

MRS. BRADMAN [*laughing*]:   Perhaps it was one of those what you may call 'ems that Madame Arcati was talking about.

DR. BRADMAN: Elementals.

RUTH [*also laughing again*]:   Oh no, it couldn't be—she distinctly said that it was the wrong time of the year for Elementals.

[CHARLES *comes in again.*

CHARLES: Well, the old girl's gone pedalling off down the drive at the hell of a speed—we had a bit of trouble lighting her lamp.

MRS. BRADMAN: Poor thing.

CHARLES: I've got a theory about her, you know—I believe she is completely sincere.

RUTH: Charles! How could she be?

CHARLES: Wouldn't it be possible, Doctor? Some form of self-hypnotism?

DR. BRADMAN: It might be . . . as I was explaining to your wife just now, there are certain types of hysterical subjects . . .

MRS. BRADMAN: George dear—it's getting terribly late, we really must go home—you have to get up so early in the morning.

DR. BRADMAN: You see? The moment I begin to talk about anything that really interests me, my wife interrupts me . . .

MRS. BRADMAN: You know I'm right, darling—it's past eleven.

DR. BRADMAN [*to* CHARLES]:   I'll do a little reading up on the whole business—just for the fun of it.

CHARLES: You must have a drink before you go.

DR. BRADMAN: No, really, thank you—Violet's quite right, I'm afraid. I have got to get up abominably early tomorrow—I have a patient being operated on in Canterbury.

MRS. BRADMAN [*to* RUTH]:   It has been a thrilling evening—I shall never forget—it was sweet of you to include us.

DR. BRADMAN: Good night, Mrs. Condomine—thank you so much.

CHARLES: You're sure about the drink?

DR. BRADMAN: Quite sure, thanks.

RUTH: We'll let you know if we find any poltergeists whirling about.

DR. BRADMAN: I should never forgive you if you didn't.

MRS. BRADMAN: Come along, darling . . .

[CHARLES *leads the* BRADMANS *out into the hall.* RUTH, *passing close to* ELVIRA, *goes over to the fire and turns over a log with her foot. Then she takes a cigarette and is lighting it as* CHARLES *comes back into the room.*

RUTH: Well, darling?

CHARLES [*absently*]:   Well?

RUTH: Would you say the evening had been profitable?

CHARLES: Yes—I suppose so.

RUTH: I must say it was extremely funny at moments.

CHARLES: Yes—it certainly was.

RUTH: What's the matter?

CHARLES: The matter?

RUTH: Yes—you seem odd somehow—do you feel quite well?

CHARLES: Perfectly. I think I'll have a drink. Do you want one?

RUTH: No, thank you, dear.

CHARLES [*pouring himself out a drink*]:   It's rather chilly in this room.

RUTH: Come over by the fire.

CHARLES: I don't think I'll make any notes tonight—I'll start fresh in the morning. [*He is bringing his drink over to the fire when he sees* ELVIRA] My God!

[*He drops the drink on the floor.* RUTH *jumps up.*

RUTH: Charles!

ELVIRA: That was very clumsy, Charles dear.

CHARLES: Elvira!—then it's true—it was you!

ELVIRA: Of course it was.

RUTH [*coming to him*]: Charles—darling Charles—what are you talking about?

CHARLES [*to* ELVIRA]: Are you a ghost?

ELVIRA: I suppose I must be—it's all very confusing.

RUTH [*becoming agitated*]: Charles—what do you keep looking over there for? Look at me—what's happened?

CHARLES: Don't you see?

RUTH: See what?

CHARLES: Elvira.

RUTH [*staring at him incredulously*]: Elvira!!

CHARLES [*with an effort at social grace*]: Yes—Elvira dear, this is Ruth—Ruth, this is Elvira.

RUTH [*with forced calmness*]: Come and sit down, darling.

CHARLES. Do you mean to say you can't see her?

RUTH: Listen, Charles—you just sit down quietly by the fire and I'll mix you another drink. Don't worry about the mess on the carpet—Edith can clean it up in the morning.

[*She takes him by the arm.*

CHARLES [*breaking away*]: But you must be able to see her— she's there—look—right in front of you—there—

RUTH: Are you mad? What's happened to you?

CHARLES: You can't see her?

RUTH: If this is a joke, dear, it's gone quite far enough. Sit down for God's sake and don't be idiotic.

CHARLES [*clutching his head*]: What am I to do—what the hell am I to do!

ELVIRA: I think you might at least be a little more pleased to see me—after all, you conjured me up.

CHARLES: I didn't do any such thing. I did nothing of the sort.

ELVIRA: Nonsense, of course you did. That awful child with the cold came and told me you wanted to see me urgently.

CHARLES: It was all a mistake—a horrible mistake.

RUTH: Stop talking like that, Charles—as I told you before, the *joke's* gone far enough.

CHARLES [*aside*]: I've gone mad, that's what it is—I've just gone raving mad.

RUTH [*going to the table and quickly pouring him out some neat brandy*]:   Here—let me get you a drink.

CHARLES [*mechanically—taking it*]:   This is appalling!

RUTH: Relax.

CHARLES: How can I relax? I shall never be able to relax again as long as I live.

RUTH: Drink some brandy.

CHARLES [*drinking it at a gulp*]:   There now—are you satisfied?

RUTH: Now sit down.

CHARLES: Why are you so anxious for me to sit down—what good will that do?

RUTH: I want you to relax—you can't relax standing up.

ELVIRA: African natives can—they can stand on one leg for hours.

CHARLES: I don't happen to be an African native.

RUTH: You don't happen to be a *what*?

CHARLES [*savagely*]:   An African native!

RUTH: What's that got to do with it?

CHARLES: It doesn't matter, Ruth—really it doesn't matter—we'll say no more about it. [*He sits down*] See, I've sat down.

RUTH: Would you like some more brandy?

CHARLES: Yes, please.

ELVIRA: Very unwise—you always had a weak head.

CHARLES: I could drink you under the table.

RUTH: There's no need to be aggressive, Charles—I'm doing my best to help you.

CHARLES: I'm sorry.

RUTH [*bringing him some more brandy*]:   Here—drink this—and then we'll go to bed.

ELVIRA: Get rid of her, Charles—then we can talk in peace.

CHARLES: That's a thoroughly immoral suggestion, you ought to be ashamed of yourself.

RUTH: What is there immoral in that?

CHARLES: I wasn't talking to you.

RUTH: Who were you talking to, then?

CHARLES: Elvira, of course.

RUTH: To hell with Elvira!

ELVIRA: There now—she's getting cross.

CHARLES: I don't blame her.

RUTH: What don't you blame her for?

CHARLES: Oh, God!

RUTH: Now look here, Charles—I gather you've got some sort of plan behind all this. I'm not quite a fool. I suspected you when we were doing that idiotic séance.

CHARLES: Don't be so silly—what plan could I have?

RUTH: I don't know—it's probably something to do with the characters in your book—how they, or one of them would react to a certain situation—I refuse to be used as a guinea pig unless I'm warned beforehand what it's all about.

CHARLES [*patiently*]:   Ruth, Elvira is here—she's standing a few yards away from you.

RUTH [*sarcastically*]:   Yes, dear, I can see her distinctly—under the piano with a horse.

CHARLES: But, Ruth . . .

RUTH: I am not going to stay here arguing any longer . . .

ELVIRA: Hurray!

CHARLES: Shut up.

RUTH [*incensed*]:   How dare you speak to me like that!

CHARLES: Listen, Ruth—please listen—

RUTH: I will not listen to any more of this nonsense—I am going up to bed now. I'll leave you to turn out the lights. I shan't be asleep—I'm too upset so you can come in and say good night to me if you feel like it.

ELVIRA: That's big of her, I must say.

CHARLES: Be quiet—you're behaving like a guttersnipe.

RUTH [*icily—at door*]:   That is all I have to say. Good night, Charles.

[RUTH *walks swiftly out of the room without looking at him again.*

CHARLES: Ruth . . .

ELVIRA: That was one of the most enjoyable half-hours I have ever spent.

CHARLES: Oh, Elvira—how could you!

ELVIRA: Poor Ruth.

CHARLES [*staring at her*]:   This is obviously a hallucination, isn't it?

ELVIRA: I'm afraid I don't know the technical term for it.

CHARLES [*rising and walking about the room*]: What am I to do?

ELVIRA: What Ruth suggested—relax.

CHARLES: Where have you come from?

ELVIRA: Do you know, it's very peculiar, but I've sort of forgotten.

CHARLES: Are you here to stay indefinitely?

ELVIRA: I don't know that either.

CHARLES: Oh, my God!

ELVIRA: Why, would you hate it so much if I did?

CHARLES: Well, you must admit it would be embarrassing.

ELVIRA: I don't see why, really—it's all a question of adjusting yourself—anyhow I think it's horrid of you to be so unwelcoming and disagreeable.

CHARLES: Now look here, Elvira . . .

ELVIRA [*near tears*]: I do—I think you're mean.

CHARLES: Try to see my point, dear—I've been married to Ruth for five years, and you've been dead for seven . . .

ELVIRA: Not dead, Charles—"passed over." It's considered vulgar to say "dead" where I come from.

CHARLES: Passed over, then.

ELVIRA: At any rate, now that I'm here, the least you can do is to make a pretense of being amiable about it . . .

CHARLES: Of course, my dear, I'm delighted in one way . . .

ELVIRA: I don't believe you love me any more.

CHARLES: I shall always love the memory of you.

ELVIRA [*rising and walking about*]: You mustn't think me unreasonable, but I really am a little hurt. You called me back—and at great inconvenience I came—and you've been thoroughly churlish ever since I arrived.

CHARLES [*gently*]: Believe me, Elvira, I most emphatically did not send for you—there's been some mistake.

ELVIRA [*irritably*]: Well, somebody did—and that child said it was you—I remember I was playing backgammon with a very sweet old Oriental gentleman—I think his name was Genghis Khan—and I'd just thrown double sixes, and then that child

paged me and the next thing I knew I was in this room . . .
perhaps it was your subconscious.

CHARLES: Well, you must find out whether you are going to
stay or not, and we can make arrangements accordingly.

ELVIRA: I don't see how I can.

CHARLES: Well, try to think—isn't there anyone that you
know, that you can get in touch with over there—on the other
side, or whatever it's called—who could advise you?

ELVIRA: I can't think—it seems so far away—as though I'd
dreamed it . . .

CHARLES: You must know somebody else besides Genghis
Khan.

ELVIRA: Oh, Charles . . .

CHARLES: What is it?

ELVIRA: I want to cry, but I don't think I'm able to . . .

CHARLES: What do you want to cry for?

ELVIRA: It's seeing you again—and you being so irascible like
you always used to be . . .

CHARLES: I don't mean to be irascible, Elvira . . .

ELVIRA: Darling—I don't mind really—I never did.

CHARLES: Is it cold—being a ghost?

ELVIRA: No—I don't think so.

CHARLES: What happens if I touch you?

ELVIRA: I doubt if you can. Do you want to?

CHARLES: Oh, Elvira . . .

[*He buries his face in his hands.*

ELVIRA: What is it, darling?

CHARLES: I really do feel strange, seeing you again . . .

ELVIRA: That's better.

CHARLES [*looking up*]: What's better?

ELVIRA: Your voice was kinder.

CHARLES: Was I ever unkind to you when you were alive?

ELVIRA: Often . . .

CHARLES: Oh, how can you! I'm sure that's an exaggeration.

ELVIRA: Not at all—you were an absolute pig that time we
went to Cornwall and stayed in that awful hotel—you hit me
with a billiard cue—

CHARLES: Only very, very gently . . .

ELVIRA: I loved you very much.

CHARLES: I loved you too . . . [*He puts out his hand to her and then draws it away*] No, I can't touch you—isn't that horrible?

ELVIRA: Perhaps it's as well if I'm going to stay for any length of time . . .

CHARLES: I feel strangely peaceful—I suppose I shall wake up eventually . . .

ELVIRA: Put your head back.

CHARLES [*doing so*]:   Like that?

ELVIRA [*stroking his hair*]:   Can you feel anything . . . ?

CHARLES: Only a very little breeze through my hair . . .

ELVIRA: Well, that's better than nothing.

CHARLES [*drowsily*]:   I suppose if I'm really out of my mind they'll put me in an asylum.

ELVIRA: Don't worry about that—just relax—

CHARLES [*very drowsily indeed*]:   Poor Ruth . . .

ELVIRA [*gently and sweetly*]:   To hell with Ruth.

CURTAIN

ACT TWO

SCENE I

It is about nine-thirty the next morning. The sun is pouring in through the open French windows.

RUTH *is sitting at the breakfast table, drinking coffee and reading the* Times. *After a few moments* CHARLES *comes in. He kisses her.*

CHARLES: Good morning, darling.

RUTH [*with a certain stiffness*]: Good morning, Charles.

CHARLES [*going to the open window and taking a deep breath*]: It certainly is.

RUTH: What certainly is what?

CHARLES: A good morning—a tremendously good morning— there isn't a cloud in the sky and everything looks newly washed.

RUTH [*turning a page of the* Times]: Edith's keeping your breakfast hot—you'd better ring.

CHARLES [*pressing the bell by the fireplace*]: Anything interesting in the *Times*?

RUTH: Don't be silly, Charles.

CHARLES [*coming to the table*]: I intend to work all day.

RUTH: Good.

CHARLES: It's extraordinary about daylight, isn't it?

RUTH: How do you mean?

CHARLES: The way it reduces everything to normal.

RUTH: Does it?

CHARLES [*sits. Firmly*]: Yes—it does.

RUTH: I'm sure I'm very glad to hear it.

CHARLES: You're very glacial this morning.

RUTH: Are you surprised?

CHARLES: Frankly—yes. I expected more of *you*.

RUTH: Well, really!

CHARLES: I've always looked upon you as a woman of perception and understanding.

RUTH: Perhaps this is one of my off days.

[EDITH *comes in with some bacon and eggs and toast.*

CHARLES [*cheerfully*]: Good morning, Edith.

EDITH: Good morning, sir.

CHARLES: Feeling fit?

EDITH: Yes, sir—thank you, sir.

CHARLES: How's cook?

EDITH: I don't know, sir—I haven't asked her.

CHARLES: You should. You should begin every day by asking
everyone how they are—it oils the wheels.

EDITH: Yes, sir.

CHARLES: Greet her for me, will you?

EDITH: Yes, sir.

RUTH: That will be all for the moment, Edith.

EDITH: Yes'm.

[EDITH *goes out.*

RUTH: I wish you wouldn't be facetious with the servants,
Charles—it confuses them and undermines their morale.

CHARLES: I consider that point of view retrogressive, if not
downright feudal.

RUTH: I don't care what you consider it. I have to run the
house and you don't.

CHARLES: Are you implying that I couldn't?

RUTH: You're at liberty to try.

CHARLES: I take back what I said about it being a good
morning—it's a dreadful morning.

RUTH: You'd better eat your breakfast while it's hot.

CHARLES: It isn't.

RUTH [*putting down the* Times): Now look here, Charles—in
your younger days this display of roguish flippancy might
have been alluring—in a middle-aged novelist it's nauseating.

CHARLES: Would you like me to writhe at your feet in a frenzy
of self-abasement?

RUTH: That would be equally nauseating but certainly more
appropriate.

CHARLES: I really don't see what I've done that's so awful.

RUTH: You behaved abominably last night. You wounded me
and insulted me.

CHARLES: I was the victim of an aberration.

RUTH: Nonsense—you were drunk.

CHARLES: Drunk?

RUTH: You had four strong dry Martinis before dinner—a great
deal too much burgundy at dinner—heaven knows how much
Port and kümmel with Doctor Bradman while I was doing
my best to entertain that madwoman—and then two double
brandies later—I gave them to you myself—of course you
were drunk.

CHARLES: So that's your story, is it?

RUTH: You refused to come to bed and finally when I came
down at three in the morning to see what had happened to
you I found you in an alcoholic coma on the sofa with the
fire out and your hair all over your face.

CHARLES: I was not in the least drunk, Ruth. Something happened to me—you really must believe that—something very
peculiar happened to me.

RUTH: Nonsense.

CHARLES: It isn't nonsense—I know it looks like nonsense now
in the clear, remorseless light of day, but last night it was far
from being nonsense—I honestly had some sort of hallucination—

RUTH: I would really rather not discuss it any further.

CHARLES: But you must discuss it—it's very disturbing.

RUTH: There I agree with you. It showed you up in a most
unpleasant light—I find that extremely disturbing.

CHARLES: I swear to you that during the séance I was convinced that I heard Elvira's voice—

RUTH: Nobody else did.

CHARLES: I can't help that—I did.

RUTH: You couldn't have.

CHARLES: And later on I was equally convinced that she was
in this room—I saw her distinctly and talked to her. After
you'd gone up to bed we had quite a cosy little chat.

RUTH: And you seriously expect me to believe that you weren't
drunk?

CHARLES: I *know* I wasn't drunk. If I'd been all that drunk, I should have a dreadful hangover now, shouldn't I?

RUTH: I'm not at all sure that you haven't.

CHARLES: I haven't got a trace of a headache—my tongue's not coated—look at it.

[*He puts out his tongue.*

RUTH: I've not the least desire to look at your tongue; kindly put it in again.

CHARLES: I know what it is—you're frightened.

RUTH: Frightened? Rubbish! What is there to be frightened of?

CHARLES: Elvira. You wouldn't have minded all that much even if I had been drunk—it's only because it was all mixed up with Elvira.

RUTH: I seem to remember last night before dinner telling you that your views of female psychology were rather didactic. I was right. I should have added that they were puerile.

CHARLES: That was when it all began.

RUTH: When what all began?

CHARLES: We were talking too much about Elvira—it's dangerous to have somebody very strongly in your mind when you start dabbling with the occult.

RUTH: She certainly wasn't strongly in my mind.

CHARLES: She was in mine.

RUTH: Oh, she was, was she?

CHARLES: You tried to make me say that she was more physically attractive than you, so that you could hold it over me.

RUTH: I did not. I don't give a hoot how physically attractive she was.

CHARLES: Oh yes, you do—your whole being is devoured with jealousy.

RUTH [*rises and starts to clear table*]: This is *too* much!

CHARLES: Women! My God, what I think of women!

RUTH: Your view of women is academic to say the least of it—just because you've always been dominated by them it doesn't necessarily follow that you know anything about them.

CHARLES: I've never been dominated by anyone.

RUTH: You were hag-ridden by your mother until you were twenty-three—then you got into the clutches of that awful Mrs. Whatever-her-name-was—

CHARLES: Mrs. Winthrop-Lewellyn.

RUTH: I'm not interested. Then there was Elvira—she ruled you with a rod of iron.

CHARLES: Elvira never ruled anyone, she was much too elusive —that was one of her greatest charms.

[*Sits.*

RUTH: Then there was Maud Charteris—

CHARLES: My affair with Maud Charteris lasted exactly seven and a half weeks and she cried all the time.

RUTH: The tyranny of tears! Then there was—

CHARLES: If you wish to make an inventory of my sex life, dear, I think it only fair to tell you that you've missed out several episodes—I'll consult my diary and give you the complete list after lunch.

RUTH: It's no use trying to impress me with your routine amorous exploits—

CHARLES: The only woman in my whole life who's ever attempted to dominate me is you—you've been at it for years.

RUTH: That is completely untrue.

CHARLES: Oh no, it isn't. You boss me and bully me and order me about—you won't even allow me to have an hallucination if I want to.

RUTH: Alcohol will ruin your whole life if you allow it to get a hold on you, you know.

CHARLES: Once and for all, Ruth, I would like you to understand that what happened last night was nothing whatever to do with alcohol. You've very adroitly rationalized the whole affair to your own satisfaction, but your deductions are based on complete fallacy. I am willing to grant you that it was an aberration, some sort of odd psychic delusion brought on by suggestion or hypnosis. I was stone cold sober from first to last and extremely upset into the bargain.

RUTH: *You* were upset indeed! What about me?

CHARLES: You behaved with a stolid, obtuse lack of compre-
hension that frankly shocked me!

RUTH: I consider that I was remarkably patient. I shall know
better next time.

CHARLES: Instead of putting out a gentle, comradely hand to
guide me you shouted staccato orders at me like a sergeant-
major.

RUTH: You seem to forget that you gratuitously insulted me.

CHARLES: I did not.

RUTH: You called me a guttersnipe—you told me to shut up—
and when I quietly suggested that we should go up to bed
you said, with the most disgusting leer, that it was an immoral suggestion.

CHARLES [*exasperated*]:   I was talking to Elvira!

RUTH: If you were I can only say that it conjures up a fragrant
picture of your first marriage.

CHARLES: My first marriage was perfectly charming and I think
it's in the worst possible taste for you to sneer at it.

RUTH: I am not nearly so interested in your first marriage as
you think I am. It's your second marriage that is absorbing
me at the moment—it seems to me to be on the rocks.

CHARLES: Only because you persist in taking up this ridiculous
attitude.

RUTH: My attitude is that of any normal woman whose
husband gets drunk and hurls abuse at her.

CHARLES [*shouting*]:   I was not drunk!

RUTH: Be quiet, they'll hear you in the kitchen.

CHARLES: I don't care if they hear me in the Folkestone Town
Hall—I was not drunk!

RUTH: Control yourself, Charles.

CHARLES: How can I control myself in the face of your idiotic
damned stubbornness? It's giving me claustrophobia.

RUTH [*quietly*]: You'd better ring up Doctor Bradman.

[EDITH *comes in with a tray to clear away the breakfast things.*

EDITH: Can I clear, please'm?

RUTH: Yes, Edith.

EDITH: Cook wants to know about lunch, mum.

RUTH [*coldly*]:   Will you be in to lunch, Charles?

CHARLES: Please don't worry about me—I shall be perfectly happy with a bottle of gin in my bedroom.

RUTH: Don't be silly, dear. [*To* EDITH] Tell cook we shall both be in.

EDITH: Yes'm.

RUTH [*conversationally—after a long pause*]:   I'm going into Hythe this morning—is there anything you want?

CHARLES: Yes—a great deal—but I doubt if you could get it in Hythe.

RUTH: Tell cook to put Alka-Seltzer down on my list, will you, Edith?

EDITH: Yes'm.

RUTH [*at the window—after another long pause*]:   It's clouding over.

CHARLES: You have a genius for understatement.

[*In silence, but breathing heavily,* EDITH *staggers out with the tray.*

RUTH [*as she goes*]:   Don't worry about the table, Edith—I'll put it away.

EDITH: Yes'm.

[*When* EDITH *has gone* CHARLES *goes over to* RUTH.

CHARLES: Please, Ruth—be reasonable.

RUTH: I'm perfectly reasonable.

CHARLES: I wasn't pretending—I really did believe that I saw Elvira and when I heard her voice I was appalled.

RUTH: You put up with it for five years.

[*Puts chair by gramophone.*

CHARLES [*puts table in hall*]:   Naturally when I saw her I had the shock of my life—that's why I dropped the glass.

RUTH: But you *couldn't* have seen her.

CHARLES: I know I couldn't have but I *did!*

RUTH: I'm willing to concede then that you imagined you did.

CHARLES: That's what I've been trying to explain to you for hours.

RUTH: Well, then, there's obviously something wrong with you.

CHARLES: Exactly—there is something wrong with me—something fundamentally wrong with me—that's why I've been imploring your sympathy and all I got was a sterile temperance lecture.

RUTH: You had been drinking, Charles—there's no denying that.

CHARLES: No more than usual.

RUTH: Well, how do you account for it then?

CHARLES [*frantically*]:   I can't account for it—that's what so awful.

RUTH [*practically*]:   Did you feel quite well yesterday—during the day, I mean?

CHARLES: Of course I did.

RUTH: What did you have for lunch?

CHARLES: You ought to know, you had it with me.

RUTH [*thinking*]:   Let me see now, there was lemon sole and that cheese thing—

CHARLES: Why should having a cheese thing for lunch make me see my deceased wife after dinner?

RUTH: You never know—it was rather rich.

CHARLES: Why didn't you see your dead husband then? You had just as much of it as I did.

RUTH: This is not getting us anywhere at all.

CHARLES: Of course it isn't, and it won't as long as you insist on ascribing supernatural phenomena to colonic irritation.

RUTH: Supernatural grandmother!

CHARLES: I admit she'd have been much less agitating.

RUTH [*sits*]:   Perhaps you ought to see a nerve specialist.

CHARLES: I am not in the least neurotic and never have been.

RUTH: A psychoanalyst then.

CHARLES: I refuse to endure months of expensive humiliation only to be told at the end of it that at the age of four I was in love with my rocking horse.

RUTH: What do you suggest then?

CHARLES: I don't suggest anything—I'm profoundly uneasy.

RUTH: Perhaps there's something pressing on your brain.

CHARLES: If there were something pressing on my brain, I should have violent headaches, shouldn't I?

RUTH: Not necessarily. An uncle of mine had a lump the size of a cricket ball pressing on his brain for years and he never felt a thing.

CHARLES [*rises*]:   I know I should know if I had anything like that.

RUTH: He didn't.

CHARLES: What happened to him?

RUTH: He had it taken out and he's been as bright as a button ever since.

CHARLES: Did he have any sort of delusions—did he think he saw things that weren't there?

RUTH: No, I don't think so.

CHARLES: Well, what the hell are we talking about him for then? It's sheer waste of valuable time.

RUTH: I only brought him up as an example.

CHARLES: I think I'm going mad.

RUTH: How do you feel now?

CHARLES: Physically do you mean?

RUTH: Altogether.

CHARLES [*after due reflection*]:   Apart from being worried I feel quite normal.

RUTH: Good. You're not hearing or seeing anything in the least unusual?

CHARLES: Not a thing.

[*At this moment* ELVIRA *comes in from the garden, carrying an armful of roses. The roses are as grey as the rest of her.*

ELVIRA: You've absolutely ruined that border by the sundial —it looks like a mixed salad.

CHARLES: O, my God!

RUTH: What's the matter now?

CHARLES: She's here again!

RUTH: What do you mean? Who's here again?

CHARLES: Elvira.

RUTH: Pull yourself together and don't be absurd.

ELVIRA: It's all those nasturtiums—they're so vulgar.

CHARLES: I like nasturtiums.

RUTH: You like what?

ELVIRA [*putting her grey roses into a vase*]:   They're all right in moderation but in a mass like that they look beastly.

CHARLES: Help me, Ruth—you've got to help me—

RUTH [*rises*]:   What did you mean about nasturtiums?

CHARLES: Never mind about that now—I tell you she's here again.

ELVIRA: You have been having a nice scene, haven't you? I could hear you right down the garden.

CHARLES: Please mind your own business.

RUTH: If your behaving like a lunatic isn't my business nothing is.

ELVIRA: I expect it was about me, wasn't it? I know I ought to feel sorry but I'm not—I'm delighted.

CHARLES: How can you be so inconsiderate?

RUTH [*shrilly*]:   Inconsiderate!—I like that, I must say—

CHARLES: Ruth—darling—please . . .

RUTH: I've done everything I can to help—I've controlled myself admirably—and I should like to say here and now that I don't believe a word about your damned hallucinations— you're up to something, Charles—there's been a certain furtiveness in your manner for weeks—Why don't you be honest and tell me what it is?

CHARLES: You're wrong—you're dead wrong—I haven't been in the least furtive—I—

RUTH: You're trying to upset me—for some obscure reason you're trying to goad me into doing something that I might regret—I won't stand for it any more—You're making me utterly miserable—

[*She bursts into tears and collapses on sofa.*

CHARLES: Ruth—please—

[*Sits on sofa beside* RUTH.

RUTH: Don't come near me—

ELVIRA: Let her have a nice cry—it'll do her good.

CHARLES: You're utterly heartless!

RUTH: Heartless!

CHARLES [*wildly*]:   I was not talking to you—I was talking to Elvira.

RUTH: Go on talking to her then, talk to her until you're blue in the face but don't talk to me—

CHARLES: Help me, Elvira,—

ELVIRA: How?

CHARLES: Make her see you or something.

ELVIRA: I'm afraid I couldn't manage that—it's technically the most difficult business—frightfully complicated, you know—it takes years of study—

CHARLES: You are here, aren't you? You're not an illusion?

ELVIRA: I may be an illusion but I'm most definitely here.

CHARLES: How did you get here?

ELVIRA: I told you last night—I don't exactly know—

CHARLES: Well, you must make me a promise that in future you only come and talk to me when I'm alone—

ELVIRA [*pouting*]: How unkind you are—making me feel so unwanted—I've never been treated so rudely—

CHARLES: I don't mean to be rude, but you must see—

ELVIRA: It's all your own fault for having married a woman who is incapable of seeing beyond the nose on her face—if she had a grain of real sympathy or affection for you she'd believe what you tell her.

CHARLES: How could you expect anybody to believe this?

ELVIRA: You'd be surprised how gullible people are—we often laugh about it on the other side.

[RUTH, *who has stopped crying and been staring at* CHARLES, *in horror, suddenly gets up.*

RUTH [*gently*]: Charles—

CHARLES [*surprised at her tone*]: Yes, dear—

RUTH: I'm awfully sorry I was cross—

CHARLES: But, my dear—

RUTH: I understand everything now, I do really—

CHARLES: You do?

RUTH [*patting his arm reassuringly*]: Of course I do.

ELVIRA: Look out—she's up to something—

CHARLES: Will you please be quiet?

RUTH: Of course, darling—we'll all be quiet, won't we? We'll be as quiet as little mice.

CHARLES: Ruth dear, listen—

RUTH: I want you to come upstairs with me and go to bed—

ELVIRA: The way that woman harps on bed is nothing short of erotic.

CHARLES: I'll deal with you later—

RUTH: Whenever you like, darling. Come along.

CHARLES: Ruth dear—I'd really rather not go to bed in the middle of the morning—

ELVIRA: How you've changed, darling!

CHARLES: Don't be disgusting.

RUTH [*sweetly*]:   I'm sorry, dear—I didn't mean to be.

CHARLES: What are you up to?

RUTH: I'm not up to anything—I just want you to go quietly to bed and wait there until Doctor Bradman comes—

CHARLES: No, Ruth—you're wrong—

RUTH [*firmly*]:   Come, dear—

ELVIRA: She'll have you in a straitjacket before you know where you are.

CHARLES [*frantically*]:   Help me—you must help me—

ELVIRA [*enjoying herself*]:   My dear, I would with pleasure, but I can't think how—

CHARLES: I can—listen, Ruth—

RUTH: Yes, dear?

CHARLES: If I promise to go to bed will you let me stay here for five minutes longer?

RUTH: I really think it would be better—

CHARLES: Bear with me—however mad it may seem—bear with me for just five minutes longer—

RUTH [*letting go of him*]:   Very well—what is it?

CHARLES: Sit down then.

RUTH [*sitting down*]:   All right—there.

CHARLES: Now listen—listen carefully—

ELVIRA: Have a cigarette, it will soothe your nerves.

CHARLES: I don't want a cigarette.

RUTH [*indulgently*]:   Then you shan't have one, darling.

CHARLES: Ruth, I want to explain to you clearly and without emotion that beyond any shadow of doubt the ghost or shade or whatever you like to call it of my first wife Elvira is in this room now.

RUTH: Yes, dear.

CHARLES: I know you don't believe it and are trying valiantly to humor me but I intend to prove it to you.

RUTH: Why not lie down and have a nice rest and you can prove anything you want to later on?

CHARLES: She may not be here later on.

ELVIRA: Don't worry—she will!

CHARLES: O God!

RUTH: Hush, dear.

CHARLES [*to* ELVIRA]: Promise you'll do what I ask?

ELVIRA: That all depends what it is.

CHARLES: Ruth—you see that bowl of flowers on the piano?

RUTH: Yes, dear—I did it myself this morning.

ELVIRA: / Very untidily if I may say so.

CHARLES: You may not.

RUTH: Very well—I never will again—I promise.

CHARLES: Elvira will now carry that bowl of flowers to the mantelpiece and back again. You will, Elvira, won't you—just to please me?

ELVIRA: I don't really see why I should—you've been quite insufferable to me ever since I materialized.

CHARLES: Please.

ELVIRA: All right, I will just this once—not that I approve of all these Herman the Great carryings on.

[*She goes over to the piano.*

CHARLES: Now, Ruth—watch carefully.

RUTH [*patiently*]: Very well, dear.

CHARLES: Go on, Elvira—bring it to the mantelpiece and back again.

[ELVIRA *does so, taking obvious pleasure in doing it in a very roundabout way. At one moment she brings it up to within an inch of* RUTH's *face.* RUTH *shrinks back with a scream and then jumps to her feet.*

RUTH [*furiously*]: How dare you, Charles! You ought to be ashamed of yourself!

CHARLES: What on earth for?

RUTH [*hysterically*]: It's a trick—I know perfectly well it's a trick—you've been working up to this—it's all part of some horrible plan—

CHARLES: It isn't—I swear it isn't—Elvira—do something else for God's sake—

ELVIRA: Certainly—anything to oblige.

RUTH [*becoming really frightened*]:   You want to get rid of me
—you're trying to drive me out of my mind—

CHARLES: Don't be so silly.

RUTH: You're cruel and sadistic and I'll never forgive you—
[ELVIRA *lifts up a light chair and waltzes solemnly round the
room with it, then she puts it down with a bang. Making a
dive for the door*] I'm not going to put up with this any more.

CHARLES [*holding her*]:   You must believe it—you must—

RUTH: Let me go immediately—

CHARLES: That was Elvira—I swear it was—

RUTH [*struggling*]:   Let me go—

CHARLES: Ruth—please—

[RUTH *breaks away from him and runs towards the windows.*
ELVIRA *gets there just before her and shuts them in her face.*
RUTH *starts back, appalled.*

RUTH [*looking at* CHARLES *with eyes of horror*]:   Charles—this is
madness—sheer madness! It's some sort of autosuggestion,
isn't it—some form of hypnotism, swear to me it's only that?
Swear to me it's only that.

ELVIRA [*taking an expensive vase from the mantelpiece and
crashing it into the grate*]:   Hypnotism my foot!

[RUTH *gives a scream and goes into violent hysterics as the
curtain falls.*

SCENE II

The time is late on the following afternoon.

When the curtain rises RUTH *is sitting alone at the tea table,
which is set in front of the fire. After a moment or two she gets
up and, frowning thoughtfully, goes over to the piano and takes
a cigarette out of a box. As she returns to the table the front
door bell rings. She hears it and straightens herself as though
preparing for a difficult interview.*

[EDITH *enters.*

EDITH: Madame Arcati.

[EDITH *steps aside and* MADAME ARCATI *comes in.* EDITH *goes out.*

MADAME ARCATI *is wearing a tweed coat and skirt and a great many amber beads and, possibly, a beret.*

MADAME ARCATI: My dear Mrs. Condomine, I came directly I got your message.

RUTH: That was very kind of you.

MADAME ARCATI [*briskly*]: Kind? Nonsense! Nothing kind about it—I look upon it as an outing.

RUTH: I'm so glad—will you have some tea?

MADAME ARCATI: China or Indian?

RUTH: China.

MADAME ARCATI: Good. I never touch Indian, it upsets my vibrations.

RUTH: Do sit down.

MADAME ARCATI [*turning her head and sniffing*]: I find this room very interesting—very interesting indeed. I noticed it the other night.

RUTH: I'm not entirely surprised.

[*She proceeds to pour out tea.*

MADAME ARCATI [*sitting down and pulling off her gloves*]: Have you ever been to Cowden Manor?

RUTH: No, I'm afraid I haven't.

MADAME ARCATI: That's very interesting too—strikes you like a blow between the eyes the moment you walk into the drawing room. Two lumps of sugar, please, and no milk at all.

RUTH: I am profoundly disturbed, Madame Arcati, and I want your help.

MADAME ARCATI: Aha! I thought as much. What's in these sandwiches?

RUTH: Cucumber.

MADAME ARCATI: Couldn't be better. [*She takes one*] Fire away.

RUTH: It's most awfully difficult to explain.

MADAME ARCATI: Facts first—explanations afterwards.

RUTH: It's the facts that are difficult to explain—they're so fantastic.

MADAME ARCATI: Facts very often are. Take creative talent for instance, how do you account for that? Look at Shakespeare and Michael Angelo! Try to explain Mozart snatching sounds out of the air and putting them down on paper when he was practically a baby—facts—plain facts. I know it's the fashion nowadays to ascribe it all to glands but my reply to that is fiddlededee.

RUTH: Yes, I'm sure you're quite right.

MADAME ARCATI: There are more things in heaven and earth than are dreamt of in your philosophy, Mrs. Condomine.

RUTH: There certainly are.

MADAME ARCATI: Come now—take the plunge—out with it. You've heard strange noises in the night no doubt—boards creaking—doors slamming—subdued moaning in the passages —is that it?

RUTH: No—I'm afraid it isn't.

MADAME ARCATI: No sudden gusts of cold wind, I hope?

RUTH: No, it's worse than that.

MADAME ARCATI: I'm all attention.

RUTH [*with an effort*]:   I know it sounds idiotic but the other night—during the séance—something happened—

MADAME ARCATI: I knew it! Probably a poltergeist, they're enormously cunning, you know, they sometimes lie doggo for days—

RUTH: You know that my husband was married before?

MADAME ARCATI: Yes—I have heard it mentioned.

RUTH: His first wife, Elvira, died comparatively young—

MADAME ARCATI [*sharply*]:   Where?

RUTH: Here—in this house—in this very room.

MADAME ARCATI [*whistling*]:   Whew! I'm beginning to see daylight!

RUTH: She was convalescing after pneumonia and one evening she started to laugh helplessly at one of the B.B.C. musical programmes and died of a heart attack.

MADAME ARCATI: And she materialized the other evening— after I had gone?

RUTH: Not to me, but to my husband.

MADAME ARCATI [*rising impulsively*]:   Capital—capital! Oh, but that's splendid!

RUTH [*coldly*]:   From your own professional standpoint I can see that it might be regarded as a major achievement!

MADAME ARCATI [*delighted*]:   A triumph, my dear! Nothing more nor less than a triumph!

RUTH: But from my own personal point of view you must see that, to say the least of it, it's embarrassing.

MADAME ARCATI [*walking about the room*]:   At last—at last—a genuine materialization!

RUTH: Please sit down again, Madame Arcati.

MADAME ARCATI: How could anyone sit down at a moment like this? It's tremendous! I haven't had such a success since the Sudbury case.

RUTH [*sharply*]:   Nevertheless I must insist upon you sitting down and controlling your natural exuberance. I appreciate fully your pride in your achievement but I would like to point out that it has made my position in this house untenable and that I hold you entirely responsible.

MADAME ARCATI [*contrite*]:   Forgive me, Mrs. Condomine—I am being abominably selfish—[*She sits down*]—How can I help you?

RUTH: How? By sending her back immediately to where she came from, of course.

MADAME ARCATI: I'm afraid that that is easier said than done.

RUTH: Do you mean to tell me that she is liable to stay here indefinitely?

MADAME ARCATI: It's difficult to say—I fear it depends largely on her.

RUTH: But my dear Madame Arcati—

MADAME ARCATI: Where is she now?

RUTH: My husband has driven her into Folkestone—apparently she was anxious to see an old friend of hers who is staying at the Grand.

MADAME ARCATI [*producing a notebook*]:   Forgive this formality, but I shall have to make a report to the Psychical Research people—

RUTH: I would be very much obliged if there were no names mentioned.

MADAME ARCATI: The report will be confidential.

RUTH: This is a small village you know and gossip would be most undesirable.

MADAME ARCATI: I quite understand. You say she is visible only to your husband?

RUTH: Yes.

MADAME ARCATI: "Visible only to husband." Audible too I presume?

RUTH: Extremely audible.

MADAME ARCATI: "Extremely audible." Your husband was devoted to her?

RUTH [*with slight irritation*]: I believe so—

MADAME ARCATI: "Husband devoted."

RUTH: It was apparently a reasonably happy marriage—

MADAME ARCATI: Tut, tut, Mrs. Condomine.

RUTH: I beg your pardon?

MADAME ARCATI: When did she pass over?

RUTH: Seven years ago.

MADAME ARCATI: Aha! That means she must have been on the waiting list.

RUTH: Waiting list?

MADAME ARCATI: Yes, otherwise she would have got beyond the materialization stage by now. She must have marked herself down for a return visit and she'd never have been able to manage it unless there were a strong influence at work.

RUTH: Do you mean that Charles—my husband—wanted her back all that much?

MADAME ARCATI: Possibly, or it might have been her own determination—

RUTH: That sounds much more likely.

MADAME ARCATI: Would you say that she was a woman of strong character?

RUTH [*with rising annoyance*]: I really don't know, Madame Arcati. I never met her. Nor am I particularly interested in how and why she got here. I am solely concerned with the question of how to get her away again as soon as possible.

MADAME ARCATI: I fully sympathize with you, Mrs. Condomine, and I assure you I will do anything in my power to help—but at the moment I fear I cannot offer any great hopes.

RUTH: But I always understood that there was a way of exorcising ghosts—some sort of ritual?

MADAME ARCATI: You mean the old Bell and Book method?

RUTH: Yes—I suppose I do.

MADAME ARCATI: Poppycock, Mrs. Condomine. It was quite effective in the days of genuine religious belief but that's all changed now. I believe the decline of faith in the Spirit World has been causing grave concern.

RUTH [*impatiently*]:   Has it indeed?

MADAME ARCATI: There was a time of course when a drop of holy water could send even a poltergeist scampering for cover, but not any more—"*Où sont les neiges d'Antan?*"

RUTH: Be that as it may, Madame Arcati, I must beg of you to do your utmost to dematerialize my husband's first wife as soon as possible.

MADAME ARCATI: The time has come for me to admit to you frankly, Mrs. Condomine, that I haven't the faintest idea how to set about it.

RUTH [*rises*]:   Do you mean to sit there and tell me that having mischievously conjured up this ghost or spirit or whatever she is and placed me in a hideous position you are unable to do anything about it at all?

MADAME ARCATI: Honesty is the best policy.

RUTH: But it's outrageous! I ought to hand you over to the police.

MADAME ARCATI [*rising*]:   You go too far, Mrs. Condomine.

RUTH [*furiously*]:   I go too far indeed? Do you realize what your insane amateur muddling has done?

MADAME ARCATI: I have been a professional since I was a child, Mrs. Condomine—"Amateur" is a word I cannot tolerate.

RUTH: It seems to me to be the height of amateurishness to evoke malignant spirits and not be able to get rid of them again.

MADAME ARCATI [*with dignity*]:   I was in a trance. Anything might happen when I am in a trance.

RUTH: Well, all I can suggest is that you go into another one immediately and get this damned woman out of my house.

MADAME ARCATI: I can't go into trances at a moment's notice—

it takes hours of preparation—in addition to which I have
to be extremely careful of my diet for days beforehand.
Today, for instance, I happened to lunch with friends and
had pigeon pie which, plus these cucumber sandwiches, would
make a trance out of the question.

RUTH: Well, you'll have to do something.

MADAME ARCATI: I will report the whole matter to the Society
for Psychical Research at the earliest possible moment.

RUTH: Will they be able to do anything?

MADAME ARCATI: I doubt it. They'd send an investigating
committee, I expect, and do a lot of questioning and wall
tapping and mumbo jumbo and then they'd have a con-
ference and you would probably have to go up to London to
testify—

RUTH [*near tears*]:   It's too humiliating—it really is.

MADAME ARCATI: Please try not to upset yourself—nothing can
be achieved by upsetting yourself.

RUTH: It's all very fine for you to talk like that, Madame
Arcati—you don't seem to have the faintest realization of
my position.

MADAME ARCATI: Try to look on the bright side.

RUTH: Bright side indeed! If your husband's first wife suddenly
appeared from the grave and came to live in the house with
you, do you suppose you'd be able to look on the bright side?

MADAME ARCATI: I resent your tone, Mrs. Condomine, I really
do.

RUTH: You most decidedly have no right to—you are entirely
to blame for the whole horrible situation.

MADAME ARCATI: Kindly remember that I came here the other
night on your own invitation.

RUTH: On my husband's invitation.

MADAME ARCATI: I did what I was requested to do, which was
to give a séance and establish contact with the other side—I
had no idea that there was any ulterior motive mixed up
with it.

RUTH: Ulterior motive?

MADAME ARCATI: Your husband was obviously eager to get in
touch with his former wife. If I had been aware of that at

the time I should naturally have consulted you beforehand—
after all "*Noblesse oblige*"!

RUTH: He had no intention of trying to get in touch with
anyone—the whole thing was planned in order for him to get
material for a mystery story he is writing about a homicidal
medium.

MADAME ARCATI [*drawing herself up*]: Am I to understand
that I was only invited in a spirit of mockery?

RUTH: Not at all—he merely wanted to make notes of some of
the tricks of the trade.

MADAME ARCATI [*incensed*]: Tricks of the trade! Insufferable!
I've never been so insulted in my life. I feel we have nothing
more to say to one another, Mrs. Condomine. Good-bye—

[*She goes towards the door.*

RUTH: Please don't go—please—

MADAME ARCATI: Your attitude from the outset has been most
unpleasant, Mrs. Condomine. Some of your remarks have
been discourteous in the extreme and I should like to say
without umbrage that if you and your husband were foolish
enough to tamper with the unseen for paltry motives and in a
spirit of ribaldry, whatever has happened to you is your own
fault, and, to coin a phrase, as far as I'm concerned you can
stew in your own juice!

[MADAME ARCATI *goes majestically from the room.*

RUTH [*left alone, walks about the room*]: Damn—damn—
damn!

[*After a moment or two* CHARLES *comes in with* ELVIRA.

CHARLES: What on earth was Madame Arcati doing here?

RUTH: She came to tea.

CHARLES: Did you ask her?

RUTH: Of course I did.

CHARLES: You never told me you were going to.

RUTH: You never told me you were going to ask Elvira to live
with us.

CHARLES: I didn't.

ELVIRA [*sauntering over to the tea table*]: Oh, yes, you did,
darling—it was your subconscious.

CHARLES: What was the old girl so cross about?—she practically cut me dead.

RUTH: I told her the truth about why we invited her the other
night.

CHARLES: That was quite unnecessary and most unkind.

RUTH: She needed taking down a bit, she was blowing herself
out like a pouter pigeon.

CHARLES: Why did you ask her to tea?

ELVIRA: To get me exorcised, of course. Oh dear, I wish I
could have a cucumber sandwich—I did love them so.

CHARLES: Is that true, Ruth?

RUTH: Is what true?

CHARLES: What Elvira said.

RUTH: You know perfectly well I can't hear what Elvira says.

CHARLES: She said that you got Madame Arcati here to try to
get her exorcised. Is that true?

RUTH: We discussed the possibilities.

ELVIRA: There's a snake in the grass for you.

CHARLES: You had no right to do such a thing without con-
sulting me.

RUTH: I have every right—this situation is absolutely impossible and you know it.

CHARLES: If only you'd make an effort and try to be a little
more friendly to Elvira we might all have quite a jolly time.

RUTH: I have no wish to have a jolly time with Elvira.

ELVIRA: She's certainly very bad tempered, isn't she? I can't
think why you married her.

CHARLES: She's naturally a bit upset—we must make allow-
ances.

ELVIRA: I was never bad tempered though, was I, darling? Not
even when you were beastly to me—

CHARLES: I was never beastly to you.

RUTH [exasperated]:   Where is Elvira at the moment?

CHARLES: In the chair, by the table.

RUTH: Now look here, Elvira—I shall have to call you Elvira,
shan't I? I can't very well go on saying Mrs. Condomine
all the time, it would sound too silly—

ELVIRA: I don't see why not.

RUTH: Did she say anything?

CHARLES: She said she'd like nothing better.

ELVIRA [*giggling*]:   You really are sweet, Charles darling—I worship you.

RUTH: I wish to be absolutely honest with you, Elvira—

ELVIRA: Hold on to your hats, boys!

RUTH: I admit I did ask Madame Arcati here with a view to getting you exorcised and I think that if you were in my position you'd have done exactly the same thing—wouldn't you?

ELVIRA: I shouldn't have done it so obviously.

RUTH: What did she say?

CHARLES: Nothing—she just nodded and smiled.

RUTH [*with a forced smile*]:   Thank you, Elvira—that's generous of you. I really would so much rather that there were no misunderstandings between us—

CHARLES: That's very sensible, Ruth—I agree entirely.

RUTH [*to* ELVIRA]:   I want, before we go any further, to ask you a frank question. Why did you really come here? I don't see that you could have hoped to have achieved anything by it beyond the immediate joke of making Charles into a sort of astral bigamist.

ELVIRA: I came because the power of Charles's love tugged and tugged and tugged at me. Didn't it, my sweet?

RUTH: What did she say?

CHARLES: She said that she came because she wanted to see me again.

RUTH: Well, she's done that now, hasn't she?

CHARLES: We can't be inhospitable, Ruth.

RUTH: I have no wish to be inhospitable, but I should like to have just an idea of how long you intend to stay, Elvira?

ELVIRA: I don't know—I really don't know! [*She giggles*] Isn't it awful?

CHARLES: She says she doesn't know.

RUTH: Surely that's a little inconsiderate?

ELVIRA: Didn't the old spiritualist have any constructive ideas about getting rid of me?

CHARLES: What did Madame Arcati say?

RUTH: She said she couldn't do a thing.

ELVIRA [*moving gaily over to the window*]:   Hurray!

CHARLES: Don't be upset, Ruth dear—we shall soon adjust ourselves, you know—you must admit it's a unique experience—I
can see no valid reason why we shouldn't get a great deal of
fun out of it.

RUTH: Fun? Charles, how can you—you must be out of your
mind!

CHARLES: Not at all—I thought I was at first—but now I must
say I'm beginning to enjoy myself.

RUTH [*bursting into tears*]:   Oh, Charles—Charles—

ELVIRA: She's off again.

CHARLES: You really must not be so callous, Elvira—try to see
her point a little—

RUTH: I suppose she said something insulting—

CHARLES: No, dear, she didn't do anything of the sort.

RUTH: Now look here, Elvira—

CHARLES: She's over by the window now.

RUTH: Why the hell can't she stay in the same place!

ELVIRA: Temper again—my poor Charles, what a terrible life
you must lead.

CHARLES: Do shut up, darling, you'll only make everything
worse.

RUTH: Who was that "darling" addressed to—her or me?

CHARLES: Both of you.

RUTH [*rises. Stamping her foot*]:   This is intolerable!

CHARLES: For heaven's sake don't get into another state—

RUTH [*furiously*]:   I've been doing my level best to control myself ever since yesterday morning and I'm damned if I'm
going to try any more, the strain is too much. She has the
advantage of being able to say whatever she pleases without
me being able to hear her, but she can hear me all right,
can't she, without any modified interpreting?

CHARLES: Modified interpreting? I don't know what you mean.

RUTH: Oh yes, you do—you haven't told me once what she
really said—you wouldn't dare. Judging from her photograph
she's the type who would use most unpleasant language—

CHARLES: Ruth—you're not to talk like that.

RUTH: I've been making polite conversation all through dinner
last night and breakfast and lunch today—and it's been a
nightmare—and I am not going to do it any more. I don't
like Elvira any more than she likes me and what's more I'm
certain that I never could have, dead or alive. If, since her un-
timely arrival here the other evening, she had shown the
slightest sign of good manners, the slightest sign of breeding,
I might have felt differently towards her, but all she has done
is try to make mischief between us and have private jokes
with you against me. I am now going up to my room and I
shall have my dinner on a tray. You and she can have the
house to yourselves and joke and gossip with each other to
your heart's content. The first thing in the morning I am
going up to London to interview the Psychical Research
Society and if they fail me I shall go straight to the Arch-
bishop of Canterbury—

[*She goes out.*

CHARLES [*making a movement to follow her*]:   Ruth—

ELVIRA: Let her go—she'll calm down later on.

CHARLES: It's unlike her to behave like this—she's generally so
equable.

ELVIRA: No, she isn't, not really, her mouth gives her away—
it's a hard mouth, Charles.

CHARLES: Her mouth's got nothing to do with it—I resent you
discussing Ruth as though she were a horse.

ELVIRA: Do you love her?

CHARLES: Of course I do.

ELVIRA: As much as you loved me?

CHARLES: Don't be silly—it's all entirely different.

ELVIRA: I'm so glad. Nothing could ever have been quite the
same, could it?

CHARLES: You always behaved very badly.

ELVIRA: Oh, Charles!

CHARLES: I'm grieved to see that your sojourn in the other
world hasn't improved you in the least.

ELVIRA [*curling up in sofa*]:   Go on, darling—I love it when
you pretend to be cross with me—

CHARLES: I'm now going up to talk to Ruth.

ELVIRA: Cowardly custard.

CHARLES: Don't be so idiotic. I can't let her go like that—I
must be a little nice and sympathetic to her.

ELVIRA: I don't see why! If she's set on being disagreeable I
should just let her get on with it.

CHARLES: The whole business is very difficult for her—we must
be fair.

ELVIRA: She should learn to be more adaptable.

CHARLES: She probably will in time—it's been a shock—

ELVIRA: Has it been a shock for you too, darling?

CHARLES: Of course—what did you expect?

ELVIRA: A nice shock?

CHARLES: What do you want, Elvira?

ELVIRA: Want? I don't know what you mean.

CHARLES: I remember that whenever you were overpoweringly
demure like that it usually meant that you wanted something.

ELVIRA: It's horrid of you to be so suspicious. All I want is to
be with you.

CHARLES: Well, you are.

ELVIRA: I mean alone, darling. If you go and pamper Ruth
and smalm her over, she'll probably come flouncing down
again and our lovely quiet evening together will be spoilt.

CHARLES: You're incorrigibly selfish.

ELVIRA: Well, I haven't seen you for seven years—it's only
natural that I should want a little time alone with you—to
talk over old times. I'll let you go up just for a little while if
you really think it's your duty.

CHARLES: Of course it is.

ELVIRA [smiling]: Then I don't mind.

CHARLES [rises]: You're disgraceful, Elvira.

ELVIRA: You won't be long, will you? You'll come down again
very soon?

CHARLES: I shall most likely dress for *dinner* while I'm upstairs
—you can read the *Tatler* or something.

ELVIRA: Darling, you don't have to dress—for me.

CHARLES: I always dress for dinner.

ELVIRA: What are you going to have? I should like to watch
you eat something really delicious—

CHARLES [*smiling and kissing his hand to her*]:   Be a good girl
now—you can play the gramophone if you like.

ELVIRA [*demurely*]:   Thank you, Charles.

[CHARLES *goes out.* ELVIRA *gets up, looks in the gramophone cupboard, finds the record of "Always" and puts it on. She starts
to waltz lightly round the room to it.* EDITH *comes in to fetch
the tea tray. She sees the gramophone playing by itself so she
turns it off and puts the record back in the cupboard. While
she is picking up the tray* ELVIRA *takes the record out and puts it
on again.* EDITH *gives a shriek, drops the tray and rushes out of
the room.* ELVIRA *continues to waltz gaily.*

SCENE III

The time is evening several days later.

When the curtain rises MRS. BRADMAN *is sitting in an armchair.*
RUTH *is standing by the window drumming on the pane with
her fingers.*

MRS. BRADMAN [*in armchair*]:   Does it show any signs of
clearing?

RUTH [*at window—looking out*]:   No, it's still pouring.

MRS. BRADMAN: I do sympathize with you, really I do—it's
really been quite a chapter of accidents, hasn't it?

RUTH: It certainly has.

MRS. BRADMAN: That happens sometimes, you know—everything seems to go wrong at once—exactly as though there
were some evil forces at work. I remember once when George
and I went away for a fortnight's holiday not long after we
were married—we were dogged by bad duck from beginning
to end—the weather was vile—George sprained his ankle—I
caught a terrible cold and had to stay in bed for two days—
and to crown everything the lamp fell over in the sitting
room and set fire to the treatise George had written on
hyperplasia of the abdominal glands.

RUTH [*absently*]:   How dreadful.

MRS. BRADMAN: He had to write it all over again—every single
word.

RUTH: You're sure you wouldn't like a cocktail or some sherry or anything?

MRS. BRADMAN: No, thank you—really not—George will be down in a minute and we've got to go like lightning—we were supposed to be at the Wilmots' at seven and it's nearly that now.

RUTH: I think I'll have a little sherry—I feel I need it.

[*She goes to the side table and pours herself some sherry.*

MRS. BRADMAN: Don't worry about your husband's arm, Mrs. Condomine—I'm sure it's only a sprain.

RUTH: It's not his arm I'm worried about.

MRS. BRADMAN: And I'm sure Edith will be up and about again in a few days—

RUTH: My cook gave notice this morning.

MRS. BRADMAN: Well, really! Servants are awful, aren't they? Not a shred of gratitude—at the first sign of trouble they run out on you—like rats leaving a sinking ship.

RUTH: I can't feel that your simile was entirely fortunate, Mrs. Bradman.

MRS. BRADMAN [*flustered*]: Oh, I didn't mean that, really I didn't!

[DR. BRADMAN *comes in.*

DR. BRADMAN: Nothing to worry about, Mrs. Condomine— it's only a slight strain—

RUTH: I'm so relieved.

DR. BRADMAN: He made a good deal of fuss when I examined it—men are much worse patients than women, you know— particularly highly strung men like your husband.

RUTH: Is he so highly strung, do you think?

DR. BRADMAN: Yes, as a matter of fact I wanted to talk to you about that. I'm afraid he's been overworking lately.

RUTH [*frowning*]: Overworking?

DR. BRADMAN: He's in rather a nervous condition—nothing serious, you understand—

RUTH: What makes you think so?

DR. BRADMAN: I know the symptoms. Of course the shock of his fall might have something to do with it, but I certainly should advise a complete rest for a couple of weeks—

RUTH: You mean he ought to go away?

DR. BRADMAN: I do. In cases like that a change of atmosphere can work wonders.

RUTH: What symptoms did you notice?

DR. BRADMAN: Oh, nothing to be unduly alarmed about—a certain air of strain—an inability to focus his eyes on the person he is talking to—a few rather marked irrelevancies in his conversation.

RUTH: I see. Can you remember any specific example?

DR. BRADMAN: Oh, he suddenly shouted "What are you doing in the bathroom?" and then, a little later, while I was writing him a prescription, he suddenly said "For God's sake, behave yourself!"

MRS. BRADMAN: How extraordinary.

RUTH [*nervously*]: He often goes on like that—particularly when he's immersed in writing a book—

DR. BRADMAN: Oh, I am not in the least perturbed about it really—but I do think a rest and a change would be a good idea.

RUTH: Thank you so much, Doctor. Would you like some sherry?

DR. BRADMAN: No, thank you—we really must be off.

RUTH: How is poor Edith?

DR. BRADMAN: She'll be all right in a few days—she's still recovering from the concussion.

MRS. BRADMAN: It's funny, isn't it, that both your housemaid and your husband should fall down on the same day, isn't it?

RUTH: Yes, if that sort of thing amuses you.

MRS. BRADMAN [*giggling nervously*]: Of course I didn't mean it like that, Mrs. Condomine—

DR. BRADMAN: Come along, my dear—you're talking too much as usual.

MRS. BRADMAN: You are horrid, George. Good-bye, Mrs. Condomine—

[*Rises.*

RUTH [*shaking hands*]: Good-bye.

DR. BRADMAN [*also shaking hands*]: I'll pop in and have a look at both patients sometime tomorrow morning.

RUTH: Thank you so much.

[CHARLES *comes in. His left arm is in a sling.* ELVIRA *follows him and sits down by the fire.*

DR. BRADMAN: Well—how does it feel?

CHARLES: All right.

DR. BRADMAN: It's only a slight sprain, you know.

CHARLES: Is this damned sling really essential?

DR. BRADMAN: It's a wise precaution—it will prevent you using your left hand except when it's really necessary.

CHARLES: I had intended to drive into Folkestone this evening—

DR. BRADMAN: It would be much better if you didn't.

CHARLES: It's extremely inconvenient—

RUTH: You can easily wait and go tomorrow, Charles—

ELVIRA: I can't stand another of those dreary evenings at home, Charles—it'll drive me dotty—and I haven't seen a movie for seven years—

CHARLES: Let me be the first to congratulate you.

DR. BRADMAN [*kindly*]: What's that, old man?

RUTH [*with intense meaning*]: Charles dear—try to be sensible, I implore you.

CHARLES: Sorry—I forgot.

DR. BRADMAN: You can drive the car if you promise to go very slowly and carefully. Your gear shift is on the right, isn't it?

CHARLES: Yes.

DR. BRADMAN: Well, use your left hand as little as possible.

CHARLES: All right.

RUTH: You'd much better stay at home.

DR. BRADMAN: Couldn't you drive him in?

RUTH [*stiffly*]: I'm afraid not—I have lots to do in the house and there's Edith to be attended to.

DR. BRADMAN: Well, I'll leave you to fight it out among yourselves—[*to* CHARLES]: But remember if you do insist on going—carefully does it—the roads are very slippery anyhow. Come along, Violet.

MRS. BRADMAN: Good-bye again—Good-bye, Mr. Condomine.

CHARLES: Good-bye.

[*He goes into the hall with the* BRADMANS. RUTH, *left alone, puts her sherry glass down on the table irritably.*

RUTH: You really are infuriating, Elvira—surely you could wait and go to the movies another night—[ELVIRA *gives a little laugh and, taking a rose out of a vase, throws it at* RUTH *and vanishes through the French windows. Picking up the rose and putting it back in the vase*] And stop behaving like a schoolgirl—you're old enough to know better.

CHARLES [*coming in*]: What?

RUTH: I was talking to Elvira.

CHARLES: She isn't here.

RUTH: She was a moment ago—she threw a rose at me.

CHARLES: She's been very high-spirited all day. I know this mood of old. It usually meant that she was up to something.

RUTH: You're sure she isn't here?

CHARLES: Quite sure.

RUTH: I want to talk to you.

CHARLES: O God!

RUTH: I must—it's important.

CHARLES: You've behaved very well for the last few days, Ruth —you're not going to start making scenes again, are you?

RUTH: I resent that air of patronage, Charles. I have behaved well, as you call it, because there was nothing else to do, but I think it only fair to warn you that I offer no guarantee for the future. My patience is being stretched to its uttermost.

CHARLES: As far as I can see the position is just as difficult for Elvira as it is for you—if not more so. The poor little thing comes back trustingly after all those years in the other world and what is she faced with? Nothing but brawling and hostility?

RUTH: What did she expect?

CHARLES: Surely even a protoplasmic manifestation has the right to expect a little of the milk of human kindness?

RUTH: Milk of human fiddlesticks.

CHARLES: That just doesn't make sense, dear.

RUTH: Elvira is about as trusting as a puff adder.

CHARLES: You're granite, Ruth—sheer, unyielding granite.

RUTH: And a good deal more dangerous into the bargain.

CHARLES: Dangerous? I never heard anything so ridiculous. How could a poor lonely, wistful little spirit like Elvira be dangerous?

RUTH: Quite easily—and she is. She's beginning to show her hand.

CHARLES: How do you mean—in what way?

RUTH [sits on sofa]:   This is a fight, Charles—a bloody battle—a duel to the death between Elvira and me. Don't you realize that?

CHARLES: Melodramatic hysteria.

RUTH: It isn't melodramatic hysteria—it's true. Can't you see?

CHARLES: No, I can't. You're imagining things—jealousy causes people to have the most curious delusions.

RUTH: I am making every effort not to lose my temper with you, Charles, but I must say you are making it increasingly difficult for me.

CHARLES: All this talk of battles and duels—

RUTH: She came here with one purpose and one purpose only—and if you can't see it you're a bigger fool than I thought you.

CHARLES: What purpose could she have had beyond a natural desire to see me again? After all, you must remember that she was extremely attached to me, poor child.

RUTH: Her purpose is perfectly obvious. It is to get you to herself forever.

CHARLES: That's absurd—how could she?

RUTH: By killing you off of course.

CHARLES: Killing me off? You're mad!

RUTH: Why do you suppose Edith fell down the stairs and nearly cracked her skull?

CHARLES: What's Edith got to do with it?

RUTH: Because the whole of the top stair was covered with axle grease. Cook discovered it afterwards.

CHARLES: You're making this up, Ruth—

RUTH: I'm not. I swear I'm not. Why do you suppose when

you were lopping that dead branch off the pear tree that the ladder broke? Because it had been practically sawn through on both sides.

CHARLES: But why should she want to kill me? I could understand her wanting to kill you, but why me?

RUTH: If you were dead, it would be her final triumph over me. She'd have you with her forever on her damned astral plane and I'd be left high and dry. She's probably planning a sort of spiritual remarriage. I wouldn't put anything past her.

CHARLES [*rises. Really shocked*]:   Ruth!

RUTH: Don't you see now?

CHARLES [*walking about the room*]:   She couldn't be so sly, so wicked—she couldn't.

RUTH: Couldn't she just!

CHARLES: I grant you that as a character she was always rather light and irresponsible but I would never have believed her capable of low cunning—

RUTH: Perhaps the spirit world has deteriorated her.

CHARLES: Oh, Ruth!

RUTH: For heaven's sake stop looking like a wounded spaniel and concentrate—this is serious.

CHARLES: What are we to do?

RUTH: You're not to let her know that we suspect a thing— behave perfectly ordinarily—as though nothing had happened. I'm going to Madame Arcati immediately—I don't care how cross she is she's got to help us—even if she can't get rid of Elvira she must know some technical method of rendering her harmless. If a trance is necessary she shall go into a trance if I have to beat her into it. I'll be back in a half an hour—tell Elvira I've gone to see the Vicar—

CHARLES: This is appalling—

RUTH: Never mind about that—remember now, don't give yourself away by so much as a flick of an eyelid—

[ELVIRA *comes in from the garden.*

CHARLES: Look out—

RUTH: What?

CHARLES: I merely said it's a nice lookout.

ELVIRA: What's a nice lookout?

CHARLES: The weather, Elvira—the glass is going down and down and down—it's positively macabre.

ELVIRA: I find it difficult to believe that you and Ruth, at this particular moment, can't think of anything more interesting to talk about than the weather.

RUTH [*rises*]:   I can't stand this any more. I really can't.

CHARLES: Ruth dear—please—

ELVIRA: Has she broken out again?

RUTH: What did she say?

CHARLES: She asked if you had broken out again.

RUTH: How dare you talk like that, Elvira!

CHARLES: Now then, Ruth—

RUTH [*with dignity*]:   Charles and I were not talking about the weather, Elvira, as you so very shrewdly suspected. I should loathe you to think *that we had any secrets from you* and so I will explain exactly what we were talking about. I was trying to persuade him *not* to drive you into Folkestone this evening. It will be bad for his arm and you can perfectly easily wait until tomorrow. However, as he seems to be determined to place your wishes before mine in everything, I have nothing further to say. I'm sure I hope you both enjoy yourselves.

[*She goes out and slams the door.*

CHARLES: There now.

ELVIRA: Oh, Charles—have you been beastly to her?

CHARLES: No—Ruth doesn't like being thwarted any more than you do.

ELVIRA: She's a woman of sterling character. It's a pity she's so unforgiving.

CHARLES: As I told you before—I would rather not discuss Ruth with you—it makes me uncomfortable.

ELVIRA: I won't mention her again. Are you ready?

CHARLES: What for?

ELVIRA: To go to Folkestone of course.

CHARLES [*rises from pouffe*]:   I want a glass of sherry first.

ELVIRA: I don't believe you want to take me at all.

CHARLES: Of course I want to take you, but I still think it
would be more sensible to wait until tomorrow—it's a filthy
night.

ELVIRA [*crossly*]:   How familiar this is.

CHARLES: In what way familiar?

ELVIRA: All through our married life I only had to suggest
something for you immediately to start hedging me off—

CHARLES: I'm not hedging you off, I merely said—

ELVIRA: All right—all right—we'll spend another cosy, intimate
evening at home with Ruth sewing away at that hideous table
center and snapping at us like a terrier.

CHARLES: Ruth is perfectly aware that the table center is
hideous. It happens to be a birthday present for her mother—

ELVIRA: It's no use trying to defend Ruth's taste to me—it's
thoroughly artsy craftsy and you know it.

CHARLES: It is not artsy craftsy.

ELVIRA: She's ruined this room—look at those curtains and
that awful shawl on the piano—

CHARLES: Lady Mackinley sent it to us from Burma.

ELVIRA: Obviously because it had been sent to her from Bir-
mingham.

CHARLES: If you don't behave yourself I shan't take you into
Folkestone ever.

ELVIRA [*coaxingly*]:   Please, Charles—don't be elderly and grand
with me! Please let's go now.

CHARLES: Not until I've had my sherry.

ELVIRA: You are tiresome, darling—I've been waiting about
for hours—

CHARLES: A few more minutes won't make any difference then.
[*He pours himself out some sherry.*

ELVIRA [*petulantly, flinging herself into a chair*]:   Oh, very well.

CHARLES: Besides, the car won't be back for a half an hour at
least.

ELVIRA [*sharply*]:   What do you mean?

CHARLES [*sipping his sherry nonchalantly*]:   Ruth's taken it—
she had to go and see the Vicar—

ELVIRA [*jumping up—in extreme agitation*]:   What!!

CHARLES: What on earth's the matter?

ELVIRA: You say *Ruth's* taken the car?

CHARLES: Yes—to go and see the Vicar—but she won't be long.

ELVIRA [*wildly*]:   O, my God! O, my God!

CHARLES: Elvira!—

ELVIRA: Stop her! You must stop her at once—

CHARLES: Why—what for?—

ELVIRA [*jumping up and down*]:   Stop her—go out and stop her immediately!

CHARLES: It's too late now—she's gone already.

ELVIRA [*backs away towards window*]:   Oh! Oh! Oh! Oh!!!

CHARLES: What are you going on like this for? What have you done?

ELVIRA [*frightened*]:   Done?—I haven't done anything—

CHARLES: Elvira—you're lying—

ELVIRA [*backing away from him*]:   I'm not lying. What is there to lie about?

CHARLES: What are you in such a state for?

ELVIRA [*almost hysterical*]:   I'm not in a state—I don't know what you mean—

CHARLES: You've done something dreadful—

ELVIRA [*backs away*]:   Don't look at me like that, Charles— I haven't—I swear I haven't—

CHARLES [*striking his forehead*]:   My God, the car!

ELVIRA: No, Charles—no—

CHARLES: Ruth was right—you did want to kill me—you've done something to the car—

ELVIRA [*howling like a banshee*]:   Oh—oh—oh—oh!—

CHARLES: What did you do—answer me?

[*At this moment the telephone rings.* CHARLES *stops dead; then with slow steps goes to it.*

CHARLES [*at telephone*]:   Hallo—hallo—yes, speaking—I see— the bridge at the bottom of the hill—thank you. No, I'll come at once—

[*He slowly puts back the receiver. As he does so the door bursts open.*

ELVIRA [*obviously retreating from someone*]:   Well, of all the filthy, low-down tricks—[*She shields her head with her hands and screams*] Ow—stop it—Ruth—let go—

[*She runs out of the room and slams the door. It opens again immediately and slams again.* CHARLES *stares, aghast.*

CURTAIN

ACT THREE

SCENE I

The time is evening a few days later.

CHARLES *is standing before the fire drinking his after-dinner coffee. He is in deep mourning. He finishes his coffee, puts the cup down on the mantlepiece, lights a cigarette and settles himself comfortably in an armchair. He adjusts a reading lamp and with a sigh of well-being opens a novel and begins to read it.*

There is a ring at the front doorbell. With an exclamation of annoyance he puts down the book, gets up and goes out into the hall. After a moment or so MADAME ARCATI *comes in.* CHARLES *follows her and shuts the door.* MADAME ARCATI *is wearing the strange, rather barbaric evening clothes that she wore in Act One.*

MADAME ARCATI: I hope you will not consider this an intrusion, Mr. Condomine.

CHARLES: Not at all—please sit down, won't you?

MADAME ARCATI: Thank you.

[*She does so.*

CHARLES: Would you like some coffee—or a liqueur?

MADAME ARCATI: No, thank you. I had to come, Mr. Condomine.

CHARLES [*politely*]: Yes?

MADAME ARCATI: I felt a tremendous urge—like a rushing wind, and so I hopped on my bike and here I am.

CHARLES: It was very kind of you.

MADAME ARCATI: No, no, no—not kind at all—it was my duty—I know it strongly.

CHARLES: Duty?

MADAME ARCATI: I reproach myself bitterly, you know.

CHARLES: Please don't—there is no necessity for that.
[*Sits in armchair.*

MADAME ARCATI: I allowed myself to get into a huff the other
day with your late wife. I rode all the way home in the grip
of temper, Mr. Condomine—I have regretted it ever since.

CHARLES: My dear Madame Arcati . . .

MADAME ARCATI [*holding up her hand*]:   Please let me go on.
Mine is the shame, mine is the blame—I shall never forgive
myself. Had I not been so impetuous—had I listened to the
cool voice of reason—much might have been averted . . .

CHARLES: You told my wife distinctly that you were unable
to help her—you were perfectly honest. Over and above the
original unfortunate mistake I see no reason for you to reproach yourself.

MADAME ARCATI: I threw up the sponge—in a moment of
crisis I threw up the sponge instead of throwing down the
gauntlet . . .

CHARLES: Whatever you threw, Madame Arcati, I very much
fear nothing could have been done—it seems that circumstances have been a little too strong for all of us.

MADAME ARCATI: I cannot bring myself to admit defeat so
easily—it is gall and wormwood to me—I could have at least
concentrated—made an effort.

CHARLES: Never mind.

MADAME ARCATI: I do mind. I cannot help it. I mind with
every fiber of my being. I have been thinking very carefully.
I have also been reading up a good deal during the last few
dreadful days . . . I gather that we are alone?

CHARLES [*looking around*]:   My first wife is not in the room,
she is upstairs lying down, the funeral exhausted her. I imagine
that my second wife is with her but of course I have no way
of knowing for certain.

MADAME ARCATI: You have remarked no difference in the tex-
ture of your first wife since the accident?

CHARLES: No, she seems much as usual, a little under the
weather perhaps, a trifle low-spirited, but that's all.

MADAME ARCATI: Well, that washes that out.

CHARLES: I'm afraid I don't understand.

MADAME ARCATI: Just a little theory I had. In the nineteenth
  century there was a pretty widespread belief that a ghost who
  participated in the death of a human being disintegrated
  automatically—

CHARLES: How do you know that Elvira was in any way responsible for Ruth's death?

MADAME ARCATI: Elvira—such a pretty name—it has a definite
  lilt to it, hasn't it? [*She hums for a moment. Singing the
  Elvi-i-ira*] Elvira—Elvi-ira . . .

CHARLES [*rather agitated*]:   You haven't answered my question.
  How did you know?

MADAME ARCATI: It came to me last night, Mr. Condomine—
  it came to me in a blinding flash—I had just finished my
  Ovaltine and turned the light out when I suddenly started
  up in bed with a loud cry—"Great Scott. I've got it!" I said—
  after that I began to put two and two together. At three in
  the morning—with my brain fairly seething—I went to work
  on my crystal for a little but it wasn't very satisfactory—
  cloudy, you know—

CHARLES [*moving about uneasily*]:   I would be very much
  obliged if you would keep any theories you have regarding
  my wife's death to yourself, Madame Arcati . . .

MADAME ARCATI: My one desire is to help you. I feel I have
  been dreadfully remiss over the whole affair—not only remiss
  but untidy.

CHARLES: I am afraid there is nothing whatever to be done.

MADAME ARCATI [*triumphantly*]:   But there is—there is! [*She
  produces a piece of paper from her bag and brandishes it*]
  I have found a formula—here it is! I copied it out of Ed-
  mondson's Witchcraft and Its Byways.

CHARLES [*irritably*]:   What the hell are you talking about?

MADAME ARCATI [*rises*]:   Pluck up your heart, Mr. Condomine
  . . . all is not lost!

CHARLE [*rises*]:   Now look here, Madame Arcati—

MADAME ARCATI: You are still anxious to dematerialize your
  first wife, I suppose?

CHARLES [*in a lower voice, with a cautious look towards the*

door]:   Of course I am—I'm perfectly furious with her, but—
MADAME ARCATI: But what?
CHARLES: Well—she's been very upset for the last few days—
you see apart from me being angry with her which she always hated even when she was alive, Ruth, my second wife,
has hardly left her side for a moment—you must see that she's
been having a pretty bad time what with one thing and another . . .
MADAME ARCATI: Your delicacy of feeling does you credit but
I must say, if you will forgive my bluntness, that you are a
damned fool, Mr. Condomine.
CHARLES [*stiffly*]:   You are at liberty to think whatever you
please.
MADAME ARCATI: Now, now, now—don't get on your high
horse—there's no sense in that, is there? I have a formula
here that I think will be able to get rid of her without hurting her feelings in the least. It's extremely simple and requires
nothing more than complete concentration from you and
minor trance from me—I may even be able to manage it without lying down.
CHARLES: Honestly I would rather—
[*At this moment the door opens and* ELVIRA *enters, coming
quickly into the room. She is obviously very upset.*
ELVIRA: Charles—
CHARLES: What on earth's the matter?
ELVIRA [*seeing* MADAME ARCATI]:   Oh! What's she doing here?
CHARLES: She came to offer me her condolences.
ELVIRA: They should have been congratulations.
CHARLES: Please don't say things like that, Elvira—it is in the
worst possible taste. Madame Arcati—allow me to introduce
my first wife Elvira—
MADAME ARCATI: How do you do?
ELVIRA: What does she want, Charles? Send her away—
[*She walks about the room.*
MADAME ARCATI: In what part of the room is she at the
moment?
CHARLES: She's moving about rather rapidly. I'll tell you when
and where she settles.

ELVIRA: She's the one who got me here in the first place, isn't she?

CHARLES: Yes.

ELVIRA: Well, please tell her to get me away again as soon as possible—I can't stand this house another minute.

CHARLES: Really, Elvira—I'm surprised at you.

ELVIRA [*nearly in tears*]:   I don't care how surprised you are—I want to go home—I'm sick of the whole thing.

CHARLES: Don't be childish, Elvira.

ELVIRA: I'm not being childish—I mean it.

MADAME ARCATI [*sniffing*]:   Very interesting—very interesting—I smell protoplasm strongly!

ELVIRA: What a disgusting thing to say.

MADAME ARCATI [*very excited*]:   Where is she now?

CHARLES: Here—close to me.

MADAME ARCATI [*mystically—stretching out her hands*]:   Are you happy, my dear—?

ELVIRA [*stamping her foot*]:   Tell the silly old bitch to mind her own business.

MADAME ARCATI [*in a singsong voice*]:   Was the journey difficult? Are you weary?

ELVIRA: She's dotty.

CHARLES: Just a moment, Madame Arcati . . .

MADAME ARCATI [*with her eyes shut*]:   This is wonderful—wonderful—

ELVIRA: For God's sake tell her to go into the other room, Charles. I've got to talk to you.

CHARLES: Madame Arcati . . .

MADAME ARCATI: Just a moment. I almost have contact—I can sense the vibrations—this is magnificent . . .

CHARLES: Go on, Elvira—don't be a spoilsport—give her a bit of encouragement.

ELVIRA: If you'll promise to get her into the other room.

CHARLES: All right.

[ELVIRA *goes up to* MADAME ARCATI *and blows gently into her ear*.

MADAME ARCATI [*jumping*]:   Yes, yes—again—again—

ELVIRA [*blowing in the other ear behind* MADAME ARCATI]: How's that?

MADAME ARCATI [*clasping and unclasping her hands in a frenzy of excitement*]: This is first rate—it really is first rate. Absolutely stunning!

CHARLES: I'm so glad you're pleased.

ELVIRA: Please get rid of her. Ruth will be in in a minute.

CHARLES: Madame Arcati, would you think it most frightfully rude if I asked you to go into the dining room for a moment? My first wife wishes to speak to me alone.

MADAME ARCATI: Oh, must I? It's so lovely being actually in the room with her.

CHARLES: Only for a few minutes—I promise she'll be here when you come back.

MADAME ARCATI: Very well. Hand me my bag, will you?—It's on the sofa.

ELVIRA [*picking it up and handing it to her*]: Here you are.

MADAME ARCATI [*taking it and blowing her a kiss*]: Oh, you darling—you little darling.

[MADAME ARCATI, *humming ecstatically, goes into the dining room and shuts the door.*

ELVIRA: How good is she really?

CHARLES: I don't know.

ELVIRA: Do you think she really could get me back again?

CHARLES: But my dear child . . .

ELVIRA: And don't call me your dear child—it's smug and supercilious.

CHARLES: There's no need to be rude.

ELVIRA [*turning away*]: The whole thing's been a failure—a miserable, dreary failure—and oh! what *high hopes* I started out with.

CHARLES: You can't expect much sympathy from me, you know. I am perfectly aware that your highest hope was to murder me.

ELVIRA: Don't put it like that, it sounds so beastly.

CHARLES: It is beastly. It's one of the beastliest ideas I've ever heard.

ELVIRA: There was a time when you'd have welcomed the chance of being with me forever.

CHARLES: Your behavior has shocked me immeasurably, Elvira, I had no idea you were so unscrupulous.

ELVIRA [*bursting into tears*]: Oh, Charles.

CHARLES: Stop crying.

ELVIRA: They're only ghost tears—they don't mean anything really—but they're very painful.

CHARLES: You've brought all this on yourself, you know.

[*Sits on sofa.*

ELVIRA: That's right—rub it in. Anyhow, it was only because I loved you—the silliest thing I ever did in my whole life was to love you—you were always unworthy of me.

CHARLES: That remark comes perilously near impertinence, Elvira.

ELVIRA: I sat there, on the other side, just longing for you day after day. I did really—all through your affair with that brassy-looking woman in the South of France I went on loving you and thinking truly of you—then you married Ruth and even then I forgave you and tried to understand because all the time I believed deep inside that you really loved me best . . . that's why I put myself down for a return visit and had to fill in all those forms and wait about in draughty passages for hours—if only you'd died before you met Ruth everything might have been all right—she's absolutely ruined you—I hadn't been in the house a day before I realized that. Your books aren't a quarter as good as they used to be either.

CHARLES [*incensed. Rises*]: That is entirely untrue . . . Ruth helped me and encouraged me with my work which is a damned sight more than you ever did.

ELVIRA: That's probably what's wrong with it.

CHARLES: All you ever thought of was going to parties and enjoying yourself.

ELVIRA: Why shouldn't I have fun? I died young, didn't I?

CHARLES: You needn't have died at all if you hadn't been idiotic enough to go out on the river with Guy Henderson and get soaked to the skin—

ELVIRA: So we're back at Guy Henderson again, are we?

CHARLES: You behaved abominably over Guy Henderson and it's no use pretending that you didn't.

ELVIRA [*sits on arm of chair*]: Guy adored me—and anyhow he was very attractive.

CHARLES: You told me distinctly that he didn't attract you in the least.

ELVIRA: You'd have gone through the roof if I'd told you that he did.

CHARLES: Did you have an affair with Guy Henderson?

ELVIRA: I would rather not discuss it if you don't mind.

CHARLES: Answer me—did you or didn't you?

ELVIRA: Of course I didn't.

CHARLES: You let him kiss you though, didn't you?

ELVIRA: How could I stop him? He was bigger than I was.

CHARLES [*furiously*]: And you swore to me—

ELVIRA: Of course I did. You were always making scenes over nothing at all.

CHARLES: Nothing at all.

ELVIRA: You never loved me a bit really—it was only your beastly vanity.

CHARLES: You seriously believe that it was only vanity that upset me when you went out in the punt with Guy Henderson?

ELVIRA: It was not a punt—it was a little launch.

CHARLES: I don't care if it was a three-masted schooner, you had no right to go!

ELVIRA: You seem to forget *why* I went! You seem to forget that you had spent the entire evening making sheep's eyes at that overblown-looking harridan with the false pearls.

CHARLES: A woman in Cynthia Cheviot's position would hardly wear false pearls.

ELVIRA: They were practically all she was wearing.

CHARLES: I am pained to observe that seven years in the echoing vaults of eternity have in no way impaired your native vulgarity.

ELVIRA: That was the remark of a pompous ass.

CHARLES: There is nothing to be gained by continuing this discussion.

ELVIRA: You always used to say that when you were thoroughly worsted.

CHARLES: On looking back on our married years, Elvira, I see now, with horrid clarity, that they were nothing but a mockery.

ELVIRA: You invite mockery, Charles—it's something to do with your personality I think, a certain seedy grandeur.

CHARLES: Once and for all, Elvira—

ELVIRA: You never suspected it but I laughed at you steadily from the altar to the grave—all your ridiculous petty jealousies and your fussings and fumings—

CHARLES: You were feckless and irresponsible and morally unstable—I realized that before we left Budleigh Salterton.

ELVIRA: Nobody but a monumental bore would have thought of having a honeymoon at Budleigh Salterton.

CHARLES: What's the matter with Budleigh Salterton?

ELVIRA: I was an eager young bride, Charles—I wanted glamor and music and romance—all I got was potted palms, seven hours of every day on a damp golf course and a three-piece orchestra playing "Merrie England."

CHARLES: It's a pity you didn't tell me so at the time.

ELVIRA: I did—but you wouldn't listen—that's why I went out on the moors that day with Captain Bracegirdle. I was desperate.

CHARLES: You swore to me that you'd gone over to see your aunt in Exmouth!

ELVIRA: It was the moors.

CHARLES: With Captain Bracegirdle?

ELVIRA: With Captain Bracegirdle.

CHARLES [furiously]:   I might have known it—what a fool I was—what a blind fool! Did he make love to you?

ELVIRA [sucking her finger and regarding it thoughtfully]:   Of course.

CHARLES: Oh, Elvira!

ELVIRA: Only very discreetly—he was in the cavalry, you know—

CHARLES: Well, all I can say is that I'm well rid of you.

ELVIRA: Unfortunately you're not.

CHARLES: Oh yes, I am—you're dead and Ruth's dead—I shall sell this house lock, stock and barrel and go away.

ELVIRA: I shall follow you.

CHARLES: I shall go a long way away—I shall go to South America—you'll hate that, you were always a bad traveller.

ELVIRA [*at piano*]:   That can't be helped—I shall have to follow you—you called me back.

CHARLES: I did *not* call you back!

ELVIRA: Well, somebody did—and it's hardly likely to have been Ruth.

CHARLES: Nothing in the world was further from my thoughts.

ELVIRA: You were talking about me before dinner that evening.

CHARLES: I might just as easily have been talking about Joan of Arc but that wouldn't necessarily mean that I wanted her to come and live with me.

ELVIRA: As a matter of fact she's rather fun.

CHARLES: Stick to the point.

ELVIRA: When I think of what might have happened if I'd succeeded in getting you to the other world after all—it makes me shudder, it does honestly . . . it would be nothing but bickering and squabbling forever and ever and ever . . . I swear I'll be better off with Ruth—at least she'll find her own set and not get in my way.

CHARLES: So I get in your way, do I?

ELVIRA: Only because I was idiotic enough to imagine that you loved me, and I sort of felt sorry for you.

CHARLES: I'm sick of these insults—please go away.

ELVIRA: There's nothing I should like better—I've always believed in cutting my losses. That's why I died.

CHARLES [*rises*]:   Of all the brazen sophistry—

ELVIRA: Call that old girl in again—set her to work—I won't tolerate this any longer—I want to go home.

[*She starts to cry.*

CHARLES: For heaven's sake don't snivel.

ELVIRA [*stamping her foot*]:   Call her in—she's got to get me out of this.

CHARLES [*going to the dining-room door*]:   I quite agree—and

the sooner the better. [*He opens the door*] Madame Arcati—
would you please come in now?

[MADAME ARCATI *comes in eagerly.*

MADAME ARCATI: Is the darling still here?

CHARLES [*grimly*]:   Yes, she is.

MADAME ARCATI: Where—tell me where?

CHARLES: Over by the piano—blowing her nose.

MADAME ARCATI [*approaching the piano*]:   My dear—oh, my
dear—

ELVIRA: Stop her fawning on me, Charles, or I shall break
something.

CHARLES: Elvira and I have discussed the whole situation,
Madame Arcati, and she wishes to go home immediately.

MADAME ARCATI: Home?

CHARLES: Wherever she came from.

MADAME ARCATI: You don't think she would like to stay a few
days longer—while I try to get things a little more organized?

ELVIRA: No—no—I want to go now.

MADAME ARCATI: I could come and be here with her—I could
bring my crystal—

ELVIRA: God forbid!

CHARLES: We are both agreed that she must go as soon as possible. Please strain every nerve, Madame Arcati—make every
effort—you said something about a formula—what is it?

MADAME ARCATI [*reluctantly*]:   Well—if you insist.

CHARLES: I most emphatically do insist.

ELVIRA [*wailing*]:   Oh, Charles . . .

CHARLES: Shut up.

MADAME ARCATI: I can't guarantee anything, you know—I'll
do my best but it may not work.

CHARLES: What is the formula?

MADAME ARCATI: Nothing more than a little verse really—it
fell into disuse after the seventeenth century—I shall need
some pepper and salt—

CHARLES: There's some pepper and salt in the dining room—
I'll get it.

[*He goes.*

MADAME ARCATI: We ought of course to have some Shepherd's

Wort and a frog or two, but I think I can manage without. You won't be frightened, dear, will you? It's absolutely painless.

CHARLES [*coming back with the cruet*]:   Will this be enough?

MADAME ARCATI: Oh yes—I only need a little—put it on the table please. Now then, let me see—[*She fumbles in her bag for the paper and her glasses*] Ah yes—[*To* CHARLES] Sprinkle it, will you—just a soupçon—there, right in the middle— [CHARLES *does so.*

ELVIRA: This is going to be a flop—I can tell you that here and now.

MADAME ARCATI: Now a few snapdragons out of that vase, there's a good chap.

ELVIRA [*contemptuously*]:   Merlin does all this sort of thing at parties and bores us all stiff with it, only he always uses blackthorn and a great deal of whimsy!

CHARLES: Here you are.

MADAME ARCATI: Now then—the gramophone—in the old days of course they used a zither or reed pipes—[*She goes to the gramophone*] We'd better have the same record we had before, I think.

ELVIRA: I'll get it.

[*She takes out the record and puts it on the gramophone.*

MADAME ARCATI [*watching, fascinated*]:   Oh, if only that Mr. Emsworth of the Psychical Research Society could see this— he'd have a fit, he would really! Don't start it yet, dear. Now then—[CHARLES *gets piano chair and brings it down to table*] Sit down, please, Mr. Condomine, rest your hands on the table but don't put your fingers in the pepper—I shall turn out the lights myself. Oh, shucks, I'd nearly forgotten— [*She goes to the table and makes designs in the sprinkled pepper and salt with her forefinger*] One triangle—[*She consults the paper*] One half circle and one little dot—there!

ELVIRA: This is waste of time—she's a complete fake.

CHARLES: Anything's worth trying.

ELVIRA: I'm as eager for it to succeed as you are—don't make any mistake about that. But I'll lay you ten to one it's a dead failure.

MADAME ARCATI: Now, if your wife would be kind enough to lie down on the sofa—

CHARLES: Go on, Elvira.

ELVIRA [*lies down on sofa*]:   This is sheer nonsense—don't blame me if I get the giggles.

CHARLES: Concentrate—think of nothing.

MADAME ARCATI: That's right—quite right—hands at the sides —legs extended—breathe steadily—one two—one two—one two—is she comfortable?

CHARLES: Are you comfortable, Elvira?

ELVIRA: No.

CHARLES: She's quite comfortable.

MADAME ARCATI: I shall join you in a moment, Mr. Condomine—I may have to go into a slight trance but if I do, pay no attention—Now first the music and away we go!

[MADAME ARCATI *turns on the gramophone and stands quite still by the side of it with her hands behind her head for a little— then suddenly, with great swiftness, she runs to the door and switches out the lights. Her form can dimly be discerned moving about in the darkness.* CHARLES *gives a loud sneeze.*]

ELVIRA [*giggling*]:   Oh, dear—it's the pepper.

CHARLES: Damn!

MADAME ARCATI: Hold on to yourself—concentrate—[MADAME ARCATI *recites in a singsong voice*]

> "Ghostly spectre—ghoul or fiend
> Never more be thou convened
> Shepherd's Wort and Holy Rite
> Banish thee into the night."

ELVIRA: What a disagreeable little verse.

CHARLES: Be quiet, Elvira.

MADAME ARCATI: *Shhh!* [*There is silence*] Is there anyone there? . . . Is there anyone there?—one rap for yes—two raps for no. Is there anyone there? . . . [*The table gives a loud bump*] Aha! Good stuff! Is it Daphne? . . . [*The table gives another bump*] I'm sorry to bother you, dear, but Mrs. Condomine wants to return. [*The table bumps several times very quickly*] Now then, Daphne . . . Did you hear what I said? [*After a pause the table gives one bump*] Can you help

us? . . . [*There is another pause, then the table begins to
bump violently without stopping*] Hold tight, Mr. Condomine—it's trying to break away. Oh! Oh! Oh—
[*The table falls over with a crash.*

CHARLES: What's the matter, Madame Arcati? Are you hurt?

MADAME ARCATI [*wailing*]:   Oh! Oh! Oh—

CHARLES [*turns on lights*]:   What on earth's happening?
[MADAME ARCATI *is lying on the floor with the table upside
down on her back.* CHARLES *hurriedly lifts it off. Shaking her*]
Are you hurt, Madame Arcati?

ELVIRA: She's in one of her damned trances again and I'm here
as much as ever I was.

CHARLES [*shaking* MADAME ARCATI]:   For God's sake, wake up.

MADAME ARCATI [*moaning*]:   Oh! Oh! Oh—

ELVIRA: Leave her alone—she's having a whale of a time. If I
ever do get back I'll strangle that bloody little Daphne . . .

CHARLES: Wake up!

MADAME ARCATI [*sitting up suddenly*]:   What happened?

CHARLES: Nothing—nothing at all.

MADAME ARCATI [*rising and dusting herself*]:   Oh yes, it did—
I know something happened.

CHARLES: You fell over—that's all that happened.

MADAME ARCATI: Is she still here?

CHARLES: Of course she is.

MADAME ARCATI: Something must have gone wrong.

ELVIRA: Make her do it properly. I'm sick of being messed
about like this.

CHARLES: She's doing her best. Be quiet, Elvira.

MADAME ARCATI: Something happened—I sensed it in my
trance—I felt it—it shivered through me.

[*Suddenly the window curtains blow out almost straight and*
RUTH *walks into the room. She is still wearing the brightly
colored clothes in which we last saw her but now they are entirely grey. So is her hair and her skin.*

RUTH: Once and for all, Charles, what the hell does this
mean?

The lights fade

SCENE II

When the lights go up again several hours have elapsed. The whole room is in slight disarray. There are birch branches and evergreens laid on the floor in front of the doors and crossed birch branches pinned rather untidily onto the curtains. The furniture has been moved about a bit. On the bridge table there is a pile of playing cards, MADAME ARCATI'S *crystal and a Ouija board. Also a plate of sandwiches and two empty beer mugs.*

MADAME ARCATI *is stretched out on the sofa with her eyes shut.* ELVIRA *is seated at the bridge table looking despondently at the debris.* RUTH *is by the fireplace.* CHARLES *is walking irritably about the room.*

RUTH: Well—we've done all we can—I must say I couldn't be more exhausted.

ELVIRA: It will be daylight soon.

[*The clock strikes five, very slowly.*

RUTH: That clock's always irritated me—it strikes far too slowly.

CHARLES: It was a wedding present from Uncle Walter.

RUTH: Whose Uncle Walter?

CHARLES: Elvira's.

RUTH: Well, all I can say is he might have chosen something a little more decorative.

ELVIRA: If that really were all you could say, Ruth, I'm sure it would be a great comfort to us all.

RUTH [*grandly*]:   You can be as rude as you like, Elvira, I don't mind a bit—as a matter of fact I should be extremely surprised if you weren't.

ELVIRA [*truculently*]:   Why?

RUTH: The reply to that is really too obvious.

CHARLES: I wish you two would stop bickering for one minute.

RUTH: This is quite definitely one of the most frustrating nights I have ever spent.

ELVIRA: The reply to that is pretty obvious, too.

RUTH: I'm sure I don't know what you mean.

ELVIRA: Skip it.

RUTH: Now listen to me, Elvira. If you and I have got to stay together indefinitely in this house—and it looks unpleasantly —[*Turns to* MADAME ARCATI]—likely—we had better come to some sort of an arrangement.

ELVIRA: What sort of an arrangement?

CHARLES: You're *not* going to stay indefinitely in this house.

RUTH: With you then—we shall have to be with you.

CHARLES: I don't see why—why don't you take a cottage somewhere?

RUTH: You called us back.

CHARLES: I've already explained until I'm black in the face that I did nothing of the sort.

RUTH: Madame Arcati said you did.

CHARLES: Madame Arcati's a muddling old fool.

ELVIRA: I could have told you that in the first place.

RUTH: I think you're behaving very shabbily, Charles.

CHARLES: I don't see what I've done.

RUTH: We have all agreed that as Elvira and I are dead that it would be both right and proper for us to dematerialize again as soon as possible. That, I admit. We have allowed ourselves to be subjected to the most humiliating hocus-pocus for hours and hours without complaining—

CHARLES: Without complaining?

RUTH: We've stood up—we've lain down—we've concentrated. We've sat interminably while that tiresome old woman recited extremely unflattering verses at us. We've endured five séances—we've watched her fling herself in and out of trances until we're dizzy and at the end of it all we find ourselves exactly where we were at the beginning . . .

CHARLES: Well, it's not my fault.

RUTH: Be that as it may, the least you could do is to admit failure gracefully and try and make the best of it—your manners are boorish to a degree.

CHARLES: I'm just as exhausted as you are. I've had to do all the damned table tapping, remember.

RUTH: If she can't get us back, she can't and that's that. We shall have to think of something else.

CHARLES: She *must* get you back—anything else is unthinkable.

ELVIRA: There's gratitude for you!

CHARLES: Gratitude?

ELVIRA: Yes, for all the years we've both devoted to you—you ought to be ashamed.

CHARLES: What about all the years I've devoted to you?

ELVIRA: Nonsense—we've waited on you hand and foot—haven't we, Ruth? You're exceedingly selfish and always were.

CHARLES: In that case I fail to see why you were both so anxious to get back to me.

RUTH: You called us back. And you've done nothing but try to get rid of us ever since we came—hasn't he, Elvira?

ELVIRA: He certainly has.

RUTH: And now, owing to your idiotic inefficiency, we find ourselves in the most mortifying position—we're neither fish, flesh nor fowl nor whatever it is.

ELVIRA: Good red herring.

RUTH: It can't be.

CHARLES: Well, why don't you do something about it? Why don't you go back on your own?

RUTH: We can't—you know perfectly well we can't.

CHARLES: Isn't there anybody on the other side who can help?

RUTH: How do I know? I've only been there a few days . . . ask Elvira.

ELVIRA: I've already told you, that's no good—if we got Cagliostro, Mesmer, Merlin, Gil de Retz and the Black Douglas in a row they couldn't do a thing—the impetus has got to come from here. . . . Perhaps darling Charles doesn't want us to go quite enough.

CHARLES: I certainly do.

ELVIRA: Well, you must have a very weak will then. I always suspected it.

RUTH: It's no use arguing any more—wake up Madame Arcati.

ELVIRA: Oh, not another séance—please, not another séance!

CHARLES [*loudly—bending over* MADAME ARCATI]:   Please wake up, Madame Arcati . . .

RUTH: Shake her.

CHARLES: It might upset her.

RUTH: I don't care if it kills her.

CHARLES: Please wake up, Madame Arcati . . .

MADAME ARCATI [*waking*]:   What time is it?

CHARLES: Ten past five!

MADAME ARCATI: What time did I go off?
[*She sits up.*

CHARLES: Over an hour ago.

MADAME ARCATI [*reaching for her bag*]:   Curious . . . very curious. Forgive me for a moment, I must just make a note of that for my diary. [*She takes a book out of her bag and scribbles in it*] Are they still here?

CHARLES: Yes.

MADAME ARCATI: How disappointing.

CHARLES: Have you any suggestions?

MADAME ARCATI [*rising briskly*]:   We mustn't give up hope. Chin up—never give in—that's my motto.

RUTH: This schoolgirl phraseology's driving me mad.

MADAME ARCATI: Now then . . .

CHARLES: Now then what?

MADAME ARCATI: What do you say we have another séance and really put our shoulders to the wheel?—Make it a real rouser!

ELVIRA: For God's sake not another séance.

MADAME ARCATI: I might be able to materialize a trumpet if I tried hard enough—better than nothing, you know—I feel as fit as a fiddle after my rest.

ELVIRA: I don't care if she materializes a whole symphony orchestra—I implore you not to let her have another séance.

CHARLES: Don't you think, Madame Arcati, that perhaps we've had enough séances? After all they haven't achieved much have they?

MADAME ARCATI: Rome wasn't built in a day, you know.

CHARLES: I know it wasn't, but . . .

MADAME ARCATI: Well then—cheer up—away with melancholy.

CHARLES: Now listen, Madame Arcati . . . before you go off into any further trances, I really think we ought to discuss the situation a little.

MADAME ARCATI: Good—an excellent idea—and while we're

doing it I shall have another of these delicious sandwiches—
I'm as hungry as a hunter.

CHARLES: Would you like some more beer?

MADAME ARCATI: No, thank you—better not.

CHARLES: Very well—I think I'll have a small whisky and soda.

MADAME ARCATI: Make it a double and enjoy yourself.

[CHARLES *goes to the drinks table and mixes himself a whisky and soda.*

RUTH: One day I intend to give myself the pleasure of telling Madame Arcati exactly what I think of her.

CHARLES: She's been doing her best.

MADAME ARCATI: Are the girls getting despondent?

CHARLES: I'm afraid they are *rather.*

MADAME ARCATI: We'll win through yet—don't be downhearted.

RUTH: If we're not very careful she'll materialize a hockey team.

MADAME ARCATI: Now then, Mr. Condomine—the discussion —fire away.

CHARLES: Well, my wives and I have been talking it over and they are both absolutely convinced that I somehow or other called them back.

MADAME ARCATI: Very natural.

CHARLES: I am equally convinced that I did not.

MADAME ARCATI: Love is a strong psychic force, Mr. Condomine—it can work untold miracles. A true love call can encompass the universe—

CHARLES [*hastily*]:   I'm sure it can, but I must confess to you frankly that, although my affection for both Elvira and Ruth is of the warmest, I cannot truthfully feel that it would come under the heading that you describe.

ELVIRA: I should just think not indeed.

MADAME ARCATI: You may not know your own strength, Mr. Condomine.

CHARLES [*firmly*]:   I did *not* call them back—either consciously or subconsciously.

MADAME ARCATI: But, Mr. Condomine . . .

CHARLES: That is my final word on the subject.

MADAME ARCATI: Neither of them could have appeared unless there had been somebody—a psychic subject—in the house, who wished for them . . .

CHARLES: Well, it wasn't me.

ELVIRA: Perhaps it was Doctor Bradman—I never knew he cared.

MADAME ARCATI: Are you sure?—Are you really sure?

CHARLES: Absolutely positive.

MADAME ARCATI [*snapping her fingers*]:   Great Scott, I believe we've been barking up the wrong tree!

CHARLES: How do you mean?

MADAME ARCATI: The Sudbury case!

CHARLES: I don't understand.

MADAME ARCATI: There's no reason why you should—it was before your day—I wonder—oh, I wonder . . .

CHARLES: What was the Sudbury case? I wish you'd explain.

MADAME ARCATI: It was the case that made me famous, Mr. Condomine—it was what you might describe in theatrical parlance as my first smash hit! I had letters from all over the world about it—especially India.

CHARLES: What did you do?

MADAME ARCATI: I dematerialized old Lady Sudbury after she'd been firmly entrenched in the private chapel for over seventeen years.

CHARLES [*rises*]:   How?—Can't you remember how?

MADAME ARCATI: Chance—a fluke—I happened on it by the merest coincidence.

CHARLES: What fluke—what was it?

MADAME ARCATI: Wait—all in good time. [*She begins to walk about the room*] Now let me see—who was in the house during our first séance?

CHARLES: Only the Bradmans, Ruth and me and yourself.

MADAME ARCATI: Ah, yes—yes—to be sure—but the Bradmans weren't here last night, were they?

CHARLES: No.

MADAME ARCATI: Quickly . . . my crystal—

CHARLES [*handing it to her*]:   Here . . .

MADAME ARCATI [*shaking it crossly*]:   Damn the thing, it's

cloudy again—[*She looks again*] Ah!—that's better—it's there
again—it's there again—I'm beginning to understand.

CHARLES: I wish I was. What's there again?

MADAME ARCATI: A bandage—a white bandage—hold on to a
white bandage . . .

CHARLES: I haven't got a white bandage.

MADAME ARCATI: Shhh!

[*She puts the crystal down and stands silent for a moment.*

ELVIRA: She's too good, you know—she ought to be in a circus.

[MADAME ARCATI *advances to the middle of the room and raises
her arms slowly—she begins to intone.*

MADAME ARCATI:

Be you in nook or cranny answer me
Do you in Still-room or closet answer me
Do you behind the panel, above the stairs
Beneath the eaves—waking or sleeping
Answer me!

That ought to do it or I'm a Dutchman.

CHARLES: Do what?

MADAME ARCATI: Hush—wait—

[*She picks up one of the birch branches and waves it solemnly
to and fro.*

RUTH: For God's sake don't let her throw any more of that gar-
lic about. It nearly made me sick last time.

CHARLES: Would you like the gramophone on or the lights out
or anything?

MADAME ARCATI: No, no—it's near—it's very near—

ELVIRA: If it's a ghost I shall scream.

RUTH: I hope it's nobody we know—I shall feel so silly.

[*Suddenly the door opens and* EDITH *comes into the room. She
is wearing a pink flannel dressing gown and bedroom slippers.
Her head is bandaged.*

EDITH: Did you ring, sir?

MADAME ARCATI: The bandage! The white bandage!

CHARLES: No, Edith.

EDITH: I'm sorry, sir—I could have sworn I heard the bell—
or somebody calling—I was asleep—I don't rightly know
which it was . . .

MADAME ARCATI: Come here, child.

EDITH: Oh!

[*She looks anxiously at* CHARLES.

CHARLES: Go on—go to Madame Arcati—it's quite all right.

MADAME ARCATI: Who do you see in this room, child?

EDITH: Oh, dear . . .

MADAME ARCATI: Answer please.

EDITH [*falteringly*]:   You; madame—

[*She stops.*

MADAME ARCATI: Go on.

EDITH: The Master.

MADAME ARCATI: Anyone else?

EDITH: Oh no, madame . . .

MADAME ARCATI [*inflexibly*]:   Look again.

EDITH [*imploringly, to* CHARLES]:   I don't understand, sir—I—

MADAME ARCATI: Come, child—don't beat about the bush—
look again.

[ELVIRA *begins to move about the room almost as though she
were being pulled.* EDITH *follows with her eyes.*

RUTH: Do concentrate, Elvira, and keep still.

ELVIRA: I can't . . .

MADAME ARCATI: Do you see anyone else now?

EDITH [*slyly*]:   Oh, no, madame.

MADAME ARCATI: She's lying.

EDITH: Oh, madame!

MADAME ARCATI: They always do.

CHARLES: They?

MADAME ARCATI [*sharply*]:   Where are they now?

EDITH: By the fireplace. Oh!

CHARLES: She can see them—do you mean she can see them?

MADAME ARCATI: Probably not very clearly—but enough—

EDITH [*bursting into tears*]:   Let me go—I haven't done nothing
nor seen nobody—let me go back to bed.

MADAME ARCATI: Give her a sandwich.

EDITH [*drawing away*]:   I don't want a sandwich. I want to go
back to bed . . .

CHARLES [*handing* EDITH *the plate*]:   Here, Edith.

MADAME ARCATI: Nonsense—a big healthy girl like you saying

no to a delicious sandwich—I never heard of such a thing—
sit down.

EDITH [*to* CHARLES]:   Please, sir, I . . .

CHARLES: Please do as Madame Arcati says, Edith.

EDITH [*sitting down and sniffing*]:   I haven't done nothing
wrong.

CHARLES: It's all right—nobody said you had.

RUTH: If she's been the cause of all this unpleasantness I'll
give her a week's notice tomorrow.

ELVIRA: You may not be here tomorrow—

MADAME ARCATI: Look at me, Edith. [EDITH *obediently does so*]
Cuckoo—cuckoo—cuckoo—

EDITH [*jumping*]:   Oh, dear—what's the matter with her? Is she
barmy?

MADAME ARCATI: Here, Edith—this is my finger—look—
[*She waggles it*] Have you ever seen such a long, long, long
finger? Look now it's on the right—now it's on the left—
backwards and forwards it goes—see—very quietly backwards
and forwards—tic-toc—tic—toc—tic-toc.

ELVIRA: The mouse ran up the clock.

RUTH: Be *quiet*—you'll ruin everything.

[MADAME ARCATI *whistles a little tune close to* EDITH's *face—
then she snaps her fingers.* EDITH *looks stolidly in front of her
without flinching.* MADAME ARCATI *stands back.*

MADAME ARCATI: Well—so far so good—she's off all right.

CHARLES: Off?

MADAME ARCATI: She's a Natural—just the same as the Sudbury case—it really is the most amusing coincidence. Now
then—would you ask your wives to stand close together please?

CHARLES: Where?

MADAME ARCATI: Over there by you.

CHARLES: Elvira—Ruth—

RUTH: I resent being ordered about like this.

ELVIRA: I don't like this at all—I don't like any of it—I feel
peculiar.

CHARLES: I'm afraid I must insist.

ELVIRA: It would serve you right if we flatly refused to do
anything at all.

MADAME ARCATI: Are you sorry for having been so mischievous, Edith?

EDITH [*cheerfully*]:   Oh yes, madame.

MADAME ARCATI: You know what you have to do now, don't you, Edith?

EDITH: Oh yes, madame.

RUTH: I believe it's going to work whatever it is. Oh, Charles.

CHARLES: Shhh!

RUTH: This is good-bye, Charles.

ELVIRA: Tell her to stop for a minute—there's something I want to say before I go.

CHARLES: You should have thought of that before—it's too late now.

ELVIRA: Of all the mean, ungracious—

RUTH: Charles, listen a moment . . .

MADAME ARCATI [*in a shrill voice*]:   Lights!

[MADAME ARCATI *rushes to the door and switches off the lights. In the dark* EDITH *is singing "Always" in a very high cockney voice.*

ELVIRA [*in the dark*]:   I saw Captain Bracegirdle again, Charles —several times—I went to the Four Hundred with him twice when you were in Nottingham. And I must say I couldn't have enjoyed it more.

RUTH: Don't think you're getting rid of us quite so easily, my dear—you may not be able to see us but we shall be here all right—I consider that you have behaved atrociously over the whole miserable business. And I should like to say here and now—

[*Her voice fades into a whisper and then disappears altogether.*

MADAME ARCATI [*exultantly*]:   Splendid! Hurrah! We've done it! That's quite enough singing for the moment, Edith.

CHARLES [*after a pause*]:   Shall I put on the lights?

MADAME ARCATI: No—I will.

[CHARLES *pulls the curtains and daylight floods into the room.* RUTH *and* ELVIRA *have disappeared.* EDITH *is still sitting on the chair.*

CHARLES: They've gone—they've really gone.

MADAME ARCATI: Yes—I think we've really pulled it off this time.

CHARLES: You'd better wake her up, hadn't you? She might bring them back again.

MADAME ARCATI [*clapping her hands in* EDITH's *face*]:   Wake up, child!

EDITH [*nearly jumping out of the chair*]:   Good 'eavens! Where am I?

CHARLES: It's all right, Edith—you can go back to bed now.

EDITH: Why, it's morning.

CHARLES: Yes—I know it is.

EDITH: But I *was* in bed—how did I get down 'ere?

CHARLES: I rang, Edith—I rang the bell and you answered it— didn't I, Madame Arcati?

EDITH: Did I drop off? Do you think it's my concussion again? Oh, dear!

CHARLES: Off you go, Edith, and thank you very much. [*He presses a pound note into her hand*] Thank you very much indeed.

EDITH: Oh, sir, whatever for? [*She looks at him in sudden horror*] Oh, sir!!

[*She bolts from the room.*

CHARLES [*surprised*]:   What on earth did she mean by that?

MADAME ARCATI: Golly, what a night! I'm ready to drop in my tracks.

CHARLES: Would you like to stay here?—there's the spare room, you know.

MADAME ARCATI: No, thank you—each to his own nest—I'll pedal home in a jiffy—it's only seven miles.

CHARLES: I'm deeply grateful to you, Madame Arcati. I don't know what arrangements you generally make but I trust you will send in your account in due course.

MADAME ARCATI: Good heavens, Mr. Condomine—it was a pleasure—I wouldn't dream of such a thing.

CHARLES: But really I feel that all those trances . . .

MADAME ARCATI: I enjoy them, Mr. Condomine, thoroughly. I always have since a child.

CHARLES: Perhaps you'd give me the pleasure of lunching with me one day soon?

MADAME ARCATI: When you come back—I should be delighted.

CHARLES: Come back?

MADAME ARCATI [*lowering her voice*]:   Take my advice, Mr. Condomine, and go away immediately.

CHARLES: But, Madame Arcati! You don't mean that . . . ?

MADAME ARCATI [*clearing her stuff from table*]:   This must be an unhappy house for you—there must be memories both grave and gay in every corner of it—also—

[*She pauses.*

CHARLES: Also what?

MADAME ARCATI [*thinking better of it*]:   There are more things in heaven and earth, Mr. Condomine. [*She places her finger to her lips*] Just go—pack your traps and go as soon as possible.

CHARLES [*also in lowered tones*]:   Do you mean that they may still be here?

MADAME ARCATI [*she nods and then nonchalantly whistles a little tune*]:   Quien sabe, as the Spanish say.

[*She collects her bag and her crystal.*

CHARLES [*looking furtively round the room*]:   I wonder—I wonder. I'll follow your advice, Madame Arcati. Thank you again.

MADAME ARCATI: Well, good-bye, Mr. Condomine—it's been fascinating—from first to last—fascinating. Do you mind if I take just one more sandwich to munch on my way home?

[*Comes down to table for sandwich.*

CHARLES: By all means.

[MADAME ARCATI *goes to the door.* CHARLES *follows her to see her safely out.*

MADAME ARCATI [*as they go*]:   Don't trouble—I can find my way. Cheerio once more and good hunting!

[CHARLES *watches her into the hall and then comes back into the room. He prowls about for a moment as though he were not sure that he was alone.*

CHARLES [*softly*]:   Ruth—Elvira—are you there? [*A pause*] Ruth—Elvira—I know damn well you're there—[*Another pause*] I just want to tell you that I'm going away so there's no point in your hanging about any longer—I'm going a long way away—somewhere where I don't believe you'll be able to follow me. In spite of what Elvira said I don't think spirits can travel over water. Is that quite clear, my darlings? You said in one of your more acid moments, Ruth, that I had been hag-ridden all my life! How right you were—but now I'm free, Ruth dear, not only of Mother and Elvira and Mrs. Winthrop-Lewellen, but free of you too, and I should like to take this farewell opportunity of saying I'm enjoying it immensely—[A *vase crashes into the fireplace*] Aha—I thought so—you were very silly, Elvira, to imagine that I didn't know all about you and Captain Bracegirdle—I did. But what you didn't know was that I was extremely attached to Paula Westlake at the time! [*The clock strikes sixteen viciously and very quickly*] I was reasonably faithful to you, Ruth, but I doubt if it would have lasted much longer—you were becoming increasingly domineering, you know, and there's nothing more off putting than that, is there? [A *large picture falls down with a crash*] Good-bye for the moment, my dears. I expect we are bound to meet again one day, but until we do I'm going to enjoy myself as I've never enjoyed myself before. You can break up the house as much as you like—I'm leaving it anyhow. Think kindly of me and send out good thoughts— [*The overmantel begins to shake and tremble as though someone were tugging at it*] Nice work, Elvira—persevere. Good-bye again—parting is such *sweet* sorrow!

[*He goes out of the room just as the overmantel crashes to the floor and the curtain pole comes tumbling down.*

CURTAIN

HAY FEVER

A Light Comedy in Three Acts

To
LORN LORAINE

Produced by the author at The Ambassadors' Theatre, London, June 8, 1925.

Original British Cast

JUDITH BLISS	Marie Tempest
DAVID BLISS	W. Graham Browne
SOREL BLISS	Helen Spencer
SIMON BLISS	Robert Andrews
MYRA ARUNDEL	Hilda Moore
RICHARD GREATHAM	Athole Stewart
JACKIE CORYTON	Ann Trevor
SANDY TYRELL	Patrick Susands
CLARA	Minnie Rayner

Produced by the Messrs. Shubert at the Maxine Elliott Theatre, New York, October 5, 1925.

Original American Cast

SOREL BLISS	Frieda Inescourt
SIMON BLISS	Gavin Muir
CLARA	Alice Belmore Cliffe
JUDITH BLISS	Laura Hope Crews
DAVID BLISS	Harry Davenport
SANDY TYRELL	Reginald Sheffield
MYRA ARUNDEL	Phyllis Joyce
RICHARD GREATHAM	George Thorpe
JACKIE CORYTON	Margot Lester

Staged by Noel Coward and Laura Hope Crews

CHARACTERS

JUDITH BLISS
DAVID BLISS
SOREL BLISS
SIMON BLISS
MYRA ARUNDEL
RICHARD GREATHAM
JACKIE CORYTON
SANDY TYRELL
CLARA

The action of the play takes place in the hall of the BLISSES' *house at Cookham, in June*

ACT I.   Saturday afternoon

ACT II.   Saturday evening

ACT III.   Sunday morning

16?

ACT ONE

Scene: The hall of DAVID BLISS'S *house is very comfortable and extremely untidy. There are several of* SIMON'S *cartoons scattered about the walls, masses of highly colored American and classical music strewn about the piano, and lots of flowers and comfortable furniture. A staircase ascends to a small balcony leading to the bedrooms,* DAVID'S *study and* SIMON'S *room. There is a door leading to the library down R. A service door above it under the stairs. There are French windows at back, and the front door on the L.*

When the curtain rises it is about three o'clock on a Saturday afternoon in June.

SIMON, *in an extremely dirty tennis shirt and baggy gray-flannel trousers, is crouched in the middle of the floor, cutting out squares from cartridge paper.*

SOREL, *more neatly dressed, is stretched on the sofa, reading a very violently bound volume of poems which has been sent to her by an aspiring friend.*

SOREL: Listen to this, Simon. [*She reads*] "Love's a Trollop stained with wine—Clawing at the breasts of Adolescence—Nuzzling, tearing, shrieking, beating—God, why were we fashioned so!"

[*She laughs.*

SIMON: The poor girl's potty.

SOREL: I wish she hadn't sent me the beastly book. I must say something nice about it.

SIMON: The binding's very dashing.

SOREL: She used to be such fun before she married that gloomy little man.

SIMON: She was always a fierce *poseuse*. It's so silly of people to try and cultivate the artistic temperament. *Au fond* she's just a normal, bouncing Englishwoman.

SOREL: You didn't shave this morning.

SIMON: I know I didn't, but I'm going to in a minute, when I've finished this.

SOREL: I sometimes wish we were more normal and bouncing, Simon.

SIMON: Why?

SOREL: I should like to be a fresh, open-air girl with a passion for games.

SIMON: Thank God you're not.

SOREL: It would be so soothing.

SIMON: Not in this house.

SOREL: Where's mother?

SIMON: In the garden, practicing.

SOREL: Practicing?

SIMON: She's learning the names of the flowers by heart.

SOREL: What's she up to?

SIMON: I don't know—Damn! that's crooked.

SOREL: I always distrust her when she becomes the Squire's lady.

SIMON: So do I.

SOREL: She's been at it hard all day—she tapped the barometer this morning.

SIMON: She's probably got a plan about impressing somebody.

SOREL [*taking a cigarette*]: I wonder who.

SIMON: Some dreary, infatuated young man will appear soon, I expect.

SOREL: Not today? You don't think she's asked anyone down today, do you?

SIMON: I don't know. Has father noticed anything?

SOREL: No; he's too immersed in work.

SIMON: Perhaps Clara will know.

SOREL: Yell for her.

SIMON [*calling*]: Clara! Clara! . . .

SOREL: Oh, Simon, I *do* hope she hasn't asked anyone down today.

SIMON: Why? Have you?

SOREL: Yes.

SIMON [*crossly*]: Why on earth didn't you tell me?

SOREL: I didn't think you'd care one way or another.

SIMON: Who is it?

SOREL: Richard Greatham.

SIMON: How exciting! I've never heard of him.

SOREL: I shouldn't flaunt your ignorance if I were you—it makes you look silly.

SIMON [*rising*]:   Well, that's done.

[*He rolls up the cartridge paper.*

SOREL: Everybody's heard of Richard Greatham.

SIMON [*amiably*]:   How lovely for them.

SOREL: He's a frightfully well-known diplomatist—I met him at the Mainwarings' dance.

SIMON: He'll need all his diplomacy here.

SOREL: I warned him not to expect good manners, but I hope you'll be as pleasant to him as you can.

SIMON [*gently*]:   I've never met any diplomatists, Sorel, but as a class I'm extremely prejudiced against them. They're so suave and polished and debonair.

SOREL: You could be a little more polished without losing caste.

SIMON: Will he have the papers with him?

SOREL: What papers?

SIMON [*vaguely*]:   Oh, any papers.

SOREL: I wish you'd confine your biting irony to your caricatures, Simon.

SIMON: And I wish you'd confine your girlish infatuations to London, and not force them on your defenseless family.

SOREL: I shall keep him out of your way as much as possible.

SIMON: Do, darling.

[*Enter* CLARA. *She is a hot, round, untidy little woman.*

SIMON: Clara, has mother asked anyone down this weekend?

CLARA: I don't know, dear. There isn't much food in the house, and Amy's got toothache.

SOREL: I've got some oil of cloves somewhere.

CLARA: She tried that, but it only burnt her tongue. The poor girl's been writhing about in the scullery like one o'clock.

SOREL: You haven't forgotten to put those flowers in the Japanese room?

SIMON: The Japanese room is essentially feminine, and entirely unsuited to the Pet of the Foreign Office.

SOREL: Shut up, Simon.

CLARA: The room looks lovely, dear—you needn't worry. Just like your mother's dressing room on a first night.

SIMON: How restful!

CLARA [to SOREL]:   Have you told her about your boy friend?

SOREL [pained]:   Not boy friend, Clara.

CLARA [going round, picking up things]:   Oh, well, whatever he is.

SIMON: I think Sorel's beginning to be ashamed of us all, Clara—I don't altogether blame her; we are very slapdash.

CLARA: Are you going to leave that picture in the guests' bathroom, dear? I don't know if it's quite the thing—lots of pink, naked women rolling about in a field.

SIMON [severely]:   Nudity can be very beautiful, Clara.

CLARA: Oh, can it! Perhaps being a dresser for so long 'as spoilt me eye for it.

[She goes out.

SIMON: Clara's looking tired. We ought to have more servants and not depend on her so much.

SOREL: You know we can never keep them. You're right about us being slapdash, Simon. I wish we weren't.

SIMON: Does it matter?

SOREL: It must, I think—to other people.

SIMON: It's not our fault—it's the way we've been brought up.

SOREL: Well, if we're clever enough to realize that, we ought to be clever enough to change ourselves.

SIMON: I'm not sure that I want to.

SOREL: We're so awfully bad-mannered.

SIMON: Not to people we like.

SOREL: The people we like put up with it because they like us.

SIMON: What do you mean, exactly, by bad manners? Lack of social tricks and small talk?

SOREL: We never attempt to look after people when they come here.

SIMON: Why should we? It's loathsome being looked after.

SOREL: Yes, but people like little attentions. We've never once asked anyone if they've slept well.

SIMON: I consider that an impertinence, anyhow.

SOREL: I'm going to try to improve.

SIMON: You're only going on like this because you've got a mania for a diplomatist. You'll soon return to normal.

SOREL [*earnestly*]: Abnormal, Simon—that's what we are. Abnormal. People stare in astonishment when we say what we consider perfectly ordinary things. I just remarked at Freda's lunch the other day how nice it would be if some one invented something to make all our faces go up like the Chinese, because I was so bored with them going down— and they all thought I was mad!

SIMON: It's no use worrying, darling; we see things differently, I suppose, and if people don't like it they must lump it.

SOREL: Mother's been awfully restless lately.

SIMON: Yes, I know.

SOREL: Life must be terribly dull for her now, with nothing to do.

SIMON: She'll go back soon, I expect; people never retire from the stage for long.

SOREL: Father will be livid if she does.

SIMON: That won't matter.

[*Enter* JUDITH *from the garden. She is carrying an armful of flowers and wearing a teagown, a large garden hat, gauntlet gloves, and galoshes.*

JUDITH: You look awfully dirty, Simon. What have you been doing?

SIMON [*nonchalantly*]: Not washing very much.

JUDITH: You should, darling, really. It's so bad for your skin to leave things about on it.

[*She proceeds to take off her goloshes.*

SOREL: Clara says Amy's got toothache.

JUDITH: Poor dear! There's some oil of cloves in my medicine cupboard. Who is Amy?

SOREL: The scullery maid, I think.

JUDITH: How extraordinary! She doesn't look Amy a bit, does she? Much more Flossie—Give me a cigarette. [SOREL *gives her a cigarette and lights it*] Delphiniums are those stubby red flowers, aren't they?

SIMON: No, darling, they're tall and blue.

JUDITH: Yes, of course. The red ones are somebody's name—

asters, that's it. I knew it was something opulent. I do hope Clara has remembered about the Japanese room.

SOREL: Japanese room!

JUDITH: Yes; I told her to put some flowers in it and take Simon's flannels out of the wardrobe drawer.

SOREL: So did I.

JUDITH [*ominously*]: Why?

SOREL [*airily*]: I've asked Richard Greatham down for the weekend—I didn't think you'd mind.

JUDITH: Mind! How dared you do such a thing?

SOREL: He's a diplomatist.

JUDITH: That makes it much worse. We must wire and put him off at once.

SOREL: It's too late.

JUDITH: Well, we'll tell Clara to say we've been called away.

SOREL: That would be extremely rude, and, anyhow, I *want* to see him.

JUDITH: You mean to stand there in cold blood and tell me you've asked a complete stranger down for the weekend, and that you want to see him!

SOREL: I've often done it before.

JUDITH: I fail to see how that helps matters. Where's he going to sleep?

SOREL: The Japanese room.

JUDITH: Oh no, he isn't—Sandy Tyrell is sleeping in it.

SIMON: There now! What did I tell you?

SOREL: Sandy—what?

JUDITH: Tyrell, dear.

SIMON: Why didn't you tell us, mother?

JUDITH: I did. I've talked of nothing but Sandy Tyrell for days. I adore Sandy Tyrell.

SIMON: You've never mentioned him.

SOREL: Who is he, mother?

JUDITH: He's a perfect darling, and madly in love with me— at least, it isn't me really, it's my Celebrated Actress glamor —but it gives me a divinely cozy feeling. I met him at Nora Trent's.

SOREL: Mother, I wish you'd give up this sort of thing.

JUDITH: What exactly do you mean by "this sort of thing,"
Sorel?

SOREL: You know perfectly well what I mean.

JUDITH: Are you attempting to criticize me?

SOREL: I should have thought you'd be above encouraging silly,
callow young men who are infatuated by your name.

JUDITH: That may be true, but I shall allow nobody but myself to say it. I hoped you'd grow up a good daughter to me,
not a critical aunt.

SOREL: It's so terribly cheap.

JUDITH: Cheap! Nonsense! What about your diplomatist?

SOREL: Surely that's a little different, dear?

JUDITH: If you mean that because you happen to be a vigor-
ous *ingénue* of nineteen you have the complete monopoly of
any amorous adventure there may be about, I feel it my
firm duty to disillusion you.

SOREL: But, mother—

JUDITH: Anyone would think I was eighty, the way you go on.
It was a great mistake not sending you to boarding schools,
and you coming back and me being your elder sister.

SIMON: It wouldn't have been any use. Everyone knows we're
your son and daughter.

JUDITH: Only because I was stupid enough to dandle you
about in front of cameras when you were little. I knew I
should regret it.

SIMON: I don't see any point in trying to be younger than
you are.

JUDITH: At your age, dear, it would be indecent if you did.

SOREL: But, Mother darling, don't you see, it's awfully un-
dignified for you to go flaunting about with young men?

JUDITH: I don't flaunt about—I never have. I've been morally
an extremely nice woman all my life—more or less—and if
dabbling gives me pleasure, I don't see why I shouldn't
dabble.

SOREL: But it oughtn't to give you pleasure any more.

JUDITH: You know, Sorel, you grow more damnably feminine
every day. I wish I'd brought you up differently.

SOREL: I'm proud of being feminine.

JUDITH [*kissing her*]:   You're a darling, and I adore you; and you're very pretty, and I'm madly jealous of you.

SOREL [*with her arms round her*]:   Are you really? How lovely.

JUDITH: You will be nice to Sandy, won't you?

SOREL [*breaking away*]:   Can't he sleep in "Little Hell"?

JUDITH: My dear, he's frightfully athletic, and all those hot-water pipes will sap his vitality.

SOREL: They'll sap Richard's vitality, too.

JUDITH: He won't notice them; he's probably used to scorching tropical embassies with punkahs waving and everything.

SIMON: He's sure to be deadly, anyhow.

SOREL: You're getting far too blasé and exclusive, Simon.

SIMON: Nothing of the sort. Only I loathe being hearty with your men friends.

SOREL: You've never been even civil to any of my friends, men or women.

JUDITH: Don't bicker.

SIMON: Anyhow, the Japanese room's a woman's room, and a woman ought to have it.

JUDITH: I promised it to Sandy—he loves anything Japanese.

SIMON: So does Myra.

JUDITH: Myra!

SIMON: Myra Arundel. I've asked her down.

JUDITH: You've—what?

SIMON: I've asked Myra down for the weekend—she's awfully amusing.

SOREL: Well, all I can say is, it's beastly of you. You might have warned me. What on earth will Richard say?

SIMON: Something exquisitely noncommittal, I expect.

JUDITH: This is too much! Do you mean to tell me, Simon—

SIMON [*firmly*]:   Yes, Mother, I do. I've asked Myra down, and I have a perfect right to. You've always grought us up to be free about things.

JUDITH: Myra Arundel is straining freedom to its utmost limits.

SIMON: Don't you like her?

JUDITH: No, dear, I detest her. She's far too old for you, and she goes about using Sex as a sort of shrimping net.

SIMON: Really, Mother—!

JUDITH: It's no use being cross. You know perfectly well I dislike her, and that's why you never told me she was coming until too late to stop her. It's intolerable of you.

SOREL [*grandly*]: Whether she's here or not is a matter of extreme indifference to me, but I'm afraid Richard won't like her very much.

SIMON: You're afraid he'll like her too much.

SOREL: That was an offensive remark, Simon, and rather silly.

JUDITH [*plaintively*]: Why on earth don't you fall in love with nice young girls, instead of self-conscious vampires?

SIMON: She's not a vampire, and I never said I was in love with her.

SOREL: He's crazy about her. She butters him up and admires his sketches.

SIMON: What about you picking up old gentlemen at dances?

SOREL [*furiously*]: He's *not* old!

JUDITH: You've both upset me thoroughly. I wanted a nice, restful weekend, with moments of Sandy's ingenuous affection to warm the cockles of my heart when I felt in the mood, and now the house is going to be full of discord—not enough food, everyone fighting for the bath—perfect agony! I wish I were dead!

SIMON: You needn't worry about Myra and me. We shall keep out of everyone's way.

SOREL: I shall take Richard on the river all day tomorrow.

JUDITH: In what?

SOREL: The punt.

JUDITH: I absolutely forbid you to go near the punt.

SIMON: It's sure to rain, anyhow.

JUDITH: What your father will say I tremble to think. He needs complete quiet to finish off *The Sinful Woman*.

SOREL: I see no reason for there to be any noise, unless Sandy What's-his-name is given to shouting.

JUDITH: If you're rude to Sandy I shall be extremely angry.

[*Together.*

SOREL: Now, look here, Mother—

SIMON: Why you should expect—

JUDITH: He's coming all the way down specially to be nice to me—

[*Enter* DAVID *down stairs. He looks slightly irritable.*

DAVID: Why are you all making such a noise?

JUDITH: I think I'm going mad.

DAVID: Why hasn't Clara brought me my tea?

JUDITH: I don't know.

DAVID: Where is Clara?

JUDITH: Do stop firing questions at me, David.

DAVID: Why are you all so irritable? What's happened?

[*Enter* CLARA, *with a tray of tea for one.*

CLARA: Here's your tea. I'm sorry I'm late with it. Amy forgot to put the kettle on—she's got terrible toothache.

DAVID: Poor girl! Give her some oil of cloves.

SOREL: If anyone else mentions oil of cloves, I shall do something desperate.

DAVID: It's wonderful stuff. Where's Zoe?

SIMON: She was in the garden this morning.

DAVID: I suppose no one thought of giving her any lunch?

CLARA: I put it down by the kitchen table as usual, but she never came in for it.

SOREL: She's probably mousing.

DAVID: She isn't old enough yet. She might have fallen into the river, for all you care. I think it's a shame!

CLARA: Don't you worry your head—Zoe won't come to any harm; she's too wily.

DAVID: I don't want to be disturbed. [*He takes his tray and goes upstairs; then he turns*] Listen, Simon. There's a perfectly sweet flapper coming down by the four-thirty. Will you go and meet her and be nice to her? She's an abject fool, but a useful type, and I want to study her a little in domestic surroundings. She can sleep in the Japanese room.

[*He goes off, leaving behind him a deathly silence.*

JUDITH: I should like some one to play something very beautiful to me on the piano.

SIMON: Damn everything! Damn! Damn! Damn!

SOREL: Swearing doesn't help.

SIMON: It helps me a lot.

SOREL: What does Father mean by going on like that?

JUDITH: In view of the imminent reception, you'd better go and shave, Simon.

SOREL [bursting into tears of rage]: It's perfectly beastly! Whenever I make any sort of plan about anything it's always done in by some one. I wish I were earning my own living somewhere—a free agent—able to do whatever I liked without being cluttered up and frustrated by the family—

JUDITH [picturesquely]: It grieves me to hear you say that, Sorel.

SOREL: Don't be infuriating, Mother.

JUDITH [sadly]: A change has come over my children of late. I have tried to shut my eyes to it, but in vain. At my time of life one must face bitter facts!

SIMON: This is going to be the blackest Saturday till Monday we've ever spent.

JUDITH [tenderly]: Sorel, you mustn't cry.

SOREL: Don't sympathize with me; it's only temper.

JUDITH [clasping her]: Put your head on my shoulder, dear.

SIMON [bitterly]: Your head like the golden fleece . . .

SOREL: Richard'll have to have "Little Hell" and that horrible flapper the Japanese room.

JUDITH: Over my dead body!

SIMON: Mother, what are we to do?

JUDITH [drawing him forcibly into her arms so that there is a charming little motherly picture]: We must be all be very, very kind to everyone!

SIMON: Now then, Mother, none of that!

JUDITH [aggrieved]: I don't know what you mean, Simon.

SIMON: You were being beautiful and sad.

JUDITH: But I am beautiful and sad.

SIMON: You're not particularly beautiful, darling, and you never were.

JUDITH [glancing at herself in the glass]: Never mind; I made thousands think I was.

SIMON: And as for being sad—

JUDITH: Now, Simon, I will not be dictated to like this. If I say I'm sad, I am sad. You don't understand, because you're precocious and tiresome . . . There comes a time in all women's lives—

SOREL: Oh, dear!

JUDITH: What did you say, Sorel?

SOREL [*recovering*]: I said, "Oh, dear!"

JUDITH: Well, please don't say it again, because it annoys me.

SOREL: You're such a lovely hypocrite.

JUDITH [*casting up her eyes*]: I'm sure I don't know what I've done to be cursed with such ungrateful children. It's very cruel at my time of life—

SIMON: There you go again!

JUDITH [*inconsequently*]: You're getting far too tall, Sorel.

SOREL: Sorry, Mother.

JUDITH: Give me another of those disgusting cigarettes—I don't know where they came from.

SIMON [*giving her one*]: Here.

[*He lights it for her.*

JUDITH: I'm going to forget entirely about all these dreadful people arriving. My mind henceforward shall be a blank on the subject.

SOREL: It's all very fine, Mother, but—

JUDITH: I made a great decision this morning.

SIMON: What kind of decision?

JUDITH: It's a secret.

SOREL: Aren't you going to tell us?

JUDITH: Of course. I meant it was a secret from your father.

SIMON: What is it?

JUDITH: I'm going back to the stage.

SIMON: I knew it!

JUDITH: I'm stagnating, you see. I won't stagnate as long as there's breath left in my body.

SOREL: Do you think it's wise? You retired so very finally last year. What excuse will you give for returning so soon?

JUDITH: My public, dear—letters from my public!

SIMON: Have you had any?

JUDITH: One or two. That's what decided me, really—I ought to have had hundreds.

SOREL: We'll write some lovely ones, and you can publish them in the papers.

JUDITH: Of course.

SOREL: You will be dignified about it all, won't you, darling?

JUDITH: I'm much more dignified on the stage than in the country—it's my *milieu*. I've tried terribly hard to be "landed gentry," but without any real success. I long for excitement and glamor. Think of the thrill of a first night; all those ardent playgoers willing one to succeed; the critics all leaning forward with glowing faces, receptive and exultant—emitting queer little inarticulate noises as some witty line tickles their fancy. The satisfied grunt of the *Daily Mail*, the abandoned gurgle of the *Sunday Times*, and the shrill, enthusiastic scream of the *Daily Express*! I can distinguish them all—

SIMON: Have you got a play?

JUDITH: I think I shall revive "Love's Whirlwind."

SOREL [*collapsing on to sofa*]: Oh, Mother!

[*She gurgles with laughter.*

SIMON [*weakly*]: Father will be furious.

JUDITH: I can't help that.

SOREL: It's such a fearful play.

JUDITH: It's a marvelous part. You mustn't say too much against it, Sorel! I'm willing to laugh at it a little myself, but, after all, it *was* one of my greatest successes.

SIMON: Oh, it's appalling—but I love it. It makes me laugh.

JUDITH: The public love it too, and it doesn't make them laugh—much. [*She recites*] "You are a fool, a blind, pitiable fool. You think because you have bought my body that you have bought my soul!" You must say that's dramatic—"I've dreamed of love like this, but I never realized, I never knew how beautiful it could be in reality!" That line always brought a tear to my eye.

SIMON: The second act *is* the best, there's no doubt about that.

JUDITH: From the moment Victor comes in it's strong—tremendously strong . . . Be Victor a minute, Sorel—

SOREL: Do you mean when he comes in at the end of the act?

JUDITH: Yes, you know—"Is this a game?"

SOREL [*with feeling*]:   "Is this a game?"

JUDITH [*with spirit*]:   "Yes—and a game that must be played to the finish."

SIMON: "Zara, what does this mean?"

JUDITH: "So many illusions shattered—so many dreams trodden in the dust!"

SOREL: I'm George now—"I don't understand! You and Victor —My God!"

JUDITH: "Sssh! Isn't that little Pam crying?"

SIMON [*savagely*]:   "She'll cry more, poor mite, when she realizes her mother is a—"

JUDITH [*shrieking*]:   "Don't say it—don't say it!"

SOREL: "Spare her that."

JUDITH: "I've given you all that makes life worth living—my youth, my womanhood, and now my child. Would you tear the very heart out of me? I tell you that it's infamous that men like you should be allowed to pollute society. You have ruined my life—I have nothing left—nothing. God in heaven, where am I to turn for help . . ."

SOREL [*through clenched teeth*]:   "Is this true? Answer me—is this true?"

JUDITH [*wailing*]:   "Yes, yes!"

SOREL [*springing at* SIMON]:   "You cur!"

[*The front doorbell rings.*

JUDITH: Damn! There's the bell.

SOREL [*rushing to the glass*]:   I look hideous!

SIMON: Yes, dear.

[CLARA *enters.*

JUDITH: Clara—before you open the door—we shall be eight for dinner.

CLARA: My God!

SIMON: And for breakfast, lunch, tea, and dinner tomorrow.

JUDITH [*vaguely*]:   Will you get various rooms ready?

CLARA: I shall have to—they can't sleep in the passage.

SOREL: How we've upset Clara.

JUDITH: It can't be helped—nothing can be helped. It's fate—
everything that happens is fate. That's always a great comfort to me.

CLARA: More like arrant selfishness.

JUDITH: You mustn't be pert, Clara.

CLARA: Pert I may be, but I'ave got some thought for others.
Eight for dinner—Amy going home early. It's more nor less
than an imposition.

[*The bell rings again.*

SIMON: Hadn't you better let them all in?

[CLARA *goes to the front door and admits* SANDY TYRELL, *who is
a fresh-looking young man; he has an unspoiled, youthful sense
of honor and rather big hands, owing to a misplaced enthusiasm
for amateur boxing.* CLARA *goes out.*

SANDY [*to* JUDITH]:   I say, it's perfectly ripping of you to let
me come down.

JUDITH: Are you alone?

SANDY [*surprised*]:   Yes.

JUDITH: I mean, you didn't meet anyone at the station?

SANDY: I motored down; my car's outside. Would you like me
to meet anybody?

JUDITH: Oh no. I must introduce you. This is my daughter
Sorel, and my son Simon.

SANDY [*shaking hands*]:   How-do-you-do.

SOREL [*coldly*]:   I'm extremely well, thank you, and I hope you
are.

SIMON: So do I.

[*They both go upstairs rather grandly.* SANDY *looks shattered.*

JUDITH: You must forgive me for having rather peculiar children. Have you got a bag or anything?

SANDY: Yes; it's in the car.

JUDITH: We'd better leave it there for the moment, as Clara
has to get the tea. We'll find you a room afterwards.

SANDY: I've been looking forward to this most awfully.

JUDITH: It is nice, isn't it? You can see as far as Marlow on
a clear day, they tell me.

SANDY: I meant I've been looking forward to seeing you.

JUDITH: How perfectly sweet of you. Would you like a drink?

SANDY: No, thanks. I'm in training.

JUDITH [*sitting on sofa and motioning him to sit beside her*]: How lovely. What for?

SANDY: I'm boxing again in a couple of weeks.

JUDITH: I must come to your first night.

SANDY: You look simply splendid.

JUDITH: I'm so glad. You know, you mustn't mind if Simon and Sorel insult you a little—they've been very bad-tempered lately.

SANDY: It's awfully funny you having a grown-up son and daughter at all. I can hardly believe it.

JUDITH [*quickly*]: I was married very young.

SANDY: I don't wonder. You know, it's frightfully queer the way I've been planning to know you for ages, and I never did until last week.

JUDITH: I liked you from the first, really, because you're such a nice shape.

SANDY [*slightly embarrassed*]: Oh, I see . . .

JUDITH: Small hips and lovely long legs—I wish Simon had smaller hips. Do you think you could teach him to box?

SANDY: Rather—if he likes.

JUDITH: That's just the trouble—I'm afraid he won't like. He's so dreadfully un—that sort of thing. But never mind; you must use your influence subtly. I'm sure David would be pleased.

SANDY: Who's David?

JUDITH: My husband.

SANDY [*surprised*]: Oh!

JUDITH: Why do you say "Oh" like that? Didn't you know I had a husband?

SANDY: I thought he was dead.

JUDITH: No, he's not dead; he's upstairs.

SANDY: You're quite different from what you were the other day.

JUDITH: It's this garden hat—I'll take it off. [*She does so*] There. I've been pruning the calceolarias.

SANDY [*puzzled*]: Oh?—

JUDITH: I love my garden, you know—it's so peaceful and

quaint. I spend long days dreaming away in it—you know
how one dreams.

SANDY: Oh, yes.

JUDITH [*warming up*]:   I always longed to leave the brittle
glamor of cities and theaters and find rest in some Old World
nook. That's why we came to Cookham.

SANDY: It's awfully nice—Cookham.

JUDITH: Have you ever seen me on the stage?

SANDY: Rather!

JUDITH: What in?

SANDY: That thing when you pretended to cheat at cards to
save your husband's good name.

JUDITH: Oh, "The Bold Deceiver." That play was never quite
right.

SANDY: You were absolutely wonderful. That was when I
first fell in love with you.

JUDITH [*delighted*]:   Was it, really?

SANDY: Yes; you were so frightfully pathetic and brave.

JUDITH [*basking*]:   Was I?

SANDY: Rather!

[*There is a pause.*

JUDITH: Well, go on . . .

SANDY: I feel such a fool, telling you what I think, as though
it mattered.

JUDITH: Of course it matters—to me, anyhow.

SANDY: Does it—honestly?

JUDITH: Certainly.

SANDY: It seems too good to be true—sitting here and talking
as though we were old friends.

JUDITH: We *are* old friends—we probably met in another life.
Reincarnation, you know—fascinating!

SANDY: You do say ripping things.

JUDITH: Do I? Give me a cigarette and let's put our feet up.

SANDY: All right.

[*They settle themselves comfortably at opposite ends of the
sofa, smoking.*

JUDITH: Can you punt?

SANDY: Yes—a bit.

JUDITH: You must teach Simon—he always gets the pole stuck.

SANDY: I'd rather teach you.

JUDITH: You're so gallant and chivalrous—much more like an American than an Englishman.

SANDY: I should like to go on saying nice things to you for-ever.

JUDITH [*giving him her hand*]:   Sandy! [*There comes a loud ring at the bell.* JUDITH *jumps*] There now!

SANDY: Is anyone else coming to stay?

JUDITH: Anyone else! You don't know—you just don't know. Give me my hat.

SANDY [*giving it to her*]:   You said it would be quite quiet, with nobody at all.

JUDITH: I was wrong. It's going to be very noisy, with herds of angry people stamping about.

[CLARA *enters and opens the front door.* MYRA ARUNDEL *is posed outside, consciously well dressed, with several suitcases and a tennis racquet.*

MYRA [*advancing*]:   Judith—my—dear—this is divine!

JUDITH [*emptily*]:   Too, too lovely—Where are the others?

MYRA: What others?

[CLARA *goes out.*

JUDITH: Did you come by the four-thirty?

MYRA: Yes.

JUDITH: Didn't you see anyone at the station?

MYRA: Yes; several people, but I didn't know they were coming here.

JUDITH: Well, they are.

MYRA: Sorel said it was going to be just ourselves this weekend.

JUDITH [*sharply*]:   Sorel?

MYRA: Yes—didn't she tell you she'd asked me? Weren't you expecting me?

JUDITH: Simon muttered something about your coming, but Sorel didn't mention it. Wasn't that odd of her?

MYRA: You're a divinely mad family. [*To* SANDY] How do-you-do? It's useless to wait for introductions with the Blisses. My name's Myra Arundel.

JUDITH [*airily*]:   Sandy Tyrell, Myra Arundel; Myra Arundel, Sandy Tyrell. There.

MYRA: Is that your car outside?

SANDY: Yes.

MYRA: Well, Judith, I *do* think you might have told me someone was motoring down. A nice car would have been so much comfortable than that beastly train.

JUDITH: I never knew you were coming until a little while ago.

MYRA: It's heavenly here—after London. The heat was terrible when I left. You look awfully well, Judith. Rusticating obviously agrees with you.

JUDITH: I'm glad you think so. Personally, I feel that a nervous breakdown is imminent.

MYRA: My dear, how ghastly! What's the matter?

JUDITH: Nothing's the matter yet, Myra, but I have presentiments. Come upstairs, Sandy, and I'll show you your room. [*She begins to go upstairs, followed by* SANDY. *Then she turns.*] I'll send Simon down to you. He's shaving, I think, but you won't mind that, will you?

[*She goes off.* MYRA *makes a slight grimace after her, then she helps herself to a cigarette and wanders about the hall—she might almost play the piano a little; anyhow, she is perfectly at home.* SIMON *comes downstairs very fast, putting on his coat. He has apparently finished his toilet.*

SIMON: Myra, this is marvelous!

[*He tries to kiss her.*

MYRA [*pushing him away*]: No, Simon dear; it's too hot.

SIMON: You look beautifully cool.

MYRA: I'm more than cool really, but it's not climatic coolness. I've been mentally chilled to the marrow by Judith's attitude.

SIMON: Why, what did she say?

MYRA: Nothing very much. She was bouncing about on the sofa with a hearty young thing in flannels, and seemed to resent my appearance rather.

SIMON: You mustn't take any notice of Mother.

MYRA: I'll try not to, but it's difficult.

SIMON: She adores you, really.

MYRA: I'm sure she does.

SIMON: She's annoyed today because Father and Sorel have been asking people down without telling her.

MYRA: Poor dear! I quite see why.

SIMON: You look enchanting.

MYRA: Thank you, Simon.

SIMON: Are you pleased to see me?

MYRA: Of course. That's why I came.

SIMON: Darling!

MYRA: Sssh! Don't shout.

SIMON: I feel most colossally temperamental—I should like to kiss you and kiss you and kiss you and break everything in the house and then jump into the river.

MYRA: Dear Simon!

SIMON: You're everything I want you to be—absolutely everything. Marvelous clothes, marvelous looks, marvelous brain—Oh, God, it's terrible . . .

MYRA: I dined with Charlie Templeton last night.

SIMON: Well, you're a devil. You only did it to annoy me. He's far too plump, and he can't do anything but dither about the Embassy in badly cut trousers. You loathe him, really; you know you do—you're too intelligent not to. You couldn't like him and me at the same time—it's impossible!

MYRA: Don't be so conceited.

SIMON: Darling—I adore you.

MYRA: That's right.

SIMON: But you're callous—that's what it is, callous! You don't care a damn. You don't love me a bit, do you?

MYRA: Love's a very big word, Simon.

SIMON: It isn't—it's tiny. What are we to do?

MYRA: What do you mean?

SIMON: We can't go on like this.

MYRA: I'm not going on like anything.

SIMON: Yes, you are; you're going on like Medusa, and there are awful snakes popping their heads out at me from under your hat—I shall be turned to stone in a minute, and then you'll be sorry.

MYRA [laughing]: You're very sweet, and I'm very fond of you.

SIMON: Tell me what you've been doing—everything.

MYRA: Nothing.

SIMON: What did you do after you'd dined with Charlie Templeton?

MYRA: Supped with Charlie Templeton.

SIMON: Well, I don't mind a bit. I hope you ate a lot and enjoyed yourself—there!

MYRA: Generous boy! Come and kiss me.

SIMON: You're only playing up to me now; you don't really want to a bit.

MYRA: I'm aching for it.

SIMON [*kissing her violently*]:   I love you.

MYRA: This weekend's going to be strenuous.

SIMON: Hell upon earth—fifteen million people in the house. We'll get up at seven and rush away down the river.

MYRA: No, we won't.

SIMON: Don't let either of us agree to anything we say—we'll both be difficult. I love being difficult.

MYRA: You certainly do.

SIMON: But I'm in the most lovely mood now. Just seeing you makes me feel grand—

MYRA: Is your father here?

SIMON: Yes; he's working on a new novel.

MYRA: He writes brilliantly.

SIMON: Doesn't he? He drinks too much tea, though.

MYRA: It can't do him much harm, surely?

SIMON: It tans the stomach.

MYRA: Who is Sandy Tyrell?

SIMON: Never heard of him.

MYRA: He's here, with Judith.

SIMON: Oh, that poor thing with hot hands! We'll ignore him.

MYRA: I thought he looked rather nice.

SIMON: You must be mad. He looked disgusting.

MYRA [*laughing*]:   Idiot!

SIMON [*flinging himself on the sofa*]:   Smooth my hair with your soft white hands.

MYRA [*ruffling it*]:   It's got glue on it.

SIMON [*catching her hand and kissing it*]:   You smell heavenly. What is it?

MYRA: Borgia of Rosine.

SIMON: How appropriate.

[*He pulls her down and kisses her.*

MYRA [*breaking away*]: You're too demonstrative today, Simon.
[*The front doorbell rings.*

SIMON: Damn, damn! It's those drearies.

[MYRA *powders her nose as* CLARA *crosses to open door.* RICHARD
GREATHAM *and* JACKIE CORYTON *come in. There is, by this time, a
good deal of luggage on the step.* RICHARD *is iron-gray and tall;*
JACKIE *is small and shingled, with an ingenuous manner which
will lose its charm as she grows older.*

RICHARD: This is Mrs. Bliss's house.

CLARA [*offhand*]: Oh yes, this it it.

RICHARD: Is Miss Sorel Bliss in?

CLARA: I expect so. I'll see if I can find her.

[*She goes upstairs, humming a tune.*

SIMON: Hallo. Did you have a nice journey?

RICHARD: Yes, thank you, very nice. I met Miss Coryton at the
    station. We introduced ourselves while we were waiting for
    the only taxi to come back.

MYRA: Oh, *I* took the only taxi. How maddening of me.

RICHARD: Mrs. Arundel! How-do-you-do. I never recognized
    you.

[*They shake hands.*

JACKIE: I did.

MYRA: Why? Have we met anywhere?

JACKIE: No; I mean I recognized you as the one who took
    the taxi.

RICHARD [*to* SIMON]: You are Sorel's brother?

SIMON: Yes; she'll be down in a minute. Come out into the
    garden, Myra—

MYRA: But, Simon, we can't . . .

SIMON [*grabbing her hand and dragging her off*]: Yes, we can.
    I shall go mad if I stay in the house a moment longer. [*Over
    his shoulder to* RICHARD *and* JACKIE] Tea will be here soon.

[*He and* MYRA *go off.*

JACKIE: Well!

RICHARD: A strange young man.

JACKIE: Very rude, I think.

RICHARD: Have you ever met him before?

JACKIE: No; I don't know any of them except Mr. Bliss—he's
    a wonderful person.

RICHARD: I wonder if he knows you're here.

JACKIE: Perhaps that funny woman who opened the door will tell him.

RICHARD: It was fortunate that we met at the station.

JACKIE: I'm frightfully glad. I should have been terrified arriving all by myself.

RICHARD: I do hope the weather will keep good over Sunday —the country round here is delightful.

JACKIE: Yes.

RICHARD: There's nowhere like England in the spring and summer.

JACKIE: No, there isn't, is there?

RICHARD: There's a sort of *quality* you find in no other countries.

JACKIE: Have you traveled a lot?

RICHARD [*modestly*]:   A good deal.

JACKIE: How lovely.

[*There is a pause.*

RICHARD: Spain is very beautiful.

JACKIE: Yes, I've always heard Spain was awfully nice.

RICHARD: Except for the bullfights. No one who ever really loved horses could enjoy a bullfight.

JACKIE: Nor anyone who loved bulls, either.

RICHARD: Exactly.

JACKIE: Italy's awfully nice, isn't it?

RICHARD: Oh yes, charming.

JACKIE: I've always wanted to go to Italy.

RICHARD: Rome is a beautiful city.

JACKIE: Yes, I've always heard Rome was lovely.

RICHARD: And Naples and Capri—Capri's enchanting.

JACKIE: It must be.

RICHARD: Have you ever been abroad at all?

JACKIE·   Oh yes; I went to Dieppe once—we had a house there for the summer.

RICHARD [*kindly*]:   Dear little place—Dieppe.

JACKIE: Yes, it was lovely.

[JUDITH *comes downstairs, followed by* SANDY, *with his arms full of cushions. She motions him out into the garden, sits down and puts on her goloshes, and then follows him.*

JACKIE: Well!

RICHARD: Russia used to be a wonderful country before the war.

JACKIE: It must have been . . . Was that her?

RICHARD: Who?

JACKIE: Judith Bliss.

RICHARD: Yes, I expect it was.

JACKIE: I wish I'd never come.

RICHARD: You mustn't worry. They're a very Bohemian family, I believe.

JACKIE: I wonder if Mr. Bliss knows I'm here.

RICHARD: I wonder.

JACKIE: Couldn't we ring a bell, or anything?

RICHARD: Yes, perhaps we'd better.

[*He finds bell and presses it.*

JACKIE: I don't suppose it rings.

RICHARD: You mustn't be depressed.

JACKIE: I feel horrid.

RICHARD: It's always a little embarrassing coming to a strange house for the first time. You'll like Sorel—she's charming.

JACKIE [*desperately*]:   I wonder where she is.

RICHARD [*consolingly*]:   I expect tea will be here soon.

JACKIE: Do you think they *have* tea?

RICHARD [*alarmed*]:   Oh, yes—they must.

JACKIE: Oh, well, we'd better go on waiting, then.

[*She sits down.*

RICHARD: Do you mind if I smoke?

JACKIE: Not a bit.

RICHARD: Will you?

JACKIE: No, thank you.

RICHARD [*sitting down*]:   I got this case in Japan. It's pretty, isn't it?

JACKIE: Awfully pretty.

[*They lapse into hopeless silence. Enter* SOREL, *down stairs.*

SOREL: Oh, Richard, I'm dreadfully sorry. I didn't know you were here.

RICHARD: We've been here a good while.

SOREL: How awful! Please forgive me. I was upstairs.

RICHARD: This is Miss Coryton.

SOREL: Oh!

JACKIE: How-do-you-do.

SOREL: Have you come to see father?

JACKIE: Yes.

SOREL: He's in his study—you'd better go up.

JACKIE: I don't know the way.

SOREL [*irritably*]: Oh, well—I'll take you. Come on. Wait a
   minute, Richard [*She takes her to the top of the stairs*] It's
   along that passage, and the third door on the right.

JACKIE: Oh, thank you.

[*She goes out despondently.*

SOREL [*coming down again*]: The poor girl looks half-witted.

RICHARD: She's shy, I think.

SOREL: I hope father will find her a comfort.

RICHARD: Tell me one thing, Sorel, did your father and mother
   know I was coming?

SOREL: Oh yes; they were awfully pleased.

RICHARD: A rather nice-looking woman came down, in a big
   hat, and went into the garden with a young man, without
   saying a word.

SOREL: That was mother, I expect. We're an independent
   family—we entertain our friends sort of separately.

RICHARD: Oh, I see.

SOREL: It was sweet of you to come.

RICHARD: I wanted to come—I've thought about you a lot.

SOREL: Have you, really? That's thrilling.

RICHARD: I mean it. You're so alive and vital and different
   from other people.

SOREL: I'm so frightened that you'll be bored here.

RICHARD: Why should I be?

SOREL: Oh, I don't know. But you won't be, will you?—or if
   you are, tell me at once, and we'll do something quite different.

RICHARD: You're rather a dear, you know.

SOREL: I'm not—I'm devastating, entirely lacking in restraint.
   So's Simon. It's Father's and Mother's fault, really; you see,
   they're so vague—they've spent their lives cultivating their

arts and not devoting any time to ordinary conventions and
manners and things. I'm the only one who sees that, so I'm
trying to be better. I'd love to be beautifully poised and carry
off difficult situations with a lift of the eyebrows—

RICHARD: I'm sure you could carry off anything.

SOREL: There you are, you see, saying the right thing! You
always say the right thing, and no one knows a bit what you're
really thinking. That's what I adore.

RICHARD: I'm afraid to say anything now, in case you think
I'm only being correct.

SOREL: But you are correct. I wish you'd teach Simon to be
correct too.

RICHARD: It would be uphill work, I'm afraid.

SOREL: Why, don't you like him?

RICHARD: I've only met him for a moment.

SOREL: Would you like to see the garden?

RICHARD: Very much indeed.

SOREL: As a matter of fact, we'd better wait until after tea.
Shall I sing you something?

RICHARD: Please—I should love it.

SOREL: I don't want to really a bit—only I'm trying to entertain you. It's as easy as pie to talk in some one else's house,
like at the dance the other night, but here on my own ground
I'm finding it difficult.

RICHARD [*puzzled*]:   I'm sorry.

SOREL: Oh, it isn't your fault; honestly, it isn't—you're awfully
kind and responsive. What shall we do?

RICHARD: I'm quite happy talking—to you.

SOREL: Can you play Mah Jong?

RICHARD: No, I'm afraid I can't.

SOREL: I'm *so* glad—I *do* hate it so. [CLARA *enters, with prep-
arations for tea.* SOREL *sighs with relief*] Here's tea.

CLARA: Where's your mother, dear?

SOREL: Out in the garden, I think.

CLARA: It's starting to rain.

SOREL: Oh, everyone will come dashing in, then. How awful!

RICHARD: Won't the luggage get rather wet, out there?

SOREL: What luggage?

CLARA: I'll bring it in when I've made the tea.

RICHARD [*rising*]:   Oh, don't trouble; I'll do it now.

SOREL: We ought to have got William up from the village.

CLARA: It's Saturday.

SOREL: I know it is.

CLARA: He's playing cricket.

[RICHARD *opens the front door and proceeds to bring the luggage in.* SOREL *rushes to help him.*

SOREL: Do sit down and smoke. I can easily manage it.

RICHARD: Certainly not.

SOREL: How typical of Myra to have so many bags . . . Ooh!
   [*She staggers with a suitcase.* RICHARD *goes to her assistance, and they both drop it*] There now!—We've probably broken something.

RICHARD: This is the last one . . .

[*He brings in a dressing-case, and wipes his hand on his handkerchief.*

SOREL: Do you know where to wash if you want to?

RICHARD: No—but I'm all right.

[*Re-enter* CLARA, *with tea and hot-water jug.* SIMON *and* MYRA *come in from the garden.*

MYRA: Hullo, Sorel, how are you?

SOREL: I'm splendid. Do you know Mr. Greatham?

MYRA: Oh, yes; we've met several times.

SIMON: Come and sit down, Myra.

[DAVID *and* JACKIE *come downstairs.*

DAVID: Is tea ready?

SOREL: Yes; just.

DAVID: Simon, come and be nice to Miss Coryton.

SIMON: We've met already.

DAVID: That's no reason for you not to be nice to her.

MYRA [*firmly*]:   How-do-you-do.

DAVID: How-do-you-do. Are you staying here?

MYRA: I hope so.

DAVID: You must forgive me for being rather frowsy, but I've been working hard.

SOREL: Father, this is Mr. Greatham.

DAVID: How are you? When did you arrive?

RICHARD: This afternoon.

DAVID: Good. Have some tea. [*He begins to pour it out*] Everyone had better put their own sugar and milk in, or we shall
get muddled. Where's your mother, Simon?

SIMON: She was last seen in the punt.

DAVID: How extraordinary! She can't punt.

SOREL: Sandy Tyrell's with her.

DAVID: Oh, well, she'll be all right then. Who is he?

SOREL: I don't know.

DAVID: Do sit down, everybody.

[*Enter* JUDITH *and* SANDY *from the garden.*

JUDITH: There's going to be a thunderstorm. I felt sick this
morning. This is Sandy Tyrell—everybody—

RICHARD [*shaking hands*]:   How-do-you-do.

SOREL: Mother, I want you to meet Mr. Greatham.

JUDITH: Oh, yes. You were here before, weren't you?

SIMON: Before *what*, darling?

JUDITH: Before I went out in the punt. There was somebody
else here too—a fair girl—[*She sees* JACKIE] Oh, there you are.
How-do-you-do. Sit down, Sandy, and eat anything you want.
Give Sandy some bread-and-butter, Simon.

[*Everybody sits down.*

SIMON [*ungraciously*]:   Here you are.

SANDY: Thanks.

[*There is a long pause; then* MYRA *and* RICHARD *speak together.*

RICHARD: How far are you from Maidenhead exactly?

MYRA: What a pity it's raining—we might have had some
tennis—

[*They both stop, to let the other go on. There is another terrible
silence.*

MYRA: I adore the shape of this hall—it's so—

RICHARD: The train was awfully crowded coming down—

[*They both stop again, and there is another dead silence, during
which the curtain slowly falls.*

ACT TWO

It is after dinner on the Saturday evening. Everyone is talking and arguing. The following scene should be played with great speed.

SIMON: Who'll go out?

SOREL: I don't mind.

SIMON: No; you always guess it too quickly.

JACKIE: What do we have to do?

JUDITH: Choose an adverb, and then—

SIMON: Someone goes out, you see, and comes in, and you've chosen a word among yourselves, and she or he or whoever it is asks you some sort of question and you have to—

SOREL: Not an ordinary question, Simon; they have to ask them to do something in the manner of the word, and then—

SIMON: Then, you see, you act whatever it is—

SOREL: The answer to the question, you see?

RICHARD [*apprehensively*]: What sort of thing is one expected to do?

JUDITH: Quite usual things, like reciting "If," or playing the piano—

RICHARD: I can't play the piano.

SIMON: Never mind; you can fake it, as long as it conveys an idea of the word.

JACKIE: The word we've all thought of?

SOREL [*impatiently*]: Yes, the word we've chosen when whoever it is is out of the room.

JACKIE: I'm afraid I don't quite understand yet.

SIMON: Never mind; I'll explain. You see, some one goes out . . .

SOREL: I'll go out the first time, just to show her.

JUDITH: It's quite simple—all you have to do is just act in the manner of the word.

SOREL: Look here, everybody, I'm going out.

SIMON: All right; go on.

MYRA: The History game's awfully good—when two people go

out, and come back as Queen Elizabeth and Crippen or
somebody.

SANDY [*despondently*]: I'm no earthly good at this sort of
thing.

SOREL: I'll show you, Sandy. You see . . .

JUDITH: There's always "How, When and Where?" We
haven't played that for ages.

SIMON: We will afterwards. We'll do this one first—Go on,
Sorel.

SOREL: Don't be too long.

[*She goes out.*

SIMON: Now then.

JUDITH: "Bitterly."

SIMON: No, we did that last week; she'll know.

DAVID: "Intensely."

JUDITH: Too difficult.

RICHARD: There was an amusing game I played once at the
Harringtons' house. Everyone was blindfolded except—

SIMON: This room's not big enough for that. What about
"winsomely"?

JACKIE: I wish I knew what we had to do.

JUDITH: You'll see when we start playing.

MYRA: *If* we start playing.

SIMON: Mother's brilliant at this. Do you remember when we
played it at the Mackenzies'?

JUDITH: Yes, and Blanche was so cross when I kissed Freddie's
ear in the manner of the word.

RICHARD: What was the word?

JUDITH: I can't remember.

MYRA: Perhaps it's as well.

DAVID: What about "dearily"?

JUDITH: Not definite enough.

SIMON: "Winsomely" is the best.

JUDITH: She's sure to guess it straight off.

SIMON [*confidentially to* JACKIE]: These games are much too
brainy for me.

DAVID: Young Norman Robertson used to be marvelous—do
you remember?

SIMON: Yes, wonderful sense of humor.

MYRA: He's lost it all since his marriage.

JUDITH: I didn't know you knew him.

MYRA: Well, considering he married my cousin—

RICHARD: We don't seem to be getting on with the game.

JUDITH: We haven't thought of a word yet.

MYRA: "Brightly."

SIMON: Too obvious.

MYRA: Very well—don't snap at me!

JUDITH: "Saucily." I've got a lovely idea for "saucily."

MYRA [at SIMON]:   I should think "rudely" would be the easiest.

SIMON: Don't be sour, Myra.

JUDITH: The great thing is to get an obscure word.

SIMON: What a pity Irene isn't here—she knows masses of obscure words.

MYRA: She's probably picked them up from her obscure friends.

SIMON: It's no use being catty about Irene; she's a perfect darling.

MYRA: I wasn't being catty at all.

SIMON: Yes, you were.

SOREL [off]:   Hurry up!

JUDITH: Quickly, now! We must think—

JACKIE [helpfully]:   "Appendicitis."

JUDITH [witheringly]:   That's not an adverb.

SIMON: You're thinking of charades.

SANDY: Charades are damned good fun.

SIMON: Yes, but we don't happen to be doing them at the moment.

SANDY: Sorry.

JUDITH: "Saucily."

SIMON: No, "winsomely's" better.

JUDITH: All right. Call her in.

SIMON [calling]: Sorel—come on; we're ready.

[Re-enter SOREL.

SANDY [hoarsely to SIMON]: Which is it?—"saucily" or "winsomely"?

SIMON [whispering]:   "Winsomely."

SOREL [*to* JUDITH]:   Go and take a flower out of that vase and
  give it to Richard.

JUDITH: Very well.

[*She trips lightly over to the vase, gurgling with coy laughter,
selects a flower, then goes over to* RICHARD; *pursing her lips into
a mock smile, she gives him the flower, with a little girlish gasp
at her own daring, and wags her finger archly at him.*

SIMON: Marvelous, Mother!

SOREL [*laughing*]:   Oh, lovely! . . . Now, Myra, get up and say
  good-by to everyone in the manner of the word.

MYRA [*rises and starts with* DAVID]:   Good-by. It really has been
  most delightful—

JUDITH: No, no, no!

MYRA: Why—what do you mean?

JUDITH: You haven't got the right intonation a bit.

SIMON: Oh, Mother darling, do shut up!

MYRA [*acidly*]:   Remember what an advantage you have over
  we poor amateurs, Judith, having been a professional for so
  long.

JUDITH: I don't like "so long" very much.

SOREL: Do you think we might go on now?

MYRA: Go to the next one; I'm not going to do any more.

SIMON: Oh, please do. You were simply splendid.

SOREL: It doesn't matter. [*To* RICHARD] Light a cigarette in the
  manner of the word.

RICHARD: I've forgotten what it is. ·

JUDITH [*grimacing at him violently*]: ˙ You remember . . .

RICHARD: Oh, yes.

[*He proceeds to light a cigarette with great abandon, winking
his eye and chuckling* SOREL *under the chin.*

JUDITH: Oh, no, no, no!

MYRA: I can't think *what* that's meant to be.

RICHARD [*offended*]:   I was doing my best.

JUDITH: It's so *frightfully* easy, and nobody can do it right.

SIMON: I believe you've muddled it up.

RICHARD: You'd better go on to the next one.

JUDITH: Which word were you doing? Whisper—

RICHARD [*whispering*]:   "Saucily."

JUDITH: I knew it!—He was doing the wrong word.
[*She whispers to him.*
RICHARD: Oh, I see. I'm so sorry.
JUDITH: Give him another chance.
SIMON: No, it's Jackie's turn now; it will come round to him
again, I'm afraid.
SOREL [*to* JACKIE]:   Do a dance in the manner of the word.
JACKIE [*giggling*]:   I can't.
JUDITH: Nonsense! Of course you can.
JACKIE: I can't—honestly—I . . .
SIMON [*pulling her to her feet*]:   Go on; have a shot at it.
JACKIE: No, I'd much rather not. Count me out.
JUDITH: Really, the ridiculous fuss everyone makes—
JACKIE: I'm awfully stupid at anything like this.
SOREL: It's only a game, after all.
DAVID: Come along—try.
JACKIE [*dragging back*]:   I couldn't—please don't ask me to. I
simply couldn't.
SIMON: Leave her alone if she doesn't want to.
SOREL [*irritably*]:   What's the use of playing at all, if people
won't do it properly?
JUDITH: It's *so* simple.
SANDY: It's awfully difficult if you haven't done it before.
SIMON: Go on to the next one.
SOREL [*firmly*]:   Unless everyone's in it we won't play at all.
SIMON: Now don't lose your temper.
SOREL: Lose my temper! I like that! No one's given me the
slightest indication of what the word is—you all argue and
squabble—
DAVID: Talk, talk, talk! Everybody talks too much.
JUDITH: It's so surprising to me when people won't play up.
After all—
JACKIE [*with spirit*]:   It's a hateful game, anyhow, and I don't
want to play it again ever.
SOREL: You haven't played it at all yet.
SIMON: Don't be rude, Sorel.
SOREL: Really, Simon, the way you go on is infuriating!

SIMON: It's always the way; whenever Sorel goes out she gets quarrelsome.

SIMON: Don't worry, Jackie; you needn't do anything you don't want to.

JUDITH: I think, for the future, we'd better confine our efforts to social conversation and not attempt anything in the least intelligent.

SIMON: How can you be so unkind, Mother?

JUDITH [*sharply*]:   Don't speak to me like that.

JACKIE: It's all my fault—I know I'm awfully silly, but it embarrasses me so terribly doing anything in front of people.

SOREL [*with acidity*]:   I should think the word was "winsomely."

SIMON: You must have been listening outside the door, then.

SOREL: Not at all—Miss Coryton gave it away.

SIMON: Why "Miss Coryton" all of a sudden? You've been calling her Jackie all the evening. You're far too grand, Sorel.

SOREL: And you're absolutely maddening—I'll never play another game with you as long as I live.

SIMON: That won't break my heart.

JUDITH: Stop, stop, stop!

SIMON [*grabbing* JACKIE's *hand*]:   Come out in the garden. I'm sick of this.

SOREL: Don't let him take you on the river; he isn't very good at it.

SIMON [*over his shoulder*]:   Ha, ha!—very funny.

[*He drags* JACKIE *off.*

JUDITH: Sorel, you're behaving disgracefully.

SOREL: Simon ought to go into the army, or something.

DAVID: You both ought to be in reformatories.

SOREL: This always happens whenever we play a game. We're a beastly family, and I hate us.

JUDITH: Speak for yourself, dear.

SOREL: I can't, without speaking for everyone else too—we're all exactly the same, and I'm ashamed of us—Come into the library, Sandy.

She drags SANDY *off.*

MYRA: Charming! It's all perfectly charming.

DAVID: I think it would be better, Judith, if you exercised a little more influence over the children.

JUDITH: That's right—blame it all on me.

DAVID: After all, dear, you started it, by snapping everybody up.

JUDITH: You ought never to have married me, David; it was a great mistake.

DAVID: The atmosphere of this house is becoming more unbearable every day, and all because Simon and Sorel are allowed to do exactly what they like.

JUDITH: You sit upstairs all day, writing your novels.

DAVID: Novels which earn us our daily bread.

JUDITH: "Daily bread" nonsense! We've got enough money to keep us in comfort until we die.

DAVID: That will be very soon, if we can't get a little peace. [*To* MYRA] Come out into the garden—

JUDITH: I sincerely hope the night air will cool you.

DAVID: I don't know what's happened to you lately, Judith.

JUDITH: Nothing's happened to me—nothing ever does. You're far too smug to allow it.

DAVID: Smug! Thank you.

JUDITH: Yes, smug, smug, smug! And pompous!

DAVID: I hope you haven't been drinking, dear.

JUDITH: Drinking! Huh! that's very amusing!

DAVID: I think it's rather tragic, at your time of life.

[*He goes out with* MYRA.

JUDITH: David's been a good husband to me, but he's wearing a bit thin now.

RICHARD: Would you like me to go? To leave you alone for a little?

JUDITH: Why? Are you afraid I shall become violent?

RICHARD [*smiling*]: No; I merely thought perhaps I was in the way.

JUDITH: I hope you're not embarrassed—I couldn't bear you to be embarrassed.

RICHARD: Not in the least.

JUDITH: Marriage is a hideous affair altogether, don't you think?

RICHARD: I'm really hardly qualified to judge, you see.

JUDITH: Do stop being noncommittal, just for once; it's doubly annoying in the face of us all having lost control so lamentably.

RICHARD: I'm sorry.

JUDITH: There's nothing to be sorry for, really, because, after all, it's your particular "thing," isn't it?—observing everything and not giving yourself away an inch.

RICHARD: I suppose it is.

JUDITH: You'll get used to us in time, you know, and then you'll feel cozier. Why don't you sit down?

[*She sits on sofa.*

RICHARD: I'm enjoying myself very much.

JUDITH: It's very sweet of you to say so, but I don't see how you can be.

RICHARD [*laughing suddenly*]:   But I am!

JUDITH: There now! That was quite a genuine laugh. We're getting on. Are you in love with Sorel?

RICHARD [*surprised and embarrassed*]:   In love with Sorel?

JUDITH [*repentantly*]:   Now I've killed it—I've murdered the little tender feeling of comfort that was stealing over you, by sheer tactlessness! Will you teach me to be tactful?

RICHARD: Did you really think I was in love with Sorel?

JUDITH: It's so difficult to tell, isn't it?—I mean, you might not know yourself. She's very attractive.

RICHARD: Yes, she is—very.

JUDITH: Have you heard her sing?

RICHARD: No, not yet.

JUDITH: She sings beautifully. Are you susceptible to music?

RICHARD: I'm afraid I don't know very much about it.

JUDITH: You probably are, then. I'll sing you something.

RICHARD: Please do.

JUDITH [*rising*]:   It's awfully sad for a woman of my temperament to have a grown-up daughter, you know. I have to put my pride in my pocket and develop in her all the charming little feminine tricks which will eventually cut me out altogether.

RICHARD: That wouldn't be possible.

JUDITH: I do hope you meant that, because it was a sweet remark.

[*She is at the piano, turning over music.*

RICHARD [*following her*]: Of course I meant it.

JUDITH: Will you lean on the piano in an attentive attitude? It's such a help.

RICHARD: You're an extraordinary person.

JUDITH [*beginning to play*]: In what way extraordinary?

RICHARD: When I first met Sorel, I guessed what you'd be like.

JUDITH: Did you, now? And am I?

RICHARD [*smiling*]: Exactly.

JUDITH: Oh, well . . .

[*She plays and sings a little French song. There is a slight pause when it is finished.*

RICHARD [*with feeling*]: Thank you.

JUDITH [*rising from the piano*]: It's pretty, isn't it?

RICHARD: Perfectly enchanting.

JUDITH: Shall we sit down again?

[*She reseats herself on sofa.*

RICHARD: Won't you sing any more?

JUDITH: No, no more—I want you to talk to me and tell me all about yourself, and the things you've done.

RICHARD: I've done nothing.

JUDITH: What a shame! Why not?

RICHARD: I never realize how dead I am until I meet people like you. It's depressing, you know.

JUDITH: What nonsense! You're not a bit dead.

RICHARD: Do you always live here?

JUDITH: I'm going to, from now onwards. I intend to sink into a very beautiful old age. When the children marry, I shall wear a cap.

RICHARD [*smiling*]: How absurd!

JUDITH: I don't mean a funny cap.

RICHARD: You're far too full of vitality to sink into anything.

JUDITH: It's entirely spurious vitality. If you troubled to look below the surface, you'd find a very wistful and weary spirit. I've been battling with life for a long time.

RICHARD: Surely such successful battles as yours have been are not wearying?

JUDITH: Yes, they are—frightfully. I've reached an age now when I just want to sit back and let things go on around me —and they do.

RICHARD: I should like to know exactly what you're thinking about—really.

JUDITH: I was thinking of calling you Richard. It's such a nice uncompromising name.

RICHARD: I should be very flattered if you would.

JUDITH: I won't suggest you calling me Judith until you feel really comfortable about me.

RICHARD: But I do—Judith.

JUDITH: I'm awfully glad. Will you give me a cigarette?

RICHARD [*producing case*]: Certainly.

JUDITH [*taking one*]: That's a divine case.

RICHARD: It was given to me in Japan three years ago. All those little designs mean things.

JUDITH [*bending over it*]: What sort of things?

RICHARD: Charms for happiness, and luck, and—love.

JUDITH: Which is the charm for love?

RICHARD: That one.

JUDITH: What a dear!

RICHARD [*kissing her gently*]: Judith!

JUDITH [*jumping*]: Richard!

RICHARD: I'm afraid I couldn't help it.

JUDITH [*dramatically*]: What are we to do? What are we to do?

RICHARD: I don't know.

JUDITH: David must be told—everything!

RICHARD [*alarmed*]: Everything?

JUDITH [*enjoying herself*]: Yes, yes. There come moments in life when it is necessary to be honest—absolutely honest, I've trained myself always to shun the underhand methods other women so often employ—the truth must be faced fair and square—

RICHARD [*extremely alarmed*]: The truth? I don't quite understand.

JUDITH: Dear Richard, you want to spare me, I know—you're so chivalrous; but it's no use. After all, as I said before, David has been a good husband to me, according to his light. This may, of course, break him up rather, but it can't be helped; he must be told. I wonder—oh, I wonder how he'll take it. They say suffering's good for writers, it strengthens their psychology. Oh, my poor, poor David!—Never mind. You'd better go out into the garden and wait—

RICHARD [*flustered*]: Wait? What for?

JUDITH: For me, Richard, for me. I will come to you later. Wait in the summerhouse. I had begun to think that Romance was dead, that I should never know it again. Before, of course, I had my work and my life in the theater, but now, nothing—nothing! Everything is empty and hollow, like a broken shell.

RICHARD: Look here, Judith, I apologize for what I did just now. I—

JUDITH [*ignoring all interruption*]: But now you have come, and it's all changed—it's magic. I'm under a spell that I never thought to recapture again. Go along—

[*She pushes him towards the garden.*

RICHARD [*protesting*]: But, Judith—

JUDITH [*pushing him firmly*]: Don't—don't make it any harder for me. I am quite resolved—it is my self-appointed Calvary, and it's the only possible way!

[*She pushes him into the garden and waves to him bravely with her handkerchief; then she comes back into the room and powders her nose before the glass and pats her hair into place. Then, assuming an expression of restrained tragedy, she opens the library door, from which she recoils genuinely shocked. After a moment or two* SOREL *and* SANDY *come out rather sheepishly.*

SOREL: Look here, Mother, I—

JUDITH: Sorel, what am I to say to you?

SOREL: I don't know, mother.

JUDITH: Neither do I.

SANDY: It was my fault, Mrs. Bliss—Judith—

JUDITH: What a fool I've been! What a blind fool!

SOREL: Mother, are you *really* upset?

JUDITH [*with feeling*]:   I'm stunned.

SOREL: But, darling—

JUDITH [*gently*]:   Don't speak for a moment, Sorel; we must all be very quiet, and think—

SOREL: It was nothing, really. For Heaven's sake—

JUDITH: Nothing! I open the library door casually, and what do I see? I ask you, what do I see?

SANDY: I'm most awfully sorry . . .

JUDITH: Ssshh! It has gone beyond superficial apologies.

SOREL: Mother, be natural for a minute.

JUDITH: I don't know what you mean, Sorel. I'm trying to realize a very bitter truth as calmly as I can.

SOREL: There's nothing so very bitter about it.

JUDITH: My poor child!

SOREL [*suddenly*]:   Very well, then! I love Sandy, and he loves me!

JUDITH: That would be the only possible excuse for your behavior.

SOREL: Why shouldn't we love each other if we want to?

JUDITH: Sandy was in love with me this afternoon.

SOREL: Not real love—you know it wasn't.

JUDITH [*bitterly*]:   I know now.

SANDY: I say—look here—I'm most awfully sorry.

JUDITH: There's nothing to be sorry for, really; it's my fault for having been so—so ridiculous.

SOREL: Mother!

JUDITH [*sadly*]:   Yes, ridiculous. I'm getting old, old, and the sooner I face it the better.

SOREL [*hopelessly*]:   But, darling . . .

JUDITH [*splendidly*]:   Youth will be served. You're so pretty, Sorel, far prettier than I ever was—I'm very glad you're pretty.

SANDY: I feel a fearful cad.

JUDITH: Why should you? You've answered the only call that really counts—the call of Love, and Romance, and Spring. I forgive you, Sandy, completely. There.

SOREL: Well, that's all right, then.

JUDITH: I resent your tone, Sorel; you seem to be taking things too much for granted. Perhaps you don't realize that I am making a great sacrifice!

SOREL: Sorry, darling.

JUDITH: It's far from easy, at my time of life, to—

SOREL [*playing up*]: Mother—Mother, say you understand and forgive!

JUDITH: Understand! You forget, dear, I am a woman.

SOREL: I know you are, Mother. That's what makes it all so poignant.

JUDITH [*magnanimously, to* SANDY]: If you want Sorel, truly, I give her to you—unconditionally.

SANDY [*dazed*]: Thanks—awfully, Mrs. Bliss.

JUDITH: You can still call me Judith, can't you?—it's not much to ask.

SANDY: Judith.

JUDITH [*bravely*]: There, now. Away with melancholy. This is all tremendously exciting, and we must all be very happy.

SOREL: Don't tell father—yet.

JUDITH: We won't tell anybody; it shall be our little secret.

SOREL: You are splendid, mother.

JUDITH: Nonsense. I just believe in being honest with myself —it's awfully good for one, you know, so cleansing. I'm going upstairs now to have a little aspirin—[*She goes upstairs, and turns*] Ah, Youth, Youth, what a strange, mad muddle you make of things!

[*She goes off.* SOREL *heaves a slight sigh, and takes a cigarette.*

SOREL: Well, that's that.

SANDY: Yes.

SOREL: It's all right. Don't look so gloomy—I know you don't love me really.

SANDY [*startled*]: I say, Sorel—

SOREL: Don't protest; you know you don't—any more than I love you.

SANDY: But you told Judith—

SOREL [*nonchalantly*]: I was only playing up—one always plays up to mother in this house; it's a sort of unwritten law.

SANDY: Didn't she mean all she said?

SOREL: No, not really; we none of us ever mean anything.

SANDY: She seemed awfully upset.

SOREL: It must have been a slight shock for her to discover us clasped tightly in each other's arms.

SANDY: I believe I do love you, Sorel.

SOREL: A month ago I should have let you go on believing that, but now I can't—I'm bent on improving myself.

SANDY: I don't understand.

SOREL: Never mind—it doesn't matter. You just fell a victim to the atmosphere, that's all. There we were alone in the library, with the windows wide open, and probably a nightingale somewhere about—

SANDY: I only heard a cuckoo.

SOREL: Even a cuckoo has charm, in moderation. You kissed me because you were awfully nice and I was awfully nice and we both liked kissing very much. It was inevitable. Then Mother found us and got dramatic—her sense of the theater is always fatal. She knows we shan't marry, the same as you and I do. You're under absolutely no obligation to me at all.

SANDY: I wish I understood you a bit better.

SOREL: Never mind about understanding me. Let's go back into the library.

SANDY: All right.

[*They go off. After a moment's pause,* DAVID *and* MYRA *enter from the garden.*

DAVID: . . . And, you see, he comes in and finds her there waiting for him.

MYRA: She hadn't been away at all?

DAVID: No; and that's psychologically right, I'm sure. No woman, under those circumstances, *would.*

MYRA: It's brilliant of you to see that. I do think the whole thing sounds most excellent.

DAVID: I got badly stuck in the middle of the book, when the boy comes down from Oxford—but it worked out all right eventually.

MYRA [*sitting on sofa*]:   When shall I be able to read it?

DAVID: I'll send you the proofs—you can help me correct them.

MYRA: How divine! I shall feel most important.

DAVID: Would you like a cigarette, or anything?

MYRA: No, thank you.

DAVID: I think I'll have a drink.

MYRA: Very well; give me some plain soda-water, then.

DAVID [*going to side table*]: There isn't any ice—d'you mind?

MYRA: Not a bit.

DAVID [*bringing her drink*]: Here you are.

MYRA: Thank you. [*She sips it*] I wonder where everybody is.

DAVID: Not here, thank God.

MYRA: It must be dreadfully worrying for you, having a house-ful of people.

DAVID [*having poured himself out a whisky-and-soda, sits down by her side*]: It depends on the people.

MYRA: I have a slight confession to make.

DAVID: Confession?

MYRA: Yes. Do you know why I came down here?

DAVID: Not in the least. I suppose one of us asked you, didn't they?

MYRA: Oh yes, they asked me, but—

DAVID: Well?

MYRA: I was invited once before—last September.

DAVID: I was in America then.

MYRA: Exactly.

DAVID: How do you mean "exactly"?

MYRA: I didn't come. I'm a very determined woman, you know, and I made up my mind to meet you ages ago.

DAVID: That was charming of you. I'm not much to meet really.

MYRA: You see, I'd read *Broken Reeds*.

DAVID: Did you like it?

MYRA: Like it! I think it's one of the finest novels I've ever read.

DAVID: There now!

MYRA: How do you manage to know so much about women?

DAVID: I'm afraid my knowledge of them is sadly superficial.

MYRA: Oh, no; you can't call Evelyn's character superficial—it's amazing.

DAVID: Why are you being so nice to me? Have you got a

plan about something?

MYRA [*laughing*]:   How suspicious you are!

DAVID: I can't help it—you're very attractive, and I'm always suspicious of attractive people, on principle.

MYRA: Not a very good principle.

DAVID: I'll tell you something—strictly between ourselves.

MYRA: Do.

DAVID: You're wrong about me.

MYRA: Wrong? In what way?

DAVID: I write very bad novels.

MYRA: Don't be so ridiculous.

DAVID: And you *know* I do, because you're an intelligent person.

MYRA: I don't know anything of the sort.

DAVID: Tell me why you're being so nice to me?

MYRA: Because I want to be.

DAVID: Why?

MYRA: You're a very clever and amusing man.

DAVID: Splendid.

MYRA: And I think I've rather lost my heart to you.

DAVID: Shall we elope?

MYRA: David!

DAVID: There now, you've called me David!

MYRA: Do you mind?

DAVID: Not at all.

MYRA: I'm not sure that you're being very kind.

DAVID: What makes you think that?

MYRA: You're being rather the cynical author laughing up his sleeve at a gushing admirer.

DAVID: I think you're a very interesting woman, and extremely nice-looking.

MYRA: Do you?

DAVID: Yes. Would you like me to make love to you?

MYRA [*rising*]:   Really—I wish you wouldn't say things like that.

DAVID: I've knocked you off your plate—I'll look away for a minute while you climb on to it again.

[*He does so.*

MYRA [*laughing affectedly*]:   This is wonderful!
[*She sits down again.*
DAVID [*turning*]:   That's right. Now then—
MYRA: Now then, what?
DAVID: You're adorable—you're magnificent—you're tawny—
MYRA: I'm not tawny.
DAVID: Don't argue.
MYRA: This is sheer affectation.
DAVID: Affectation's very nice.
MYRA: No, it isn't—it's odious.
DAVID: You mustn't get cross.
MYRA: I'm not in the least cross.
DAVID: Yes, you are—but you're very alluring.
MYRA [*perking up*]:   Alluring?
DAVID: Terribly.
MYRA: I can hear your brain clicking—it's very funny.
DAVID: That was rather rude.
MYRA: You've been consistently rude to me for hours.
DAVID: Never mind.
MYRA: Why have you?
DAVID: I'm always rude to people I like.
MYRA: Do you like me?
DAVID: Enormously.
MYRA: How sweet of you!
DAVID: But I don't like your methods.
MYRA: Methods? What methods?
DAVID: You're far too pleasant to occupy yourself with the commonplace.
MYRA: And you spoil yourself by trying to be clever.
DAVID: Thank you.
MYRA: Anyhow, I don't know what you mean by commonplace.
DAVID: You mean you want me to explain?
MYRA: Not at all.
DAVID: Very well; I will.
MYRA: I shan't listen.
[*She stops up her ears.*

DAVID: You'll pretend not to, but you'll hear every word really.

MYRA [*sarcastically*]: You're so inscrutable and quizzical—just what a feminine psychologist should be.

DAVID: Yes, aren't I?

MYRA: You frighten me dreadfully.

DAVID: Darling!

MYRA: Don't call me darling.

DAVID: That's unreasonable. You've been trying to make me—all the evening.

MYRA: Your conceit is outrageous!

DAVID: It's not conceit at all. You've been firmly buttering me up because you want a nice little intrigue.

MYRA [*rising*]: How dare you!

DAVID [*pulling her down again*]: It's true, it's true. If it weren't, you wouldn't be so angry.

MYRA: I think you're insufferable!

DAVID [*taking her hand*]: Myra—dear Myra—

MYRA [*snatching it away*]: Don't touch me.

DAVID: Let's have that nice little intrigue. The only reason I've been so annoying is that I love to see things as they are first, and then pretend they're what they're not.

MYRA: Words! Masses and masses of words!

DAVID: They're great fun to play with.

MYRA: I'm glad you think so. Personally, they bore me stiff.

DAVID [*catching her hand again*]: Myra—don't be statuesque.

MYRA: Let go my hand!

DAVID: You're charming.

[*He gets up and stands close to her.*

MYRA [*furiously*]: Let go my hand.

DAVID: I won't.

MYRA: You will!

[*She slaps his face hard, and he seizes her in his arms and kisses her.*

DAVID [*between kisses*]: You're—perfectly—sweet.

MYRA [*giving in*]: David!

DAVID: You must say it's an entrancing amusement.

[*He kisses her again.* JUDITH *appears at the top of the stairs and sees them. They break away.*

JUDITH [*coming down*]: Forgive me for interrupting.

DAVID: Are there any chocolates in the house?

JUDITH: No, David.

DAVID: I should like a chocolate more than anything in the world, at the moment.

JUDITH: This is a very unpleasant situation, David.

DAVID [*agreeably*]: Horrible.

JUDITH: We'd better talk it all over.

MYRA [*making a movement*]: I shall do nothing of the sort.

JUDITH: Please—please don't be difficult.

DAVID: I apologize, Judith.

JUDITH: Don't apologize—I quite understand.

MYRA: Please let go of my hand, David; I should like to go to bed.

JUDITH: I should stay if I were you—it would be more dignified.

DAVID: There isn't any real necessity for a scene.

JUDITH: I don't want a scene. I just want to straighten things out.

DAVID: Very well—go ahead.

JUDITH: June has always been an unlucky month for me.

MYRA: Look here, Judith, I'd like to explain one thing—

JUDITH [*austerely*]: I don't wish to hear any explanations or excuses—they're so cheapening. This was bound to happen sooner or later—it always does, to everybody. The only thing is to keep calm.

DAVID: I am—perfectly.

JUDITH [*sharply*]: There is such a thing as being too calm.

DAVID: Sorry, dear.

JUDITH: Life has dealt me another blow, but I don't mind.

DAVID: What did you say?

JUDITH [*crossly*]: I said Life had dealt me another blow, but I didn't mind.

DAVID: Rubbish.

JUDITH [*gently*]: You're probably irritable, dear, because you're in the wrong. It's quite usual.

DAVID: Now, Judith—

JUDITH: Ssshhh! Let me speak—it is my right.

MYRA: I don't see why.

JUDITH [*surprised*]: I am the injured party, am I not?

MYRA: Injured?

JUDITH [*firmly*]: Yes, extremely injured.

DAVID [*contemptuously*]: Injured!

JUDITH: Your attitude, David, is nothing short of deplorable.

DAVID: It's all nonsense—sheer, unbridled nonsense.

JUDITH: No, David, you can't evade the real issues as calmly as that. I've known for a long time—I've realized subconsciously for years that you've stopped caring for me in "that way."

DAVID [*irritably*]: What do you mean—"that way"?

JUDITH [*with a wave of the hand*]: Just that way . . . It's rather tragic, but quite inevitable. I'm growing old now—men don't grow old like women, as you'll find to your cost, Myra, in a year or two. David has retained his youth astonishingly, perhaps because he has had fewer responsibilities and cares than I—

MYRA: This is all ridiculous hysteria.

DAVID [*looking at her and not liking her very much*]: No, Myra —Judith is right. What are we to do?

MYRA [*furious*]: Do? Nothing!

JUDITH [*ignoring her*]: Do you love her truly, David?

DAVID: Madly.

MYRA [*astounded*]: David!

DAVID [*intensely*]: You thought just now that I was joking. Couldn't you see that all my flippancy was only a mask, hiding my real emotions—crushing them down desperately—?

MYRA [*scared*]: But, David, I—

JUDITH: I knew it! The time has come for the dividing of the ways.

MYRA: What on earth do you mean?

JUDITH: I mean that I am not the sort of woman to hold a man against his will.

MYRA: You're both making a mountain out of a mole hill. David doesn't love me madly, and I don't love him. It's—

JUDITH: Ssshhh!—you *do* love him. I can see it in your eyes—
in your every gesture. David, I give you to her—freely and
without rancor. We must all be good friends, always.

DAVID: Judith, do you mean this?

JUDITH [*with a melting look*]: You know I do.

DAVID: How can we ever repay you?

JUDITH: Just by being happy. I may leave this house later on—
I have a feeling that its associations may become painful,
specially in the autumn—

MYRA: Look here, Judith—

JUDITH [*shouting her down*]: October is such a mournful
month in England. I think I shall probably go abroad—perhaps a *pension* somewhere in Italy, with cypresses in the
garden. I've always loved cypresses.

DAVID: What about the children?

JUDITH: We must share them, dear.

DAVID: I'll pay you exactly half the royalties I receive from
everything, Judith.

JUDITH [*bowing her head*]: That's very generous of you.

DAVID: You have behaved magnificently. This is a crisis in our
lives, and thanks to you—

MYRA [*almost shrieking*]: Judith—I *will* speak—I—

DAVID: Ssshhh, Myra darling—we owe it to Judith to keep
control of our emotions—a scene would be agonizing for her
now. She has been brave and absolutely splendid throughout.
Let's not make things harder for her than we can help. Come,
we'll go out into the garden.

MYRA: I will *not* go out into the garden.

JUDITH [*twisting her handkerchief*]: Please go—I don't think
I can bear any more just now.

DAVID: So this is the end, Judith?

JUDITH: Yes, my dear—the end.

[*They shake hands sadly.* SIMON *enters violently from the
garden.*

SIMON: Mother—Mother, I've got something important to tell
you.

JUDITH [*smiling bravely*]: Very well, dear.

SIMON: Where's Sorel?

JUDITH: In the library, I'm afraid.

SIMON [*opening library door*]:   Sorel, come out—I've got something vital to tell you.

DAVID [*fatherly*]:   You seem excited, my boy. What has happened?

SOREL [*entering with* SANDY]:   What's the matter?

SIMON: I wish you wouldn't all look so depressed—it's good news!

DAVID: Good news! I thought perhaps Jackie had been drowned—

SIMON: No, Jackie hasn't been drowned—she's been something else.

JUDITH: Simon, what *do* you mean?

SIMON [*calling*]:   Jackie—Jackie! [JACKIE *enters coyly from the garden*] She has become engaged—to me!

JUDITH [*in heartfelt tones*]:   Simon!

SOREL: Good heavens!

JUDITH: Simon, my dear! Oh, this is too much!

[*She cries a little.*

SIMON: What on earth are you crying about, Mother?

JUDITH [*picturesquely*]:   All my chicks leaving the nest. Now I shall only have my memories left. Jackie, come and kiss me. [JACKIE *goes to her*] You must promise to make my son happy—

JACKIE [*worried*]:   But, Mrs. Bliss—

JUDITH: Ssshhh! I understand. I have not been a mother for nothing.

JACKIE [*wildly*]:   But it's not true—we don't—

JUDITH: You're trying to spare my feelings—I know—

MYRA [*furiously*]:   Well, I'm not going to spare your feelings, or anyone else's. You're the most infuriating set of hypocrites I've ever seen. This house is a complete featherbed of false emotions—you're posing, self-centered egotists, and I'm sick to death of you.

SIMON: Myra!

MYRA: Don't speak to me. I've been working up for this, only every time I opened my mouth I've been mowed down by theatrical effects. You haven't got one sincere or genuine

feeling among the lot of you—you're artificial to the point
of lunacy. It's a great pity you ever left the stage, Judith—
it's your rightful home. You can rant and roar there as much
as ever you like—

JUDITH: Rant and roar! May God forgive you!

MYRA: And let me tell you this—You don't seem to grasp one
thing that—

SIMON [*interrupting*]:   I'm not going to allow you to say another word to Mother—

[*Together.*

SOREL: You ought to be ashamed of yourself—

MYRA: Let me speak—I will speak—

DAVID: Look here, Myra—

JUDITH: This is appalling—appalling!

SOREL: You must be stark, staring mad—

MYRA: Never again—never as long as I live—

SIMON: Why are you behaving like this, anyhow?

[*In the middle of the pandemonium of everyone talking at once,*
RICHARD *comes in from the garden. He looks extremely appre-
hensive, imagining that the noise is the outcome of* JUDITH'S
hysterical confession of their lukewarm passion. He goes to
JUDITH'S *side, summoning all his diplomatic forces. At his en-
trance everyone stops talking.*

RICHARD [*with forced calm*]:   What's happened? Is this a game?

[JUDITH'S *face gives a slight twitch; then with a meaning look
at* SOREL *and* SIMON, *she answers him.*

JUDITH [*with spirit*]:   Yes, and a game that must be played to
the finish!

SIMON [*grasping the situation*]:   Zara! What does this mean?

JUDITH [*in bell-like tones*]:   So many illusions shattered—so
many dreams trodden in the dust—

DAVID [*collapsing on to the sofa in hysterics*]:   Love's whirlwind! Dear old Love's whirlwind!

SOREL: I don't understand. You and Victor—My God!

JUDITH: Hush! Isn't that little Pam crying—?

SIMON [*savagely*]:   She'll cry more, poor mite, when she realizes
her mother is a—a—

JUDITH [*shrieking*]:   Don't say it! Don't say it!

SOREL: Spare her that.

JUDITH: I've given you all that makes life worth living—my youth, my womanhood, and now my child. Would you tear the very heart out of me? I tell you, it's infamous that men like you should be allowed to pollute Society. You have ruined my life. I have nothing left—nothing. God in heaven, where am I to turn for help . . .

SOREL [*through clenched teeth*]:   Is this true? Answer me—is this true?

JUDITH [*wailing*]:   Yes, yes!

SOREL [*springing at* SIMON]:   You cur! ! !

JUDITH [*rushing between them*]:   Don't strike! He is your father!

[*She totters and falls in a dead faint.* MYRA, JACKIE, RICHARD, *and* SANDY *look on, dazed and aghast.*

CURTAIN

All change ? ? .
Except for Clara !

ACT THREE

It is Sunday morning, about ten o'clock. There are various breakfast dishes on a side table, and a big table is laid down center.

SANDY appears at the top of the stairs. On seeing no one about, he comes down quickly and furtively helps himself to eggs and bacon and coffee, and seats himself at the table. He eats very hurriedly, casting occasional glances over his shoulder. A door bangs somewhere upstairs, which terrifies him; he chokes violently. When he has recovered, he tears a bit of toast from a rack, butters it and marmalades it and crams it into his mouth. Then, hearing somebody approaching, he darts into the library.

JACKIE comes downstairs timorously; her expression is dismal, to say the least of it. She looks miserably out of the window at the pouring rain, then, assuming an air of spurious bravado, she helps herself to some breakfast and sits down and looks at it. After one or two attempts to eat it, she bursts into tears.

SANDY opens the library door a crack and peeps out. JACKIE, seeing the door move, screams. SANDY re-enters.

JACKIE: Oh, it's only you—you frightened me!

SANDY: What's the matter?

JACKIE [*sniffing*]: Nothing.

SANDY: I say, don't cry.

JACKIE: I'm not crying.

SANDY: You were—I heard you.

JACKIE: It's this house. It gets on my nerves.

SANDY: I don't wonder—after last night.

JACKIE: What were you doing in the library just now?

SANDY: Hiding.

JACKIE: Hiding?

SANDY: Yes; I didn't want to run up against any of the family.

JACKIE: I wish I'd never come. I had horrible nightmares with all those fearful dragons crawling across the wall.

SANDY: Dragons?

JACKIE: Yes; I'm in a Japanese room—everything in it's Japanese, even the bed.

SANDY: How awful!

JACKIE: I believe they're all mad, you know.

SANDY: The Blisses?

JACKIE: Yes—they must be.

SANDY: I've been thinking that, too.

JACKIE: Do you suppose they know they're mad?

SANDY: No; people never do.

JACKIE: It was Mr. Bliss asked me down, and he hasn't paid any attention to me at all. I went into his study soon after I arrived yesterday, and he said, "Who the hell are you?"

SANDY: Didn't he remember?

JACKIE: He did afterwards; then he brought me down to tea and left me.

SANDY: Are you really engaged to Simon?

JACKIE [bursting into tears again]:   Oh, no—I hope not!

SANDY: You were, last night.

JACKIE: So were you—to Sorel.

SANDY: Not properly. We talked it over.

JACKIE: I don't know what happened to me. I was in the garden with Simon, and he was being awfully sweet, and then he suddenly kissed me, and rushed into the house and said we were engaged—and that hateful Judith asked me to make him happy!

SANDY: That's exactly what happened to me and Sorel. Judith gave us to one another before we knew where we were.

JACKIE: How frightful!

SANDY: I like Sorel, though; she was jolly decent about it afterwards.

JACKIE: I think she's a cat.

SANDY: Why?

JACKIE: Look at the way she lost her temper over that beastly game.

SANDY: All the same, she's better than the others.

JACKIE: That wouldn't be very difficult.

SANDY: Hic!

JACKIE: I beg your pardon?

SANDY [*abashed*]:   I say—I've got hiccoughs.

JACKIE: Hold your breath.

SANDY: It was because I bolted my breakfast.

[*He holds his breath.*

JACKIE: Hold it as long as you can.

[*There is a pause.*

SANDY [*letting his breath go with a gasp*]:   I can't any more—hic!

JACKIE: Eat a lump of sugar.

SANDY [*taking one*]:   I'm awfully sorry.

JACKIE: I don't mind—but it's a horrid feeling, isn't it?

SANDY: Horrid—hic!

JACKIE [*conversationally*]:   People have died from hiccoughs, you know.

SANDY [*gloomily*]:   Have they?

JACKIE: Yes. An aunt of mine once had them for three days without stopping.

SANDY: How beastly.

JACKIE [*with relish*]:   She had to have the doctor, and everything.

SANDY: I expect mine will stop soon.

JACKIE: I hope they will.

SANDY: Hic!—There!

JACKIE: Drink some water the wrong way round.

SANDY: How do you mean—the wrong way round?

JACKIE [*rising*]:   The wrong side of the glass. I'll show you. [*She goes to side table*] There isn't any water.

SANDY: Perhaps coffee would do as well.

JACKIE: I've never tried coffee, but it might. [*She pours him out some*] There you are.

SANDY [*anxiously*]:   What do I do?

JACKIE: Tip it up and drink from the opposite side, sort of upside down.

SANDY [*trying*]:   I can't reach any—

JACKIE [*suddenly*]:   Look out—somebody's coming. Bring it into the library—quick . . .

SANDY: Bring the sugar—I might need it again—hic! Oh God!

JACKIE: All right.

[*They go off into the library hurriedly.* RICHARD *comes down-stairs. He glances round a trifle anxiously; then, pulling himself together, he goes boldly to the barometer and taps it. It falls off the wall and breaks; he picks it up quickly and places it on the piano. Then he helps himself to some breakfast, and sits down.* MYRA *appears on the stairs, very smart and bright.*

MYRA [*vivaciously*]: Good morning.

RICHARD: Good morning.

MYRA: Are we the first down?

RICHARD: No, I don't think so.

MYRA [*looking out of the window*]: Isn't this rain miserable?

RICHARD: Appalling!

MYRA: Where's the barometer?

RICHARD: On the piano.

MYRA: What a queer place for it to be.

RICHARD: I tapped it, and it fell down.

MYRA: Typical of this house. [*At side table*] Are you having eggs and bacon, or haddock?

RICHARD: Haddock.

MYRA: I'll have haddock too. I simply couldn't strike out a line for myself this morning. [*She helps herself to haddock and coffee, and sits down opposite* RICHARD] Have you seen anybody?

RICHARD: No.

MYRA: Good. We might have a little peace.

RICHARD: Have you ever stayed here before?

MYRA: No, and I never will again.

RICHARD: I feel far from well this morning.

MYRA: I'm so sorry, but not entirely surprised.

RICHARD: You see, I had the boiler room.

MYRA: How terrible!

RICHARD: The window stuck, and I couldn't open it—I was nearly suffocated. The pipes made peculiar noises all night, as well.

MYRA: There isn't any sugar.

RICHARD: Oh—we'd better ring.

MYRA: I doubt if it will be the slightest use, but we'll try.

RICHARD [*ringing and ringing bell*]: Do the whole family have breakfast in bed?

MYRA: I neither know—nor care.

RICHARD: They're strange people, aren't they?

MYRA: I think "strange" is putting it mildly.

[*Enter* CLARA.

CLARA: What's the matter?

MYRA: There isn't any sugar.

CLARA: There is—I put it 'ere myself.

MYRA: Perhaps you'd find it for us, then?

CLARA [*searching*]: That's very funny. I could 'ave sworn on me Bible oath I brought it in.

MYRA: Well, it obviously isn't here now.

CLARA: Someone's taken it—that's what it is.

RICHARD: It seems a queer thing to do.

MYRA: Do you think you could get us some more?

CLARA: Oh yes, I'll fetch you some; but mark my words, there's been some 'anky-panky somewhere.

[*She goes out.*

MYRA: Clara is really more at home in a dressing room than a house.

RICHARD: Was she Judith's dresser?

MYRA: Of course. What other excuse could there possibly be for her?

RICHARD: She seems good-natured, but quaint.

MYRA: This haddock's disgusting.

RICHARD: It isn't very nice, is it?

[*Re-enter* CLARA *with sugar. She plumps it down.*

CLARA: There you are, dear.

MYRA: Thank you.

CLARA: It's a shame the weather's changed—you might 'ave 'ad such fun up the river. [*There comes the sound of a crash from the library, and a scream*] What's that? [*She opens the door*] Come out! What are you doing?

[JACKIE *and* SANDY *enter, rather shamefaced.*

JACKIE: Good morning. I'm afraid we've broken a coffee cup.

CLARA: Was there any coffee in it?

SANDY: Yes, a good deal.

CLARA [*rushing into the library*]: Oh dear! all over the carpet!

SANDY: It was my fault. I'm most awfully sorry.

[CLARA *reappears.*

CLARA: How did you come to do it?

JACKIE: Well, you see, he had the hiccoughs, and I was showing him how to drink upside down.

MYRA: How ridiculous!

CLARA: Well, thank 'Eaven it wasn't one of the Crown Derbys.
[*She goes out.*

SANDY: They've gone now, anyhow.

JACKIE: It was the sudden shock, I expect.

SANDY [*observantly*]: I say—it's raining!

MYRA: It's been raining for hours.

RICHARD: Mrs. Arundel—

MYRA: Yes?

RICHARD: What are you going to do about—about today?

MYRA: Nothing, except go up to London by the first train
possible.

RICHARD: Do you mind if I come too? I don't think I could
face another day like yesterday.

JACKIE: Neither could I.

SANDY [*eagerly*]: Let's all go away—quietly!

RICHARD: Won't it seem a little rude if we *all* go?

MYRA: Yes it will. [*To* SANDY] You and Miss Coryton must
stay.

JACKIE: I don't see why.

SANDY: I don't think they'd mind *very* much if we all went.

MYRA: Yes, they would. You must let Mr. Greatham and me
get away first, anyhow. Ring for Clara. I want to find out
about trains.

RICHARD: I hope they won't all come down now.

MYRA: You needn't worry about that; they're sure to roll
about in bed for hours—they're such a slovenly family.

RICHARD: Have you got much packing to do?

MYRA: No; I did most of it before I came down.

[*Re-enter* CLARA.

CLARA: What is it now?

MYRA: Can you tell me what trains there are up to London?

CLARA: When?

MYRA: This morning.

CLARA: Why?—You're not leaving, are you?

MYRA: Yes; Mr. Greatham and I have to be up by lunch time.

CLARA: Well, you have missed the ten-fifteen.

MYRA: Obviously.

CLARA: There isn't another till twelve-thirty.

RICHARD: Good heavens!

CLARA: And that's a slow one.

[She goes out.

SANDY [to JACKIE]: Look here; I'll take you up in my car as soon as you like.

JACKIE: All right; lovely!

MYRA: You've got a car, haven't you?

SANDY: Yes.

MYRA: Will it hold all of us?

JACKIE: You said it would be rude for us all to go. Hadn't you and Mr. Greatham better wait for the train?

MYRA: Certainly not.

RICHARD [to SANDY]: If there is room, we should be very, very grateful.

SANDY: I think I can squeeze you in.

MYRA: Then that's settled, then.

JACKIE: When shall we start?

SANDY: As soon as you're ready.

JACKIE: Mrs. Arundel, what are you going to do about tipping Clara?

MYRA: I don't know. [To RICHARD] What do you think?

RICHARD: I've hardly seen her since I've been here.

JACKIE: Isn't there a houesmaid or anything?

RICHARD: I don't think so.

SANDY: Is ten bob enough?

JACKIE: Each?

MYRA: Too much.

RICHARD: We'd better give her one pound ten between us.

MYRA: Very well, then. Will you do it, and we'll settle up in the car?

RICHARD: Must I?

MYRA: Yes. Ring for her.

RICHARD: You'd do it much better.

[SANDY *rings the bell.*

MYRA: Oh no, I shouldn't. [*To* JACKIE] Come on; we'll finish our packing.

JACKIE: All right.

[*They begin to go upstairs.*

RICHARD: Here—don't leave me.

SANDY: I'll just go and look at the car. Will you all be ready in ten minutes?

MYRA: Yes, ten minutes.

[*She goes off with* JACKIE.

SANDY: Righto.

[*He rushes out.* CLARA *re-enters.*

CLARA: 'Allo, where's everybody gone?

RICHARD: They've gone to get ready. We're leaving in Mr. Tyrell's car.

CLARA: A bit sudden, isn't it?

RICHARD [*pressing money into her hand*]: This is from all of us, Clara. Thank you very much for all your trouble.

CLARA [*surprised*]: Aren't you a dear, now! There wasn't any trouble.

RICHARD: There must have been a lot of extra work.

CLARA: One gets used to that 'ere.

RICHARD: Good-by, Clara.

[*He goes upstairs.* CLARA *proceeds to clear away the dirty break-fast things, which she takes out. She returns with a fresh pot of coffee, and meets* JUDITH *coming downstairs.*

JUDITH: Good morning, Clara. Have the papers come?

CLARA: Yes—I'll fetch them.

[*She goes out.* JUDITH *pours herself out some coffee, and sits down.* CLARA *re-enters with papers.*

JUDITH: Thank you. You've forgotten my orange juice.

CLARA: No, I 'aven't, dear; it's just outside.

[*She goes out again.* JUDITH *turns to the theatrical column of the* Sunday Times. SOREL *comes downstairs and kisses her.*

SOREL: Good morning, darling.

JUDITH: Listen to this. [*She reads*] "We saw Judith Bliss in a box at the Haymarket on Tuesday, looking as lovely as ever." There now! I thought I looked hideous on Tuesday.

SOREL: You looked sweet.

[*She goes to get herself some breakfast.* CLARA *reappears, with a glass of orange juice.*

CLARA [*placing it in front of* JUDITH]: Did you see that nice bit in the *Referee?*

JUDITH: No—the *Times.*

CLARA: The *Referee's* much better.

[*She finds the place and hands it to* SOREL.

SOREL [*reading*]: "I saw gay and colorful Judith Bliss at the Waifs and Strays matinée last week. She was talking vivaciously to Producer Basil Dean. 'I sooth,' said I to myself, 'where ignorance is Bliss, 'tis folly to be wise.' "

JUDITH [*taking it from her*]: Dear *Referee!* It's so unself-conscious.

CLARA: If you want any more coffee, ring for it.

[*She goes out.*

SOREL [*sitting down*]: I wish I were sitting on a lovely South Sea island, with masses of palm trees and cocoanuts and turtles—

JUDITH: It would be divine, wouldn't it?

SOREL: I wonder where everybody is?

JUDITH [*still reading*]: I wonder . . . Mary Saunders has got another failure.

SOREL: She must be used to it by now.

[SIMON *comes downstairs with a rush.*

SIMON [*kissing* JUDITH]: Good morning, darling—Look!

[*He shows her a newly completed sketch.*

JUDITH: Simon! How lovely! When did you do it?

SIMON: This morning—I woke early.

SOREL [*rising and craning over* JUDITH's *shoulder*]: Let's see.

SIMON [*over the other shoulder*]: I'm going to alter Helen's face; it's too pink.

SOREL [*laughing*]: It's exactly like her.

JUDITH: What a clever son I have!

SIMON: Now then, Mother!

JUDITH: It's too wonderful—when I think of you both in your perambulators . . . Oh dear, it makes me cry!
[*She sniffs.*

SOREL: . I don't believe you ever saw us in our perambulators.

JUDITH: I don't believe I did.

[DAVID *comes downstairs.*

DAVID [*hilariously*]:   It's finished!

JUDITH: What, dear?

DAVID: *The Sinful Woman.*

JUDITH: How splendid. Read it to us now.

DAVID: I've got the last chapter here.

JUDITH: Go on, then.

[SANDY *rushes in from the front door. On seeing everyone, he halts.*

SANDY: Good morning.

[*He bolts upstairs two at a time.*

JUDITH: I seem to know that boy's face.

DAVID [*preparing to read*]:   Listen. You remember when Violet was taken ill in Paris?

JUDITH: Yes, dear—Marmalade, Simon.

DAVID: Well, I'll go on from there.

JUDITH: Do, dear.

DAVID [*reading*]:   "Paris in spring, with the Champs Elysées alive and dancing in the sunlight; lightly dressed children like gay painted butterflies—"

SIMON [*whispering to* SOREL]:   What's happened to the barometer?

SOREL [*sibilantly*]:   I don't know.

DAVID: Damn the barometer!

JUDITH: Don't get cross, dear.

DAVID: Why can't you keep quiet, Simon, or go away!

SIMON: Sorry, Father.

DAVID: Well, don't interrupt again . . . [*Reading*] ". . . gay painted butterflies; the streets were thronged with hurrying vehicles, the thin peek-peek of taxi-hooters—"

SOREL: I love "peek-peek."

DAVID [*ignoring her*]:   "—seemed to merge in with the other vivid noises weaving a vast pattern of sound which was Paris.

Jane Sefton, in her scarlet Hispano, swept out of the Rue
St.-Honoré into the Place de la Concorde—"

JUDITH: She couldn't have.

DAVID: Why?

JUDITH: The Rue St.-Honoré doesn't lead into the Place de la
Concorde.

DAVID: Yes, it does.

SOREL: You're thinking of the Rue Boissy d'Anglas, Father.

DAVID: I'm not thinking of anything of the sort.

JUDITH: David darling, don't be obstinate.

DAVID [hotly]:   Do you think I don't know Paris as well as you
do?

SIMON: Never mind. Father's probably right.

SOREL: He isn't right—he's wrong!

DAVID: Go on with your food, Sorel.

JUDITH: Don't be testy, David: it's a sign of age.

DAVID [firmly]:   "Jane Sefton, in her scarlet Hispano, swept out
of the Rue St.-Honoré into the Place de la Concorde—"

JUDITH: That sounds absolutely ridiculous. Why don't you
alter it?

DAVID: It isn't ridiculous; it's perfectly right.

JUDITH: Very well, then; get a map, and I'll show you.

SIMON: We haven't got a map.

DAVID [putting his MS. down]:   Now, look here Judith—here's
the Rue Royale—[He arranges the butter-dish and marma-
lade-pot]—here's the Crillon Hotel, and here's the Rue St.-
Honoré—

JUDITH: It isn't—it's the Boissy d'Anglas.

DAVID: That runs parallel with the Rue de Rivoli.

JUDITH: You've got it all muddled.

DAVID [loudly]:   I have not got it all muddled.

JUDITH: Don't shout. You have.

SIMON: Why not let Father get on with it?

JUDITH: It's so silly to get cross at criticism—it indicates a
small mind.

DAVID: Small mind my foot!

JUDITH: That was very rude. I shall go to my room in a
minute.

DAVID: I wish you would.

JUDITH [*outraged*]:   David!

SOREL: Look here, Father, Mother's right—here's the Place de la Concorde—

SIMON: Oh, shut up, Sorel.

SOREL: Shut up yourself, you pompous little beast.

SIMON: You think you know such a lot about everything, and you're as ignorant as a frog.

SOREL: Why a frog?

JUDITH: I give you my solemn promise, David, that you're wrong.

DAVID: I don't want your solemn promise, because I *know* I'm right.

SIMON: It's no use arguing with Father, Mother.

SOREL: Why isn't it any use arguing with Father?

SIMON: Because you're both so pigheaded!

DAVID: Are you content to sit here, Judith, and let your son insult me?

JUDITH: He's your son as well as mine.

DAVID: I begin to doubt it.

JUDITH [*bursting into tears of rage*]:   David!

SIMON [*consoling her*]:   Father, how can you!

DAVID [*rising*]:   I'll never attempt to read any of you anything again as long as I live. You're not a bit interested in my work, and you don't give a damn whether I'm a success or a failure.

JUDITH: You're dead certain to be a failure if you cram your books with inaccuracies.

DAVID [*hammering the table with his fist*]:   I *am not inac-curate!*

JUDITH: Yes, you are; and you're foul-tempered and spoilt.

DAVID: Spoiled! I like that! Nobody here spoils me—you're the most insufferable family to live with—

JUDITH: Well, why in Heaven's name don't you go and live somewhere else?

DAVID: There's gratitude!

JUDITH: Gratitude for what, I'd like to know?

SOREL: Mother, keep calm.

JUDITH: Calm! I'm furious.

DAVID: What have you got to be furious about? Everyone rushing round adoring you and saying how wonderful you are—

JUDITH: I am wonderful, Heaven knows, to have stood you for all these years.

SOREL: Mother, do sit down and be quiet.

SIMON: How dare you speak to Mother like that!

[*During this scene* MYRA, JACKIE, RICHARD, *and* SANDY *creep downstairs, with their bags, unperceived by the family. They make for the front door.*

JUDITH [*wailing*]:   Oh, oh! To think that my daughter should turn against me!

DAVID: Don't be theatrical.

JUDITH: I'm not theatrical—I'm wounded to the heart.

DAVID: Rubbish—rubbish—rubbish!

JUDITH: Don't you say Rubbish to me!

DAVID: I *will* say Rubbish!

[*Together.*

SOREL: Ssshhh, Father!

SIMON: That's right! Be the dutiful daughter and encourage your father—

DAVID: Listen to me, Judith—

JUDITH: Oh, this is dreadful—dreadful!

SOREL: The whole thing doesn't really matter in the least—

SIMON: —to insult your mother—

DAVID: The Place de la Concorde—

JUDITH: I never realized how small you were, David. You're tiny—

[*The universal pandemonium is suddenly broken by the front door slamming. There is dead silence for a moment, then the noise of a car is heard.* SOREL *runs and looks out of the window.*

SIMON: There now!

SOREL: They've all gone!

JUDITH [*sitting down*]:   How very rude!

DAVID [*also sitting down*]:   People really do behave in the most extraordinary manner these days—

JUDITH: Come back and finish your breakfast, Sorel.

SOREL: All right.

[*She sits down.*

SIMON: Toast, please, Sorel.

SOREL [*passing it to him*]: Here.

JUDITH: Go on, David; I'm dying to hear the end—

DAVID [*reading*]: "Jane Sefton, in her scarlet Hispano, swept out of the Rue Boissy d'Anglas into the Place Vêndome—"

JUDITH: I meant to tell you before, David—I've made a great decision.

DAVID [*amiably*]: What is it?

JUDITH: I really am going to return to the stage!

CURTAIN

PRIVATE LIVES

An Intimate Comedy in Three Acts

For
JEFFREY
from
NOEL

Shanghai 1930

Produced by the author at The Phoenix Theatre, London, September 8, 1930.

Original British Cast

SYBIL CHASE	Adrianne Allen
ELYOT CHASE	Noel Coward
VICTOR PRYNNE	Laurence Olivier
AMANDA PRYNNE	Gertrude Lawrence
LOUISE	Everley Gregg

Produced by Charles B. Cochran at the Times Square Theatre, New York, January 27, 1931.

Original American Cast

SYBIL CHASE	Jill Esmond
ELYOT CHASE	Noel Coward
VICTOR PRYNNE	Laurence Olivier
AMANDA PRYNNE	Gertrude Lawrence
LOUISE	Therese Quadri

Noel Coward refused to play more than the three months originally scheduled for the run of the play. Mr. Selwyn arranged with Madge Kennedy and Otto Kruger to continue the run, beginning with the performance of May 11, 1931. Audrey Pointing, Robert Newman, and Juliana Taberni were also added to the cast.

CHARACTERS

AMANDA PRYNNE
VICTOR PRYNNE, her husband
LOUISE, a maid
SIBYL CHASE
ELYOT CHASE, her husband

ACT I.   The Terrace of a Hotel in France. Summer evening.

ACT II.   Amanda's flat in Paris. A few days later. Evening.

ACT III.   The same. The next morning.

Time: The Present.

ACT ONE

The scene is the terrace of a hotel in France. There are two French windows at the back opening onto two separate suites. The terrace space is divided by a line of small trees in tubs, and, downstage, running parallel with the footlights, there is a low stone balustrade. Upon each side of the line of tree tubs is a set of suitable terrace furniture, a swinging seat, two or three chairs, and a table. There are orange and white awnings shading the windows, as it is summer.

When the curtain rises it is about eight o'clock in the evening. There is an orchestra playing not very far off. SIBYL CHASE *opens the windows on the Right, and steps out on to the terrace. She is very pretty and blonde, and smartly dressed in travelling clothes. She comes downstage, stretches her arms wide with a little sigh of satisfaction, and regards the view with an ecstatic expression.*

SIBYL [*calling*]: Elli, Elli dear, do come out. It's so lovely.

ELYOT [*inside*]: Just a minute.

[*After a pause* ELYOT *comes out. He is about thirty, quite slim and pleasant looking, and also in travelling clothes. He walks right down to the balustrade and looks thoughtfully at the view.* SIBYL *stands beside him, and slips her arm through his.*

ELYOT: Not so bad.

SIBYL: It's heavenly. Look at the lights of that yacht reflected in the water. Oh dear, I'm so happy.

ELYOT [*smiling*]: Are you?

SIBYL: Aren't you?

ELYOT: Of course I am. Tremendously happy.

SIBYL: Just to think, here we are, you and I, married!

ELYOT: Yes, things have come to a pretty pass.

SIBYL: Don't laugh at me, you mustn't be blasé about honeymoons just because this is your second.

ELOYT [*frowning*]: That's silly.

SIBYL: Have I annoyed you by saying that?

ELYOT: Just a little.

SIBYL: Oh, darling, I'm so sorry. [*She holds her face up to his*] Kiss me.

ELYOT [*doing so*]: There.

SIBYL: Ummm, not so very enthusiastic.

ELYOT [*kissing her again*]: That better?

SIBYL: Three times, please, I'm superstitious.

ELYOT [*kissing her*]: You really are very sweet.

SIBYL: Are you glad you married me?

ELYOT: Of course I am.

SIBYL: How glad?

ELYOT: Incredibly, magnificently glad.

SIBYL: How lovely.

ELYOT: We ought to go in and dress.

SIBYL: Gladder than before?

ELYOT: Why do you keep harping on that?

SIBYL: It's in my mind, and yours too, I expect.

ELYOT: It isn't anything of the sort.

SIBYL: She was pretty, wasn't she? Amanda?

ELYOT: Very pretty.

SIBYL: Prettier than I am?

ELYOT: Much.

SIBYL: Elyot!

ELYOT: She was pretty and sleek, and her hands were long and slim, and her legs were long and slim, and she danced like an angel. You dance very poorly, by the way.

SIBYL: Could she play the piano as well as I can?

ELYOT: She couldn't play the piano at all.

SIBYL [*triumphantly*]: Aha! Had she my talent for organization?

ELYOT: No, but she hadn't your mother either.

SIBYL: I don't believe you like Mother.

ELYOT: Like her! I can't bear her.

SIBYL: Elyot! She's a darling, underneath.

ELYOT: I never got underneath.

SIBYL: It makes me unhappy to think you don't like Mother.

ELYOT: Nonsense. I believe the only reason you married me was to get away from her.

SIBYL: I married you because I loved you.

ELYOT: Oh dear, oh dear, oh dear, oh dear!

SIBYL: I love you far more than Amanda loved you. I'd never make you miserable like she did.

ELYOT: We made each other miserable.

SIBYL: It was all her fault, you know it was.

ELYOT [*with vehemence*]:   Yes, it was. Entirely her fault.

SIBYL: She was a fool to lose you.

ELYOT: We lost each other.

SIBYL: She lost you, with her violent tempers and carryings on.

ELYOT: Will you stop talking about Amanda?

SIBYL: But I'm very glad, because if she hadn't been uncontrolled, and wicked, and unfaithful, we shouldn't be here now.

ELYOT: She wasn't unfaithful.

SIBYL: How do you know? I bet she was. I bet she was unfaithful every five minutes.

ELYOT: It would take a far more concentrated woman than Amanda to be unfaithful every five minutes.

SIBYL [*anxiously*]:   You do hate her, don't you?

ELYOT: No, I don't hate her. I think I despise her.

SIBYL [*with satisfaction*]:   That's much worse.

ELYOT: And yet I'm sorry for her.

SIBYL: Why?

ELYOT: Because she's marked for tragedy; she's bound to make a mess of everything.

SIBYL: If it's her fault, I don't see that it matters much.

ELYOT: She has some very good qualities.

SIBYL: Considering what a hell she made of your life, I think you are very nice about her. Most men would be vindictive.

ELYOT: What's the use of that? It's all over now, such a long time ago.

SIBYL: Five years isn't very long.

ELYOT [*seriously*]:   Yes it is.

SIBYL: Do you think you could ever love her again?

ELYOT: Now then, Sibyl.

SIBYL: But could you?

ELYOT: Of course not, I love you.

SIBYL: Yes, but you love me differently; I know that.

ELYOT: More wisely perhaps.

SIBYL: I'm glad. I'd rather have that sort of love.

ELYOT: You're right. Love is no use unless it's wise, and kind, and undramatic. Something steady and sweet, to smooth out your nerves when you're tired. Something tremendously cosy; and unflurried by scenes and jealousies. That's what I want, what I've always wanted really. Oh my dear, I do hope it's not going to be dull for you.

SIBYL: Sweetheart, as tho' you could ever be dull.

ELYOT: I'm much older than you.

SIBYL: Not so very much.

ELYOT: Seven years.

SIBYL [*snuggling up to him*]: The music has stopped now and you can hear the sea.

ELYOT: We'll bathe tomorrow morning.

SIBYL: I mustn't get sunburnt.

ELYOT: Why not?

SIBYL: I hate it on women.

ELYOT: Very well, you shan't then. I hope you don't hate it on men.

SIBYL: Of course I don't. It's suitable to men.

ELYOT: You're a completely feminine little creature, aren't you?

SIBYL: Why do you say that?

ELYOT: Everything in its place.

SIBYL: What do you mean?

ELYOT: If you feel you'd like me to smoke a pipe, I'll try and master it.

SIBYL: I like a man to be a man, if that's what you mean.

ELYOT: Are you going to understand me, and manage me?

SIBYL: I'm going to try to understand you.

ELYOT: Run me without my knowing it?

SIBYL [*withdrawing slightly*]: I think you're being a little un-kind.

ELYOT: No, I don't mean to be. I was only wondering.

SIBYL: Well?

ELYOT: I was wondering what was going on inside your mind, what your plans are really?

SIBYL: Plans; Oh, Elli!

ELYOT: Apart from loving me and all that, you must have plans.

SIBYL: I haven't the faintest idea what you're talking about.

ELYOT: Perhaps it's subconscious then, age old instincts working away deep down, mincing up little bits of experience for future use, watching me carefully like a little sharp-eyed, blonde kitten.

SIBYL: How can you be so horrid.

ELYOT: I said Kitten, not Cat.

SIBYL: Kittens grow into cats.

ELYOT: Let that be a warning to you.

SIBYL [*slipping her arm through his again*]:   What's the matter, darling; are you hungry?

ELYOT: Not a bit.

SIBYL: You're very strange all of a sudden, and rather cruel. Just because I'm feminine. It doesn't mean that I'm crafty and calculating.

ELYOT: I didn't say you were either of those things.

SIBYL: I hate these half-masculine women who go banging about.

ELYOT: I hate anybody who goes banging about.

SIBYL: I should think you needed a little quiet womanliness after Amanda.

ELYOT: Why will you keep on talking about her?

SIBYL: It's natural enough, isn't it?

ELYOT: What do you want to find out?

SIBYL: Why did you really let her divorce you?

ELYOT: She divorced me for cruelty, and flagrant infidelity. I spent a whole weekend at Brighton with a lady called Vera Williams. She had the nastiest-looking hairbrush I have ever seen.

SIBYL: Misplaced chivalry, I call it. Why didn't you divorce her?

ELYOT: It would not have been the action of a gentleman, whatever that may mean.

SIBYL: I think she got off very lightly.

ELYOT: Once and for all will you stop talking about her?

SIBYL: Yes, Elli dear.

ELYOT: I don't wish to see her again or hear her name mentioned.

SIBYL: Very well, darling.

ELYOT: Is that understood?

SIBYL: Yes, darling. Where did you spend your honeymoon?

ELYOT: St. Moritz. Be quiet.

SIBYL: I hate St. Moritz.

ELYOT: So do I, bitterly.

SIBYL: Was she good on skis?

ELYOT: Do you want to dine downstairs here, or at the Casino?

SIBYL: I love you, I love you, I love you.

ELYOT: Good, let's go in and dress.

SIBYL: Kiss me first.

ELYOT [*kissing her*]: Casino?

SIBYL: Yes. Are you a gambler? You never told me.

ELYOT: Every now and then.

SIBYL: I shall come and sit just behind your chair and bring you luck.

ELYOT: That will be fatal.

[*They go off into their suite. There is a slight pause and then* VICTOR PYRNNE *enters from the Left suite. He is quite nice looking, about thirty or thirty-five. He is dressed in a light travelling suit. He sniffs the air, looks at the view, and then turns back to the window.*

VICTOR [*calling*]: Mandy.

AMANDA [*inside*]: What?

VICTOR: Come outside, the view is wonderful.

AMANDA: I'm still damp from the bath. Wait a minute— VICTOR *lights a cigarette. Presently* AMANDA *comes out on to the terrace. She is quite exquisite with a gay face and a perfect figure. At the moment she is wearing a negligee*] I shall catch pneumonia, that's what I shall catch.

VICTOR [*looking at her*]: God!

AMANDA: I beg your pardon?

VICTOR: You look wonderful.

AMANDA: Thank you, darling.

VICTOR: Like a beautiful advertisement for something.

AMANDA: Nothing peculiar, I hope.

VICTOR: I can hardly believe it's true. You and I, here alone together, married!

AMANDA [*rubbing her face on his shoulder*]: That stuff's very rough.

VICTOR: Don't you like it?

AMANDA: A bit hearty, isn't it?

VICTOR: Do you love me?

AMANDA: Of course, that's why I'm here.

VICTOR: More than—

AMANDA: Now then, none of that.

VICTOR: No, but do you love me more than you loved Elyot?

AMANDA: I don't remember, it's such a long time ago.

VICTOR: Not so very long.

AMANDA [*flinging out her arms*]: All my life ago.

VICTOR: I'd like to break his damned neck.

AMANDA [*laughing*]: Why?

VICTOR: For making you unhappy.

AMANDA: It was mutual.

VICTOR: Rubbish! It was all his fault, you know it was.

AMANDA: Yes, it was, now I come to think about it.

VICTOR: Swine!

AMANDA: Don't be so vehement, darling.

VICTOR: I'll never treat you like that.

AMANDA: That's right.

VICTOR: I love you too much.

AMANDA: So did he.

VICTOR: Fine sort of love that is. He struck you once, didn't he?

AMANDA: More than once.

VICTOR: Where?

AMANDA: Several places.

VICTOR: What a cad.

AMANDA: I struck him too. Once I broke four gramophone records over his head. It was very satisfying.

VICTOR: You must have been driven to distraction.

AMANDA: Yes, I was, but don't let's talk about it, please. After all, it's a dreary subject for our honeymoon night.

VICTOR: He didn't know when he was well off.

AMANDA: Look at the lights of that yacht reflected in the water. I wonder whose it is.

VICTOR: We must bathe tomorrow.

AMANDA: Yes. I want to get a nice sunburn.

VICTOR [reproachfully]:   Mandy!

AMANDA: Why, what's the matter?

VICTOR: I hate sunburnt women.

AMANDA: Why?

VICTOR: It's somehow, well, unsuitable.

AMANDA: It's awfully suitable to me, darling.

VICTOR: Of course if you really want to.

AMANDA: I'm absolutely determined. I've got masses of lovely oil to rub all over myself.

VICTOR: Your skin is so beautiful as it is.

AMANDA: Wait and see. When I'm done a nice crisp brown, you'll fall in love with me all over again.

VICTOR: I couldn't love you more than I do now.

AMANDA: Oh, dear. I did so hope our honeymoon was going to be progressive.

VICTOR: Where did you spend the last one?

AMANDA [warningly]:   Victor.

VICTOR: I want to know.

AMANDA: St. Moritz. It was very attractive.

VICTOR: I hate St. Moritz.

AMANDA: So do I.

VICTOR: Did he start quarrelling with you right away?

AMANDA: Within the first few days. I put it down to the high altitudes.

VICTOR: And you loved him?

AMANDA: Yes, Victor.

VICTOR: You poor child.

AMANDA: You must try not to be pompous, dear.

[She turns away.

VICTOR [hurt]:   Mandy!

AMANDA: I don't believe I'm a bit like what you think I am.

VICTOR: How do you mean?

AMANDA: I was never a poor child.

VICTOR: Figure of speech, dear, that's all.

AMANDA: I suffered a good deal, and had my heart broken.
But it wasn't an innocent girlish heart. It was jagged with
sophistication. I've always been sophisticated, far too knowing. That caused many of my rows with Elyot. I irritated
him because he knew I could see through him.

VICTOR: I don't mind how much you see through me.

AMANDA: Sweet.

[*She kisses him.*

VICTOR: I'm going to make you happy.

AMANDA: Are you?

VICTOR: Just by looking after you, and seeing that you're all
right, you know.

AMANDA [*a trifle wistfully*]:   No, I don't know.

VICTOR: I think you love me quite differently from the way
you loved Elyot.

AMANDA: Do stop harping on Elyot.

VICTOR: It's true, though, isn't it?

AMANDA: I love you much more calmly, if that's what you
mean.

VICTOR: More lastingly?

AMANDA: I expect so.

VICTOR: Do you remember when I first met you?

AMANDA: Yes. Distinctly.

VICTOR: At Marion Vale's party.

AMANDA: Yes.

VICTOR: Wasn't it wonderful?

AMANDA: Not really, dear. It was only redeemed from the
completely commonplace by the fact of my having hiccoughs.

VICTOR: I never noticed them.

AMANDA: Love at first sight.

VICTOR: Where did you first meet Elyot?

AMANDA: To hell with Elyot.

VICTOR: Mandy!

AMANDA: I forbid you to mention his name again. I'm sick of
the sound of it. You must be raving mad. Here we are

on the first night of our honeymoon, with the moon coming up, and the music playing, and all you can do is to talk about my first husband. It's downright sacrilegious.

VICTOR: Don't be angry.

AMANDA: Well, it's very annoying.

VICTOR: Will you forgive me?

AMANDA: Yes; only don't do it again.

VICTOR: I promise.

AMANDA: You'd better go and dress now, you haven't bathed yet.

VICTOR: Where shall we dine, downstairs here, or at the Casino?

AMANDA: The Casino is more fun, I think.

VICTOR: We can play boule afterwards.

AMANDA: No, we can't, dear.

VICTOR: Don't you like dear old boule?

AMANDA: No, I hate dear old boule. We'll play a nice game of chemin de fer.

VICTOR [*apprehensively*]:   Not at the big table?

AMANDA: Maybe at the biggest table.

VICROR: You're not a terrible gambler, are you?

AMANDA: Inveterate. Chance rules my life.

VICTOR: What nonsense.

AMANDA: How can you say it's nonsense. It was chance meeting you. It was chance falling in love; it's chance that we're here, particularly after your driving. Everything that happens is chance.

VICTOR: You know I feel rather scared of you at close quarters.

AMANDA: That promises to be very embarrassing.

VICTOR: You're somehow different now, wilder than I thought you were, more strained.

AMANDA: Wilder! Oh Victor, I've never felt less wild in my life. A little strained, I grant you, but that's the newly married atmosphere; you can't expect anything else. Honeymooning is a very overrated amusement.

VICTOR: You say that because you had a ghastly experience before.

AMANDA: There you go again.

VICTOR: It couldn't fail to embitter you a little.

AMANDA: The honeymoon wasn't such a ghastly experience really; it was afterwards that was so awful.

VICTOR: I intend to make you forget it all entirely.

AMANDA: You won't succeed by making constant references to it.

VICTOR: I wish I knew you better.

AMANDA: It's just as well you don't. The "woman"—in italics —should always retain a certain amount of alluring feminine mystery for the "man"—also in italics.

VICTOR: What about the man? Isn't he allowed to have any mystery?

AMANDA: Absolutely none. Transparent as glass.

VICTOR: Oh, I see.

AMANDA: Never mind, darling; it doesn't necessarily work out like that; it's only supposed to.

VICTOR: I'm glad I'm normal.

AMANDA: What an odd thing to be glad about. Why?

VICTOR: Well, aren't you?

AMANDA: I'm not so sure I'm normal.

VICTOR: Oh, Mandy, of course you are, sweetly, divinely normal.

AMANDA: I haven't any peculiar cravings for Chinamen or old boots, if that's what you mean.

VICTOR [scandalized]: Mandy!

AMANDA: I think very few people are completely normal really, deep down in their private lives. It all depends on a combination of circumstances. If all the various cosmic thingummys fuse at the same moment, and the right spark is struck, there's no knowing what one mightn't do. That was the trouble with Elyot and me, we were like two violent acids bubbling about in a nasty little matrimonial bottle.

VICTOR: I don't believe you're nearly as complex as you think you are.

AMANDA: I don't think I'm particularly complex, but I know I'm unreliable.

VICTOR: You're frightening me horribly. In what way unreliable?

AMANDA: I'm so apt to see things the wrong way round.

VICTOR: What sort of things?

AMANDA: Morals. What one should do and what one shouldn't.

VICTOR [*fondly*]:   Darling, you're so sweet.

AMANDA: Thank you, Victor, that's most encouraging. You really must have your bath now. Come along.

VICTOR: Kiss me.

AMANDA [*doing so*]:   There, dear, hurry now; I've only got to slip my dress on and then I shall be ready.

VICTOR: Give me ten minutes.

AMANDA: I'll bring the cocktails out here when they come.

VICTOR: All right.

AMANDA: Go along now, hurry.

[*They both disappear into their suite. After a moment's pause* ELYOT *steps carefully on to the terrace carrying a tray upon which are two champagne cocktails. He puts the tray down on the table.*

ELYOT [*calling*]:   Sibyl.

SIBYL [*inside*]:   Yes.

ELYOT: I've brought the cocktails out here, hurry up.

SIBYL: I can't find my lipstick.

ELYOT: Never mind, send down to the kitchen for some cochineal.

SIBYL: Don't be so silly.

ELYOT: Hurry.

[ELYOT *saunters down to the balustrade. He looks casually over on to the next terrace, and then out at the view. He looks up at the moon and sighs, then he sits down in a chair with his back towards the line of tubs, and lights a cigarette.* AMANDA *steps gingerly on to her terrace carrying a tray with two champagne cocktails on it. She is wearing a charmingly simple evening gown, her cloak is flung over her right shoulder. She places the tray carefully on the table, puts her cloak over the back of a chair, and sits down with her back towards* ELYOT. *She takes a small mirror from her handbag, and scrutinizes her face in it. The orchestra downstairs strikes up a new melody. Both* ELYOT *and* AMANDA *give a little start. After a moment,* ELYOT *pensively*

begins to hum the tune the band is playing. It is a sentimental,
romantic little tune. AMANDA *hears him, and clutches at her*
throat suddenly as though she were suffocating. Then she jumps
up noiselessly, and peers over the line of tubs. ELYOT, *with his*
back to her, continues to sing obliviously. She sits down again,
relaxing with a gesture almost of despair. Then she looks an-
xiously over her shoulder at the window in case VICTOR *should*
be listening, and then, with a little smile, she takes up the
melody herself, clearly. ELYOT *stops dead and gives a gasp, then*
he jumps up, and stands looking at her. She continues to sing,
pretending not to know that he is there. At the end of the song,
she turns slowly, and faces him.

AMANDA: Thoughtful of them to play that, wasn' it?
ELYOT [*in a stifled voice*]:   What are you doing here?
AMANDA: I'm on honeymoon.
ELYOT: How interesting, so am I.
AMANDA: I hope you're enjoying it.
ELYOT: It hasn't started yet.
AMANDA: Neither has mine.
ELYOT: Oh, my God!
AMANDA: I can't help feeling that this is a little unfortunate.
ELYOT: Are you happy?
AMANDA: Perfectly.
ELYOT: Good. That's all right, then, isn't it?
AMANDA: Are you?
ELYOT: Ecstatically.
AMANDA: I'm delighted to hear it. We shall probably meet
     again sometime. Au revoir!
[*She turns.*
ELYOT [*firmly*]:   Good-bye.
[*She goes indoors without looking back. He stands gazing after*
her with an expression of horror on his face. SIBYL *comes*
brightly on to the terrace in a very pretty evening frock.
SIBYL: Cocktail, please. [ELYOT *doesn't answer*] Elli, what's
     the matter?
ELYOT: I feel very odd.
SIBYL: Odd, what do you mean, ill?
ELYOT: Yes, ill.

SIBYL [*alarmed*]:   What sort of ill?

ELYOT: We must leave at once.

SIBYL: Leave!

ELYOT: Yes, dear. Leave immediately.

SIBYL: Elli!

ELYOT: I have a strange foreboding.

SIBYL: You must be mad.

ELYOT: Listen, darling. I want you to be very sweet, and patient, and understanding, and not be upset, or ask any questions, or anything. I have an absolute conviction that our
whole future happiness depends upon our leaving here instantly.

SIBYL: Why?

ELYOT: I can't tell you why.

SIBYL: But we've only just come.

ELYOT: I know that, but it can't be helped.

SIBYL: What's happened, what has happened?

ELYOT: Nothing has happened.

SIBYL: You've gone out of your mind.

ELYOT: I haven't gone out of my mind, but I shall if we stay
here another hour.

SIBYL: You're not not drunk, are you?

ELYOT: Of course I'm not drunk. What time have I had to
get drunk?

SIBYL: Come down and have some dinner, darling, and then
you'll feel ever so much better.

ELYOT: It's no use trying to humor me. I'm serious.

SIBYL: But darling, please be reasonable. We've only just
arrived; everything's unpacked. It's our first night together.
We can't go away now.

ELYOT: We can have our first night together in Paris.

SIBYL: We shouldn't get there until the small hours.

ELYOT [*with a great effort at calmness*]:   Now please, Sibyl, I
know it sounds crazy to you, and utterly lacking in reason
and sense, but I've got second sight over certain things. I'm
almost psychic. I've got the most extraordinary sensation of
impending disaster. If we stay here something appalling will
happen. I know it.

SIBYL [*firmly*]:   Hysterical nonsense.

ELYOT: It isn't hysterical nonsense. Presentiments are far from being nonsense. Look at the woman who cancelled her passage on the *Titanic*. All because of a presentiment.

SIBYL: I don't see what that has to do with it.

ELYOT: It has everything to do with it. She obeyed her instincts, that's what she did, and saved her life. All I ask is to be allowed to obey my instincts.

SIBYL: Do you mean that there's going to be an earthquake or something?

ELYOT: Very possibly, very possibly indeed, or perhaps a violent explosion.

SIBYL: They don't have earthquakes in France.

ELYOT: On the contrary, only the other day they felt a distinct shock at Toulon.

SIBYL: Yes, but that's in the South where it's hot.

ELYOT: Don't quibble, Sibyl.

SIBYL: And as for explosions, there's nothing here that can explode.

ELYOT: Oho, isn't there.

SIBYL: Yes, but Elli—

ELYOT: Darling, be sweet. Bear with me. I beseech you to bear with me.

SIBYL: I don't understand. It's horrid of you to do this.

ELYOT: I'm not doing anything. I'm only asking you, imploring you to come away from this place.

SIBYL: But I love it here.

ELYOT: There are thousands of others places far nicer.

SIBYL: It's a pity we didn't go to one of them.

ELYOT: Now, listen, Sibyl—

SIBYL: Yes, but why are you behaving like this, why, why, why?

ELYOT: Don't ask why. Just give in to me. I swear I'll never ask you to give into me over anything again.

SIBYL [*with complete decision*]:   I won't think of going tonight. It's utterly ridiculous. I've done quite enough travelling for one day, and I'm tired.

ELYOT: You're as obstinate as a mule.

SIBYL: I like that, I must say.

ELYOT [*hotly*]:   You've got your nasty little feet dug into the
ground, and you don't intend to budge an inch, do you?

SIBYL [*with spirit*]:   No, I do not.

ELYOT: If there's one thing in the world that infuriates me,
it's sheer wanton stubbornness. I should like to cut off your
head with a meat axe.

SIBYL: How dare you talk to me like that, on our honeymoon
night.

ELYOT: Damn our honeymoon night. Damn it, damn it, damn
it!

SIBYL [*bursting into tears*]:   Oh, Elli, Elli—

ELYOT: Stop crying. Will you or will you not come away with
me to Paris?

SIBYL: I've never been so miserable in my life. You're hateful
and beastly. Mother was perfectly right. She said you had
shifty eyes.

ELYOT: Well, she can't talk. Hers are so close together, you
couldn't put a needle between them.

SIBYL: You don't love me a little bit. I wish I were dead.

ELYOT: Will you or will you not come to Paris?

SIBYL: No, no I won't.

ELYOT: Oh, my God!

[*He stamps indoors.*

SIBYL [*following him, wailing*]:   Oh, Elli, Elli, Elli—

VICTOR *comes stamping out of the French windows on the left,
followed by* AMANDA.

VICTOR: You were certainly right when you said you weren't
normal. You're behaving like a lunatic.

AMANDA: Not at all. All I have done is to ask you a little favor.

VICTOR: Little favor indeed.

AMANDA: If we left now we could be in Paris in a few hours.

VICTOR: If we crossed Siberia by train we could be in China
in a fortnight, but I don't see any reason to do it.

AMANDA: Oh, Victor darling—please, please—be sensible, just
for my sake.

VICTOR: Sensible!

AMANDA: Yes, sensible. I shall be absolutely miserable if we stay here. You don't want me to be absolutely miserable all through my honeymon, do you?

VICTOR: But why on earth didn't you think of your sister's tragedy before?

AMANDA: I forgot.

VICTOR: You couldn't forget a thing like that.

AMANDA: I got the places muddled. Then when I saw the Casino there in the moonlight, it all came back to me.

VICTOR: When did all this happen?

AMANDA: Years ago, but it might just as well have been yesterday. I can see her now lying dead, with that dreadful expression on her face. Then all that awful business of taking the body home to England. It was perfectly horrible.

VICTOR: I never knew you had a sister.

AMANDA: I haven't any more.

VICTOR: There's something behind all this.

AMANDA: Don't be silly. What could there be behind it?

VICTOR: Well, for one thing, I know you're lying.

AMANDA: Victor!

VICTOR: Be honest. Aren't you?

AMANDA: I can't think how you can be so mean and suspicious.

VICTOR [*patiently*]: You're lying, Amanda. Aren't you?

AMANDA: Yes, Victor.

VICTOR: You never had a sister, dead or alive?

AMANDA: I believe there was a stillborn one in 1902.

VICTOR: What is your reason for all this?

AMANDA: I told you I was unreliable.

VICTOR: Why do you want to leave so badly?

AMANDA: You'll be angry if I tell you the truth.

VICTOR: What is it?

AMANDA: I warn you.

VICTOR: Tell me. Please tell me.

AMANDA: Elyot's here.

VICTOR: What!

AMANDA: I saw him.

VICTOR: When?

AMANDA: Just now, when you were in the bath.

VICTOR: Where was he?

AMANDA [*hesitatingly*]:   Down there, in a white suit.

[*She points over the balustrade.*

VICTOR [*sceptically*]:   White suit?

AMANDA: Why not? It's summer, isn't it?

VICTOR: You're lying again.

AMANDA: I'm not. He's here. I swear he is.

VICTOR: Well, what of it?

AMANDA: I can't enjoy a honeymoon with you, with Elyot liable to bounce in at any moment.

VICTOR: Really, Mandy.

AMANDA: Can't you see how awful it is? It's the most embarrassing thing that ever happened to me in my whole life.

VICTOR: Did he see you?

AMANDA: No, he was running.

VICTOR: What was he running for?

AMANDA: How on earth do I know? Don't be so annoying.

VICTOR: Well, as long as he didn't see you it's all right, isn't it?

AMANDA: It isn't all right at all. We must leave immediately.

VICTOR: But why?

AMANDA: How can you be so appallingly obstinate?

VICTOR: I'm not afraid of him.

AMANDA: Neither am I. It isn't a question of being afraid. It's just a horrible awkward situation.

VICTOR: I'm damned if I can see why our whole honeymoon should be upset by Elyot.

AMANDA: My last one was.

VICTOR: I don't believe he's here at all.

AMANDA: He is I tell you. I saw him.

VICTOR: It was probably an optical illusion. This half light is very deceptive.

AMANDA: It was no such thing.

VICTOR: I absolutely refuse to change all our plans at the last moment, just because you think you've seen Elyot. It's unreasonable and ridiculous of you to demand it. Even if he is here I can't see that it matters. He'll probably feel much more embarrassed than you, and a damned good job too; and if he annoys you in any way I'll knock him down.

AMANDA: That would be charming.

VICTOR: Now don't let's talk about it any more.

AMANDA: Do you mean to stand there seriously and imagine that the whole thing can be glossed over as easily as that?

VICTOR: I'm not going to leave, Mandy. If I start giving into you as early as this, our lives will be unbearable.

AMANDA [*outraged*]:   Victor!

VICTOR [*calmly*]:   You've worked yourself up into a state over a situation which really only exists in your mind.

AMANDA [*controlling herself with an effort*]:   Please, Victor, please, for this last time I implore you. Let's go to Paris now, tonight. I mean it with all my heart—please—

VICTOR [*with gentle firmness*]:   No, Mandy!

AMANDA: I see quite clearly that I have been foolish enough to marry a fat old gentleman in a club armchair.

VICTOR: It's no use being cross.

AMANDA: You're a pompous ass.

VICTOR [*horrified*]:   Mandy!

AMANDA [*enraged*]:   Pompous ass, that's what I said, and that's what I meant. Blown out with your own importance.

VICTOR: Mandy, control yourself.

AMANDA: Get away from me. I can't bear to think I'm married to such rugged grandeur.

VICTOR [*with great dignity*]:   I shall be in the bar. When you are ready to come down and dine, let me know.

AMANDA [*flinging herself into a chair*]:   Go away, go away.

[VICTOR *stalks off, at the same moment that* ELYOT *stamps on, on the other side, followed by* SIBYL *in tears.*

ELYOT: If you don't stop screaming, I'll murder you.

SIBYL: I wish to heaven I'd never seen you in my life, let alone married you. I don't wonder Amanda left you, if you behaved to her as you've behaved to me. I'm going down to have dinner by myself and you can just do what you like about it.

ELYOT: Do, and I hope it chokes you.

SIBYL: Oh Elli, Elli—

[*She goes wailing indoors. Elyot stamps down to the balustrade*

and lights a cigarette, obviously trying to control his nerves.
Amanda sees him, and comes down too.

AMANDA: Give me one for God's sake.

ELYOT [*hands her his case laconically*]:   Here.

AMANDA [*taking a cigarette*]:   I'm in such a rage.

ELYOT [*lighting up*]:   So am I.

AMANDA: What are we to do?

ELYOT: I don't know.

AMANDA: Whose yacht is that?

ELYOT: The Duke of Westminster's I expect. It always is.

AMANDA: I wish I were on it.

ELYOT: I wish you were too.

AMANDA: There's no need to be nasty.

ELYOT: Yes there is, every need. I've never in my life felt a greater urge to be nasty.

AMANDA: And you've had some urges in your time, haven't you?

ELYOT: If you start bickering with me, Amanda, I swear I'll throw you over the edge.

AMANDA: Try it, that's all, just try it.

ELYOT: You've upset everything, as usual.

AMANDA: I've upset everything! What about you?

ELYOT: Ever since the first moment I was unlucky enough to set eyes on you, my life has been insupportable.

AMANDA: Oh, do shut up, there's no sense in going on like that.

ELYOT: Nothing's any use. There's no escape, ever.

AMANDA: Don't be melodramatic.

ELYOT: Do you want a cocktail? There are two here.

AMANDA: There are two over here as well.

ELYOT: We'll have my two first.

[AMANDA *crosses over into* ELYOT's *part of the terrace. He gives her one, and keeps one himself.*

AMANDA: Shall we get roaring screaming drunk?

ELYOT: I don't think that would help, we did it once before and it was a dismal failure.

AMANDA: It was lovely at the beginning.

ELYOT: You have an immoral memory, Amanda. Here's to
you.

[*They raise their glasses solemnly and drink.*

AMANDA: I tried to get away the moment after I'd seen you,
but he wouldn't budge.

ELYOT: What's his name.

AMANDA: Victor, Victor Prynne.

ELYOT [*toasting*]: Mr. and Mrs. Victor Prynne. [*He drinks*]
Mine wouldn't budge either.

AMANDA: What's her name?

ELYOT: Sibyl.

AMANDA [*toasting*]: Mr. and Mrs. Elyot Chase. [*She drinks*]
God pity the poor girl.

ELYOT: Are you in love with him?

AMANDA: Of course.

ELYOT: How funny.

AMANDA: I don't see anything particularly funny about it;
you're in love with yours aren't you?

ELYOT: Certainly.

AMANDA: There you are then.

ELYOT: There we both are then.

AMANDA: What's she like?

ELYOT: Fair, very pretty, plays the piano beautifully.

AMANDA: Very comforting.

ELYOT: How's yours?

AMANDA: I don't want to discuss him.

ELYOT: Well, it doesn't matter, he'll probably come popping
out in a minute and I shall see for myself. Does he know
I'm here?

AMANDA: Yes, I told him.

ELYOT [*with sarcasm*]: That's going to make things a whole
lot easier.

AMANDA: You needn't be frightened; he won't hurt you.

ELYOT: If he comes near me I'll scream the place down.

AMANDA: Does Sibyl know I'm here?

ELYOT: No, I pretended I'd had a presentiment. I tried terribly
hard to persuade her to leave for Paris.

AMANDA: I tried too; it's lucky we didn't both succeed, isn't it?

Otherwise we should probably all have joined up in Rouen or somewhere.

ELYOT [*laughing*]:   In some frowsy little hotel.

AMANDA [*laughing too*]:   Oh dear, it would have been much, much worse.

ELYOT: I can see us all sailing down in the morning for an early start.

AMANDA [*weakly*]:   Lovely, oh lovely.

ELYOT: Glorious!

[*They both laugh helplessly.*

AMANDA: What's happened to yours?

ELYOT: Didn't you hear her screaming? She's downstairs in the dining room I think.

AMANDA: Mine is being grand, in the bar.

ELYOT: It really is awfully difficult.

AMANDA: Have you known her long?

ELYOT: About four months, we met in a house party in Norfolk.

AMANDA: Very flat, Norfolk.

ELYOT: How old is dear Victor?

AMANDA: Thirty-four, or five; and Sibyl?

ELYOT: I blush to tell you; only twenty-three.

AMANDA: You've gone a mucker alright.

ELYOT: I shall reserve my opinion of your choice until I've met dear Victor.

AMANDA: I wish you wouldn't go on calling him "Dear Victor." It's extremely irritating.

ELYOT: That's how I see him. Dumpy, and fair, and very considerate, with glasses. Dear Victor.

AMANDA: As I said before I would rather not discuss him. At least I have good taste enough to refrain from making cheap gibes at Sibyl.

ELYOT: You said Norfolk was flat.

AMANDA: That was no reflection on her, unless she made it flatter.

ELYOT: Your voice takes on an acid quality whenever you mention her name.

AMANDA: I'll never mention it again.

ELYOT: Good, and I'll keep off Victor.

AMANDA [*with dignity*]:   Thank you.

[*There is silence for a moment. The orchestra starts playing the same tune that they were singing previously.*

ELYOT: That orchestra has a remarkably small repertoire.

AMANDA: They don't seem to know anything but this, do they? [*She sits down on the balustrade, and sings it, softly. Her eyes are looking out to sea, and her mind is far away.* ELYOT *watches her while she sings. When she turns to him at the end, there are tears in her eyes. He looks away awkwardly and lights another cigarette.*

ELYOT: You always had a sweet voice, Amanda.

AMANDA [*a little huskily*]:   Thank you.

ELYOT: I'm awfully sorry about all this, really I am. I wouldn't have had it happen for the world.

AMANDA: I know. I'm sorry too. It's just rotten luck.

ELYOT: I'll go away tomorrow whatever happens, so don't you worry.

AMANDA: That's nice of you.

ELYOT: I hope everything turns out splendidly for you, and that you'll be very happy.

AMANDA: I hope the same for you, too.

[*The music, which has been playing continually through this little scene, returns persistently to the refrain. They both look at one another and laugh.*

ELYOT: Nasty insistent little tune.

AMANDA: Extraordinary how potent cheap music is.

ELYOT: What exactly were you remembering at that moment?

AMANDA: The Palace Hotel Skating Rink in the morning, bright strong sunlight, and everybody whirling round in vivid colors, and you kneeling down to put on my skates for me.

ELYOT: You'd fallen on your fanny a few moments before.

AMANDA: It was beastly of you to laugh like that, I felt so humiliated.

ELYOT: Poor darling.

AMANDA: Do you remember waking up in the morning, and standing on the balcony, looking out across the valley?

ELYOT: Blue shadows on white snow, cleanness beyond belief, high above everything in the world. How beautiful it was.

AMANDA: It's nice to think we had a few marvellous moments.

ELYOT: A few: We had heaps really, only they slip away into the background, and one only remembers the bad ones.

AMANDA: Yes. What fools we were to ruin it all. What utter, utter fools.

ELYOT: You feel like that too, do you?

AMANDA [*wearily*]:   Of course.

ELYOT: Why did we?

AMANDA: The whole business was too much for us.

ELYOT: We were so ridiculously over in love.

AMANDA: Funny, wasn't it?

ELYOT [*sadly*]:   Horribly funny.

AMANDA: Selfishness, cruelty, hatred, possessiveness, petty jealousy. All those qualities came out in us just because we loved each other.

ELYOT: Perhaps they were there anyhow.

AMANDA: No, it's love that does it. To hell with love.

ELYOT: To hell with love.

AMANDA: And yet here we are starting afresh with two quite different people. In love all over again, aren't we? [ELYOT *doesn't answer*] Aren't we?

ELYOT: No.

AMANDA: Elyot.

ELYOT: We're not in love all over again, and you know it. Good night, Amanda.

[*He turns abruptly, and goes towards the French windows.*

AMANDA: Elyot—don't be silly—come back.

ELYOT: I must go and find Sybil.

AMANDA: I must go and find Victor.

ELYOT [*savagely*]:   Well, why don't you?

AMANDA: I don't want to.

ELYOT: It's shameful, shameful of us.

AMANDA: Don't: I feel terrible. Don't leave me for a minute, I shall go mad if you do. We won't talk about ourselves any more; we'll talk about outside things, anything you like, only just don't leave me until I've pulled myself together.

ELYOT: Very well.

[*There is a dead silence.*

AMANDA: What have you been doing lately? During these last years?

ELYOT: Travelling about. I went round the world you know after—

AMANDA [*hurriedly*]: Yes, yes, I know. How was it?

ELYOT: The world?

AMANDA: Yes.

ELYOT: Oh, highly enjoyable.

AMANDA: China must be very interesting.

ELYOT: Very big, China.

AMANDA: And Japan—

ELYOT: Very small.

AMANDA: Did you eat sharks' fins, and take your shoes off, and use chopsticks and everything?

ELYOT: Practically everything.

AMANDA: And India, the burning Ghars, or Ghats, or whatever they are, and the Taj Mahal. How was the Taj Mahal?

ELYOT [*looking at her*]: Unbelievable, a sort of dream.

AMANDA: That was the moonlight, I expect; you must have seen it in the moonlight.

ELYOT [*never taking his eyes off her face*]: Yes, moonlight is cruelly deceptive.

AMANDA: And it didn't look like a biscuit box did it? I've always felt that it might.

ELYOT [*quietly*]: Darling, darling, I love you so.

AMANDA: And I do hope you met a sacred elephant. They're lint white I believe, and very, very sweet.

ELYOT: I've never loved anyone else for an instant.

AMANDA [*raising her hand feebly in protest*]: No, no, you mustn't—Elyot—stop.

ELYOT: You love me, too, don't you? There's no doubt about it anywhere, is there?

AMANDA: No, no doubt anywhere.

ELYOT: You're looking very lovely you know, in this damned moonlight. Your skin is clear and cool, and your eyes are shining, and you're growing lovelier and lovelier every second

as I look at you. You don't hold any mystery for me,
darling, do you mind? There isn't a particle of you that I
don't know, remember, and want.

AMANDA [*softly*]:   I'm glad, my sweet.

ELYOT: More than any desire anywhere, deep down in my
deepest heart I want you back again—please—

AMANDA [*putting her hand over his mouth*]:   Don't say any
more; you're making me cry so dreadfully.

[*He pulls her gently into his arms and they stand silently, completely oblivious to everything but the moment, and each other.
When finally, they separate, they sit down, rather breathlessly,
on the balustrade.*

AMANDA: What now? Oh darling, what now?

ELYOT: I don't know, I'm lost, utterly.

AMANDA: We must think quickly, oh quickly—

ELYOT: Escape?

AMANDA: Together?

ELYOT: Yes, of course, now, now.

AMANDA: We can't, we can't, you know we can't.

ELYOT: We must.

AMANDA: It would break Victor's heart.

ELYOT: And Sibyl's too probably, but they're bound to suffer
anyhow. Think of the hell we'd lead them into if we stayed.
Infinitely worse than any cruelty in the world, pretending to
love them, and loving each other, so desperately.

AMANDA: We must tell them.

ELYOT: What?

AMANDA: Call them, and tell them.

ELYOT: Oh no, no, that's impossible.

AMANDA: It's honest.

ELYOT: I can't help how honest it is, it's too horrible to think
of. How should we start? What should we say?

AMANDA: We should have to trust to the inspiration of the
moment.

ELYOT: It would be a moment completely devoid of inspiration. The most appalling moment imaginable. No, no, we
can't, you must see that, we simply can't.

AMANDA: What do you propose to do then? As it is they might appear at any moment.

ELYOT: We've got to decide instantly one way or another. Go away together now, or stay with them, and never see one another again, ever.

AMANDA: Don't be silly, what choice is there?

ELYOT: No choice at all, come—

[*He takes her hand.*

AMANDA: No, wait. This is sheer raving madness, something's happened to us, we're not sane.

ELYOT: We never were.

AMANDA: Where can we go?

ELYOT: Paris first, my car's in the garage, all ready.

AMANDA: They'll follow us.

ELYOT: That doesn't matter, once the thing's done.

AMANDA: I've got a flat in Paris.

ELYOT: Good.

AMANDA: It's in the Avenue Montaigne. I let it to Freda Lawson, but she's in Biarritz, so it's empty.

ELYOT: Does Victor know?

AMANDA: No, he knows I have one but he hasn't the faintest idea where.

ELYOT: Better and better.

AMANDA: We're being so bad, so terribly bad, we'll suffer for this, I know we shall.

ELYOT: Can't be helped.

AMANDA: Starting all those awful rows all over again.

ELYOT: No, no, we're older and wiser now.

AMANDA: What difference does that make? The first moment either of us gets a bit nervy, off we'll go again.

ELYOT: Stop shilly-shallying, Amanda.

AMANDA: I'm trying to be sensible.

ELYOT: You're only succeeding in being completely idiotic.

AMANDA: Idiotic indeed! What about you?

ELYOT: Now look here Amanda—

AMANDA [*stricken*]: Oh my God!

ELYOT [*rushing to her and kissing her*]: Darling, darling, I didn't mean it—

AMANDA: I won't move from here unless we have a compact, a sacred, sacred compact never to quarrel again.

ELYOT: Easy to make but difficult to keep.

AMANDA: No, no, it's the bickering that always starts it. The moment we notice we're bickering, either of us, we must promise on our honor to stop dead. We'll invent some phrase or catchword, which when either of us says it, automatically cuts off all conversation for at least five minutes.

ELYOT: Two minutes dear, with an option of renewal.

AMANDA: Very well, what shall it be?

ELYOT [hurriedly]: Solomon Isaacs.

AMANDA: All right, that'll do.

ELYOT: Come on, come on.

AMANDA: What shall we do if we meet either of them on the way downstairs?

ELYOT: Run like stags.

AMANDA: What about clothes?

ELYOT: I've got a couple of bags I haven't unpacked yet.

AMANDA: I've got a small trunk.

ELYOT: Send the porter up for it.

AMANDA: Oh this is terrible—terrible—

ELYOT: Come on, come on, don't waste time.

AMANDA: Oughtn't we to leave notes or something?

ELYOT: No, no, no, we'll telegraph from somewhere on the road.

AMANDA: Darling, I daren't, it's too wicked of us, I simply daren't.

ELYOT [seizing her in his arms and kissing her violently]: Now will you behave?

AMANDA: Yes, but Elyot darling—

ELYOT: Solomon Isaacs!

[They rush off together through ELYOT's suite. After a moment or so, VICTOR steps out on to the terrace and looks round anxiously. Then he goes back indoors again, and can be heard calling "Mandy." Finally he again comes out on to the terrace and comes despondently down to the balustrade. He hears SIBYL's voice calling "Elli" and looks round as she comes out of the French windows. She jumps slightly upon seeing him.

VICTOR: Good evening.

SIBYL [*rather flustered*]:   Good evening—I was—er—looking for my husband.

VICTOR: Really, that's funny. I was looking for my wife.

SIBYL: Quite a coincidence.

[*She laughs nervously.*

VICTOR [*after a pause*]:   It's very nice here isn't it?

SIBYL: Lovely.

VICTOR: Have you been here long?

SIBYL: No, we only arrived today.

VICTOR: Another coincidence. So did we.

SIBYL: How awfully funny.

VICTOR: Would you care for a cocktail?

SIBYL: Oh no, thank you—really—

VICTOR: There are two here on the table.

[SIBYL *glances at the two empty glasses on the balustrade, and tosses her head defiantly.*

SIBYL: Thanks very much, I'd love one.

VICTOR: Good, here you are.

[SIBYL *comes over to* VICTOR's *side of the terrace. He hands her one and takes one himself.*

SIBYL: Thank you.

VICTOR [*with rather forced gaiety*]:   To absent friends.

[*He raises his glass.*

SIBYL [*raising hers*]:   To absent friends. [*They both laugh rather mirthlessly and then sit down on the balustrade, pensively sipping their cocktails and looking at the view*] It's awfully pretty isn't it? The moonlight, and the lights of that yacht reflected in the water—

VICTOR: I wonder who it belongs to.

THE CURTAIN SLOWLY FALLS

ACT TWO

The Scene is AMANDA's *flat in Paris. A few days have elapsed since Act I. The flat is charmingly furnished, its principal features being a Steinway Grand on the left, facing slightly up stage. Downstage center, a very large comfortable sofa, behind which is a small table. There is also another sofa somewhere about, and one or two small tables, and a gramophone. The rest can be left to the discretion and taste of the decorator.*

When the Curtain Rises it is about ten o'clock in the evening. The windows are wide open, and the various street sounds of Paris can be heard but not very loudly as the apartment is high up.

AMANDA *and* ELYOT *are seated opposite one another at the table. They have finished dinner and are dallying over coffee and liqueurs.* AMANDA *is wearing pajamas, and* ELYOT *a comfortable dressing-gown.*

AMANDA: I'm glad we let Louise go. I am afraid she is going to have a cold.

ELYOT: Going to have a cold; she's been grunting and snorting all the evening like a whole herd of bison.

AMANDA [*thoughtfully*]: Bison never sounds right to me somehow. I have a feeling it ought to be bisons, a flock of bisons.

ELYOT: You might say a covey of bisons, or even a school of bisons.

AMANDA: Yes, lovely. The Royal London School of Bisons. Do you think Louise is happy at home?

ELYOT: No, profoundly miserable.

AMANDA: Family beastly to her?

ELYOT [*with conviction*]: Absolutely vile. Knock her about dreadfully I expect, make her eat the most disgusting food, and pull her fringe.

AMANDA [*laughing*]: Oh, poor Louise.

ELYOT: Well, you know what the French are.

AMANDA: Oh yes, indeed. I know what the Hungarians are too.

ELYOT: What are they?

AMANDA: Very wistful. It's all those pretzels I shouldn't wonder.

ELYOT: And the Poostza; I always felt the Poostza was far too big, Danube or no Danube.

AMANDA: Have you ever crossed the Sahara on a Camel?

ELYOT: Frequently. When I was a boy we used to do it all the time. My grandmother had a lovely seat on a camel.

AMANDA: There's no doubt about it, foreign travel's the thing.

ELYOT: Would you like some brandy?

AMANDA: Just a little.

[He pours some into her glass and some into his own.

ELYOT: I'm glad we didn't go out tonight.

AMANDA: Or last night.

ELYOT: Or the night before.

AMANDA: There's no reason to, really, when we're cozy here.

ELYOT: Exactly.

AMANDA: It's nice, isn't it?

ELYOT: Strangely peaceful. It's an awfully bad reflection on our characters. We ought to be absolutely tortured with conscience.

AMANDA: We are, every now and then.

ELYOT: Not nearly enough.

AMANDA: We sent Victor and Sibyl a nice note from wherever it was; what more can they want?

ELYOT: You're even more ruthless than I am.

AMANDA: I don't believe in crying over my bridge before I've eaten it.

ELYOT: Very sensible.

AMANDA: Personally I feel gratefel for a miraculous escape. I know now that I should never have been happy with Victor. I was a fool ever to consider it.

ELYOT: You did a little more than consider it.

AMANDA: Well, you can't talk.

ELYOT: I wonder whether they met each other, or whether they've been suffering alone.

AMANDA: Oh dear, don't let's go on about it, it really does make one feel rather awful.

ELYOT: I suppose one or other or both of them will turn up here eventually.

AMANDA: Bound to; it won't be very nice, will it?

ELYOT [*cheerfully*]:   Perfectly horrible.

AMANDA: Do you realize that we're living in sin?

ELYOT: Not according to the Catholics; Catholics don't recognize divorce. We're married as much as ever we were.

AMANDA: Yes, dear, but we're not Catholics.

ELYOT: Never mind, it's nice to think they'd sort of back us up. We were married in the eyes of heaven, and we still are.

AMANDA: We may be alright in the eyes of Heaven, but we look like being in the hell of a mess socially.

ELYOT: Who cares?

AMANDA: Are we going to marry again, after Victor and Sibyl divorce us?

ELYOT: I suppose so. What do you think?

AMANDA: I feel rather scared of marriage really.

ELYOT: It is a frowsy business.

AMANDA: I believe it was just the fact of our being married, and clamped together publicly, that wrecked us before.

ELYOT: That, and not knowing how to manage each other.

AMANDA: Do you think we know how to manage each other now?

ELYOT: This week's been very successful. We've hardly used Solomon Isaacs at all.

AMANDA: Solomon Isaacs is so long, let's shorten it to Sollocks.

ELYOT: All right.

AMANDA: Darling, you do look awfully sweet in your little dressing-gown.

ELYOT: Yes, it's pretty ravishing, isn't it?

AMANDA: Do you mind if I come round and kiss you?

ELYOT: A pleasure, Lady Agatha.

[AMANDA *comes round the table, kisses him, picks up the coffee pot, and returns to her chair.*

AMANDA: What fools we were to subject ourselves to five years' unnecessary suffering.

ELYOT: Perhaps it wasn't unnecessary, perhaps it mellowed and perfected us like beautiful ripe fruit.

AMANDA: When we were together, did you really think I was unfaithful to you?

ELYOT: Yes, practically every day.

AMANDA: I thought you were too; often I used to torture myself with visions of your bouncing about on divans with awful widows.

ELYOT: Why widows?

AMANDA: I was thinking of Claire Lavenham really.

ELYOT: Oh, Claire.

AMANDA [*sharply*]:   What did you say "Oh, Claire" like that for? It sounded far too careless to me.

ELYOT [*wistfully*]:   What a lovely creature she was.

AMANDA: Lovely, lovely, lovely!

ELYOT [*blowing her a kiss*]:   Darling!

AMANDA: Did you ever have an affair with her? Afterwards I mean?

ELYOT: Why do you want to know?

AMANDA: Curiosity, I suppose.

ELYOT: Dangerous.

AMANDA: Oh not now, not dangerous now. I wouldn't expect you to have been celibate during those five years, any more than I was.

ELYOT [*jumping*]:   What?

AMANDA: After all, Claire was undeniably attractive. A trifle over vivacious I always thought, but that was probably because she was fundamentally stupid.

ELYOT: What do you mean about not being celibate during those five years?

AMANDA: What do you think I mean?

ELYOT: Oh God!

[*He looks down miserably.*

AMANDA: What's the matter?

ELYOT: You know perfectly well what's the matter.

AMANDA [*gently*]:   You mustn't be unreasonable, I was only trying to stamp out the memory of you. I expect your affairs well outnumbered mine anyhow.

ELYOT: That is a little different. I'm a man.

AMANDA: Excuse me a moment while I get a caraway biscuit and change my crinoline.

ELYOT: It doesn't suit women to be promiscuous.

AMANDA: It doesn't suit men for women to be promiscuous.

ELYOT [*with sarcasm*]:   Very modern dear; really, your advanced views quite startle me.

AMANDA: Don't be cross, Elyot, I haven't been so dreadfully loose actually. Five years is a long time, and even if I did nip off with someone every now and again, they were none of them very serious.

ELYOT [*rising from the table and walking away*]:   Oh, do stop it please—

AMANDA: Well, what about you?

ELYOT: Do you want me to tell you?

AMANDA: No, no, I don't—I take everything back—I don't.

ELYOT [*viciously*]:   I was madly in love with a woman in South Africa.

AMANDA: Did she have a ring through her nose?

ELYOT: Don't be revolting.

AMANDA: We're tormenting one another. Sit down, sweet, I'm scared.

ELYOT [*slowly*]:   Very well.

[*He sits down thoughtfully.*

AMANDA: We should have said Sollocks ages ago.

ELYOT: We're in love all right.

AMANDA: Don't say it so bitterly. Let's try to get the best out of it this time, instead of the worst.

ELYOT [*stretching his hand across the table*]:   Hand, please.

AMANDA [*clasping it*]:   Here.

ELYOT: More comfortable?

AMANDA: Much more.

ELYOT [*after a slight pause*]:   Are you engaged for this dance?

AMANDA: Funnily enough I was, but my partner was suddenly taken ill.

ELYOT [*rising and going to the gramophone*]:   It's this damned smallpox epidemic.

AMANDA: No, as a matter of fact it was kidney trouble.

ELYOT: You'll dance it with me I hope?

ACT TWO

AMANDA [*rising*]:   I shall be charmed.

ELYOT [*as they dance*]:   Quite a good floor, isn't it?

AMANDA: Yes, I think it needs a little Borax.

ELYOT: I love Borax.

AMANDA: Is that the Grand Duchess Olga lying under the piano?

ELYOT: Yes, her husband died a few weeks ago, you know, on his way back from Pulborough. So sad.

AMANDA: What on earth was he doing in Pulborough?

ELYOT: Nobody knows exactly, but there have been the usual stories.

AMANDA: I see.

ELYOT: Delightful parties Lady Bundle always gives, doesn't she?

AMANDA: Entrancing. Such a dear old lady.

ELYOT: And so gay: Did you notice her at supper blowing all those shrimps through her ear trumpet?

[*The tune comes to an end.* AMANDA *sits on the edge of the sofa, pensively.*

ELYOT: What are you thinking about?

AMANDA: Nothing in particular.

ELYOT: Come on, I know that face.

AMANDA: Poor Sibyl.

ELYOT: Sibyl?

AMANDA: Yes, I suppose she loves you terribly.

ELYOT: Not as much as all that; she didn't have a chance to get really under way.

AMANDA: I expect she's dreadfully unhappy.

ELYOT: Oh, do shut up, Amanda, we've had all that out before.

AMANDA: We've certainly been pretty busy trying to justify ourselves.

ELYOT: It isn't a question of justifying ourselves; it's the true values of the situation that are really important. The moment we saw one another again we knew it was no use going on. We knew it instantly really, although we tried to pretend to ourselves that we didn't. What we've got to be thankful for is that we made the break straight away, and not later.

AMANDA: You think we should have done it anyhow?

ELYOT: Of course, and things would have been in a worse mess than they are now.

AMANDA: And what if we'd never happened to meet again. Would you have been quite happy with Sibyl?

ELYOT: I expect so.

AMANDA: Oh, Elyot!

ELYOT: You needn't look so stricken. It would have been the same with you and Victor. Life would have been smooth, and amicable, and quite charming, wouldn't it?

AMANDA: Poor dear Victor. He certainly did love me.

ELYOT: Splendid.

AMANDA: When I met him I was so lonely and depressed, I felt that I was getting old, and crumbling away unwanted.

ELYOT: It certainly is horrid when one begins to crumble.

AMANDA [*wistfully*]: He used to look at me hopelessly like a lovely spaniel, and I sort of melted like snow in the sunlight.

ELYOT: That must have been an edifying spectacle.

AMANDA: Victor really had a great charm.

ELYOT: You must tell me all about it.

AMANDA: He had a positive mania for looking after me, and protecting me.

ELYOT: That would have died down in time, dear.

AMANDA: You mustn't be rude; there's no necessity to be rude.

ELYOT: I wasn't in the least rude; I merely made a perfectly rational statement.

AMANDA: Your voice was decidedly bitter.

ELYOT: Victor had glorious legs, hadn't he? And fascinating ears.

AMANDA: Don't be silly.

ELYOT: He probably looked radiant in the morning, all flushed and tumbled on the pillow.

AMANDA: I never saw him on the pillow.

ELYOT: I'm surprised to hear it.

AMANDA [*angrily*]: Elyot!

ELYOT: There's no need to be cross.

AMANDA: What did you mean by that?

ELYOT: I'm sick of listening to you yap, yap, yap, yap, yap, yapping about Victor.

AMANDA: Now listen Elyot, once and for all—

ELYOT: Oh my dear, Sollocks! Sollocks!—two minutes—Sollocks.

AMANDA: But—

ELYOT [*firmly*]:   Sollocks! [*They sit in dead silence, looking at each other.* AMANDA *makes a sign that she wants a cigarette.* ELYOT *gets up, hands her the box, and lights one for her and himself.* AMANDA *rises and walks over to the window, and stands there, looking out for a moment. Presently* ELYOT *joins her. She slips her arm through his, and they kiss lightly. They draw the curtains and then come down and sit side by side on the sofa.* ELYOT *looks at his watch.* AMANDA *raises her eyebrows at him and he nods, then they both sigh, audibly*] That was a near thing.

AMANDA: It was my fault. I'm terribly sorry, darling.

ELYOT: I was very irritating, I know I was. I'm sure Victor was awfully nice, and you're perfectly right to be sweet about him.

AMANDA: That's downright handsome of you. Sweetheart!

[*She kisses him.*

ELYOT [*leaning back with her on the sofa*]:   I think I love you more than ever before. Isn't it ridiculous? Put your feet up.

[*She puts her legs across his, and they snuggle back together in the corner of the sofa, his head resting on her shoulder.*

AMANDA: Comfortable?

ELYOT: Almost, wait a minute.

[*He struggles a bit and then settles down with a sigh.*

AMANDA: How long, Oh Lord, how long?

ELYOT [*drowsily*]:   What do you mean, "How long, Oh Lord, how long?"

AMANDA: This is far too perfect to last.

ELYOT: You have no faith, that's what's wrong with you.

AMANDA: Absolutely none.

ELYOT: Don't you believe in—?

[*He nods upwards.*

AMANDA: No, do you?

ELYOT [*shaking his head*]:   No. What about—?

[*He points downwards.*

AMANDA: Oh, dear no.

ELYOT: Don't you believe in anything?

AMANDA: Oh yes, I believe in being kind to everyone, and giving money to old beggar women, and being as gay as possible.

ELYOT: What about after we're dead?

AMANDA: I think a rather gloomy merging into everything, don't you?

ELYOT: I hope not; I'm a bad merger.

AMANDA: You won't know a thing about it.

ELYOT: I hope for a glorious oblivion, like being under gas.

AMANDA: I always dream the most peculiar things under gas.

ELYOT: Would you be young always? If you could choose?

AMANDA: No, I don't think so, not if it meant having awful bull's glands popped into me.

ELYOT: Cows for you, dear. Bulls for me.

AMANDA: We certainly live in a marvellous age.

ELYOT: Too marvellous. It's alright if you happen to be a specialist at something, then you're too concentrated to pay attention to all the other things going on. But, for the ordinary observer, it's too much.

AMANDA [snuggling closer]:   Far, far too much.

ELYOT: Take the radio for instance.

AMANDA: Oh darling, don't let's take the radio.

ELYOT: Well, aeroplanes then, and Cosmic Atoms, and Television, and those gland injections we were talking about just now.

AMANDA: It must be so nasty for the poor animals, being experimented on.

ELYOT: Not when the experiments are successful. Why in Vienna I believe you can see whole lines of decrepit old rats carrying on like Tiller Girls.

AMANDA [laughing]:   Oh, how very, very sweet.

ELYOT [burying his face in her shoulder]:   I do love you so.

AMANDA: Don't blow, dear heart, it gives me the shivers.

ELYOT [trying to kiss her]:   Swivel your face round a bit more.

AMANDA [obliging]:   That better?

ELYOT [kissing her lingeringly]:   Very nice, thank you kindly.

AMANDA [*twining her arms round his neck*]:   Darling, you're so
terribly, terribly dear, and sweet, and attractive.
[*She pulls his head down to her again and they kiss lovingly.*
ELYOT [*softly*]:   We were raving mad, ever to part, even for an
instant.
AMANDA: Utter imbeciles.
ELYOT: I realized it almost immediately, didn't you?
AMANDA: Long before we got our decree.
ELYOT: My heart broke on that damned trip round the world.
I saw such beautiful things, darling. Moonlight shining on
old temples, strange barbaric dances in jungle villages, scarlet
flamingoes flying over deep, deep blue water. Breathlessly
lovely, and completely unexciting because you weren't there
to see them with me.
AMANDA [*kissing him again*]:   Take me please, take me at once,
let's make up for lost time.
ELYOT: Next week?
AMANDA: Tomorrow.
ELYOT: Done.
AMANDA: I must see those dear flamingoes. [*There is a pause.*]
Eight years all told, we've loved each other. Three married
and five divorced.
ELYOT: Angel. Angel. Angel.
[*He kisses her passionately.*
AMANDA [*struggling slightly*]:   No, Elyot, stop now, stop—
ELYOT: Why should I stop? You know you adore being made
love to.
AMANDA [*through his kisses*]:   It's so soon after dinner.
ELYOT [*jumping up rather angrily*]:   You really do say most
awful things.
AMANDA [*tidying her hair*]:   I don't see anything particularly
awful about that.
ELYOT: No sense of glamor, no sense of glamor at all.
AMANDA: It's difficult to feel really glamorous with a crick in
the neck.
ELYOT: Why didn't you say you had a crick in your neck?
AMANDA [*sweetly*]:   It's gone now.

ELYOT: How convenient.

[*He lights a cigarette.*

AMANDA [*holding out her hand*]:   I want one please.

ELYOT [*throwing her one*]:   Here.

AMANDA: Match?

ELYOT [*impatiently*]:   Wait a minute, can't you?

AMANDA: Chivalrous little love.

ELYOT [*throwing the matches at her*]:   Here.

AMANDA [*coldly*]:   Thank you very much indeed.

[*There is a silence for a moment.*

ELYOT: You really can be more irritating than anyone in the world.

AMANDA: I fail to see what I've done that's so terribly irritating.

ELYOT: You have no tact.

AMANDA: Tact. You have no consideration.

ELYOT [*walking up and down*]:   Too soon after dinner indeed.

AMANDA: Yes, much too soon.

ELYOT: That sort of remark shows rather a common sort of mind, I'm afraid.

AMANDA: Oh it does, does it?

ELYOT: Very unpleasant, makes me shudder.

AMANDA: Making all this fuss just because your silly vanity is a little upset.

ELYOT: Vanity: What do you mean, vanity?

AMANDA: You can't bear the thought that there are certain moments when our chemical, what d'you call 'ems, don't fuse properly.

ELYOT [*derisively*]:   Chemical what d'you call 'ems: Please try to be more explicit.

AMANDA: You know perfectly well what I mean, and don't you try to patronize me.

ELYOT [*loudly*]:   Now look here, Amanda—

AMANDA [*suddenly*]:   Darling, Sollocks! Oh, for God's sake, Sollocks!

ELYOT: But listen—

AMANDA: Sollocks, Sollocks, Oh dear—triple Sollocks!

[*They stand looking at one another in silence for a moment, then* AMANDA *flings herself down on the sofa and buries her face in the cushion.* ELYOT *looks at her, then goes over to the piano. He sits down and begins to play idly.* AMANDA *raises her head, screws herself round on the sofa, and lies there listening.* ELYOT *blows a kiss to her and goes on playing. He starts to sing softly to her, never taking his eyes off her. When he has finished the little refrain, whatever it was, he still continues to play it looking at her.*

AMANDA: Big romantic stuff, darling.

ELYOT [*smiling*]:   Yes, big romantic stuff.

[*He wanders off into another tune.* AMANDA *sits up crossed-legged on the sofa, and begins to sing it, then, still singing, she comes over and perches on the piano. They sing several old refrains from dead and gone musical comedies finishing with the song that brought them together again in the first act. Finally* AMANDA *comes down and sits next to him on the piano stool, they both therefore have their backs half turned to the audience. She rests her head on his shoulder, until finally his fingers drop off the keys, and they melt into one another's arms.*

ELYOT [*after a moment*]:   You're the most thrilling, exciting woman that was ever born.

AMANDA [*standing up, and brushing her hand lightly over his mouth*]:   Dearest, dearest heart—

[*He catches at her hand and kisses it, and then her arm, until he is standing up, embracing her ardently. She struggles a little, half laughing, and breaks away, but he catches her, and they finish up on the sofa again, clasped in each other's arms, both completely given up to the passion of the moment, until the telephone bell rings violently, and they both spring apart.*

ELYOT: Good God!

AMANDA: Do you think it's them?

ELYOT: I wonder.

AMANDA: Nobody knows we're here except Freda, and she wouldn't ring up.

ELYOT: It must be them then.

AMANDA: What are we to do?

ELYOT [*suddenly*]:   We're all right darling, aren't we—whatever happens?

AMANDA: Now and always, Sweet.

ELYOT: I don't care then.

[*He gets up and goes defiantly over to the telephone, which has been ringing incessantly during the little preceding scene.*

AMANDA: It was bound to come sooner or later.

ELYOT [*at telephone*]:   Hallo—hallo—what—comment? Madame, qui? 'allo—'allo—oui c'est ça. Oh, Madame Duvallon—Oui, oui, oui. [*He puts his hand over the mouthpiece*] It's only somebody wanting to talk to the dear Madame Duvallon.

AMANDA: Who's she?

ELYOT: I haven't the faintest idea. [*At telephone*] Je regrette beaucoup, Monsieur, mais Madame Duvallon viens de partir cette après-midi, pour Madagascar. [*He hangs up the telephone*] Whew; that gave me a fright.

AMANDA: It sent shivers up my spine.

ELYOT: What shall we do if they suddenly walk in on us?

AMANDA: Behave exquisitely.

ELYOT: With the most perfect poise?

AMANDA: Certainly, I shall probably do a Court Curtsey.

ELYOT [*sitting on the edge of the sofa*]:   Things that ought to matter dreadfully, don't matter at all when one's happy, do they?

AMANDA: What is so horrible is that one can't stay happy.

ELYOT: Darling, don't say that.

AMANDA: It's true. The whole business is a very poor joke.

ELYOT: Meaning that sacred and beautiful thing, Love?

AMANDA: Yes, meaning just that.

ELYOT [*striding up and down the room dramatically*]:   What does it all mean, that's what I ask myself in my ceaseless quest for ultimate truth. Dear God, what does it all mean?

AMANDA: Don't laugh at me, I'm serious.

ELYOT [*seriously*]:   You mustn't be serious, my dear one; it's just what they want.

AMANDA: Who's they?

ELYOT: All the futile moralists who try to make life unbearable. Laugh at them. Be flippant. Laugh at everything, all their sacred shibboleths. Flippancy brings out the acid in there damned sweetness and light.

AMANDA: If I laugh at everything, I must laugh at us too.

ELYOT: Certainly you must. We're figures of fun all right.

AMANDA: How long will it last, this ludicrous, overbearing love of ours?

ELYOT: Who knows?

AMANDA: Shall we always want to bicker and fight?

ELYOT: No, that desire will fade, along with our passion.

AMANDA: Oh dear, shall we like that?

ELYOT: It all depends on how well we've played.

AMANDA: What happens if one of us dies? Does the one that's left still laugh?

ELYOT: Yes, yes, with all his might.

AMANDA [wistfully clutching his hand]: That's serious enough, isn't it?

ELYOT: No, no, it isn't. Death's very laughable, such a cunning little mystery. All done with mirrors.

AMANDA: Darling, I believe you're talking nonsense.

ELYOT: So is everyone else in the long run. Let's be superficial and pity the poor philosophers. Let's blow trumpets and squeakers, and enjoy the party as much as we can, like very small, quite idiotic school children. Let's savour the delight of the moment. Come and kiss me darling, before your body rots, and worms pop in and out of your eye sockets.

AMANDA: Elyot, worms don't pop.

ELYOT [kissing her]: I don't mind what you do, see? You can paint yourself bright green all over, and dance naked in the Place Vendôme, and rush off madly with all the men in the world, and I shan't say a word, as long as you love me best.

AMANDA: Thank you, dear. The same applies to you, except that if I catch you so much as looking at another woman, I'll kill you.

ELYOT: Do you remember that awful scene we had in Venice?

AMANDA: Which particular one?

ELYOT: The one when you bought that little painted wooden snake on the Piazza, and put it on my bed.

AMANDA: Oh, Charles. That was his name, Charles. He did wriggle so beautifully.

ELYOT: Horrible thing, I hated it.

AMANDA: Yes, I know you did. You threw it out of the window into the Grand Canal. I don't think I'll ever forgive you for that.

ELYOT: How long did the row last?

AMANDA: It went on intermittently for days.

ELYOT: The worst one was in Cannes when your curling irons burnt a hole in my new dressing-gown.

[He laughs.

AMANDA: It burnt my comb too, and all the towels in the bathroom.

ELYOT: That was a rouser, wasn't it?

AMANDA: That was the first time you ever hit me.

ELYOT: I didn't hit you very hard.

AMANDA: The manager came in and found us rolling on the floor, biting and scratching like panthers. Oh dear, oh dear—

[She laughs helplessly.

ELYOT: I shall never forget his face.

[They both collapse with laughter.

AMANDA: How ridiculous, how utterly, utterly ridiculous.

ELYOT: We were very much younger then.

AMANDA: And very much sillier.

ELYOT: As a matter of fact the real cause of that row was Peter Burden.

AMANDA: You knew there was nothing in that.

ELYOT: I didn't know anything of the sort, you took presents from him.

AMANDA: Presents: only a trivial little brooch.

ELYOT: I remember it well, bristling with diamonds. In the worst possible taste.

AMANDA: Not at all, it was very pretty. I still have it, and I wear it often.

ELYOT: You went out of your way to torture me over Peter Burden.

AMANDA: No, I didn't, you worked the whole thing up in your jealous imagination.

ELYOT: You must admit that he was in love with you, wasn't he?

AMANDA: Just a little perhaps. Nothing serious.

ELYOT: You let him kiss you. You said you did.

AMANDA: Well, what of it?

ELYOT: What of it!

AMANDA: It gave him a lot of pleasure, and it didn't hurt me.

ELYOT: What about me?

AMANDA: If you hadn't been so suspicious and nosey you'd never have known a thing about it.

ELYOT: That's a nice point of view I must say.

AMANDA: Oh dear, I'm bored with this conversation.

ELYOT: So am I, bored stiff. [*He goes over to the table*] Want some brandy?

AMANDA: No thanks.

ELYOT: I'll have a little, I think.

AMANDA: I don't see why you want it, you've already had two glasses.

ELYOT: No particular reason, anyhow they were very small ones.

AMANDA: It seems so silly to go on, and on, and on with a thing.

ELYOT [*pouring himself out a glassful*]: You can hardly call three liqueur glasses in a whole evening going on, and on, and on.

AMANDA: It's become a habit with you.

ELYOT: You needn't be so grand, just because you don't happen to want any yourself at the moment.

AMANDA: Don't be so stupid.

ELYOT [*irritably*]: Really Amanda—

AMANDA: What?

ELYOT: Nothing. [AMANDA *sits down on the sofa, and, taking a small mirror from her bag, gazes at her face critically, and then uses some lipstick and powder. A trifle nastily*] Going out somewhere, dear?

AMANDA: No, just making myself fascinating for you.

ELYOT: That reply has broken my heart.

AMANDA: The woman's job is to allure the man. Watch me a minute, will you?

ELYOT: As a matter of fact that's perfectly true.

AMANDA: Oh, no, it isn't.

ELYOT: Yes it is.

AMANDA [*snappily*]:   Oh be quiet.

ELYOT: It's a pity you didn't have any more brandy; it might have made you a little less disagreeable.

AMANDA: It doesn't seem to have worked such wonders with you.

ELYOT: Snap, snap, snap; like a little adder.

AMANDA: Adders don't snap, they sting.

ELYOT: Nonsense, they have a little bag of venom behind their fangs and they snap.

AMANDA: They sting.

ELYOT: They snap.

AMANDA [*with exasperation*]:   I don't care, do you understand? I don't care. I don't mind if they bark, and roll about like hoops.

ELYOT [*after a slight pause*]:   Did you see much of Peter Burden after our divorce?

AMANDA: Yes, I did, quite a lot.

ELYOT: I suppose you let him kiss you a good deal more then.

AMANDA: Mind your own business.

ELYOT: You must have had a riotous time. [AMANDA *doesn't answer, so he stalks about the room*] No restraint at all— very enjoyable—you never had much anyhow.

AMANDA: You're quite insufferable; I expect it's because you're drunk.

ELYOT: I'm not in the least drunk.

AMANDA: You always had a weak head.

ELYOT: I think I mentioned once before that I have only had three minute liqueur glasses of brandy the whole evening long. A child of two couldn't get drunk on that.

AMANDA: On the contrary, a child of two could get violently drunk on only one glass of brandy.

ELYOT: Very interesting. How about a child of four, and a child of six, and a child of nine?

AMANDA [*turning her head away*]: Oh do shut up.

ELYOT [*witheringly*]: We might get up a splendid little debate about that, you know, Intemperate Tots.

AMANDA: Not very funny, dear; you'd better have some more brandy.

ELYOT: Very good idea, I will.

[*He pours out another glass and gulps it down defiantly.*

AMANDA: Ridiculous ass.

ELYOT: I beg your pardon?

AMANDA: I said ridiculous ass!

ELYOT [*with great dignity*]: Thank you. [*There is a silence. AMANDA gets up, and turns the gramophone on*] You'd better turn that off, I think.

AMANDA [*coldly*]: Why?

ELYOT: It's very late and it will annoy the people upstairs.

AMANDA: There aren't any people upstairs. It's a photographer's studio.

ELYOT: There are people downstairs, I suppose?

AMANDA: They're away in Tunis.

ELYOT: This is no time of the year for Tunis.

[*He turns the gramophone off.*

AMANDA [*icily*]: Turn it on again, please.

ELYOT: I'll do no such thing.

AMANDA: Very well, if you insist on being boorish and idiotic.

[*She gets up and turns it on again.*

ELYOT: Turn it off. It's driving me mad.

AMANDA: You're far too temperamental. Try to control yourself.

ELYOT: Turn it off.

AMANDA: I won't. [ELYOT *rushes at the gramophone.* AMANDA *tries to ward him off. They struggle silently for a moment, then the needle screeches across the record*] There now, you've ruined the record.

[*She takes it off and scrutinizes it.*

ELYOT: Good job, too.

AMANDA: Disagreeable pig.

ELYOT [*suddenly stricken with remorse*]: Amanda darling— Sollocks.

AMANDA [*furiously*]:   Sollocks yourself.

[*She breaks the record over his head.*

ELYOT [*staggering*]:   You spiteful little beast.

[*He slaps her face. She screams loudly and hurls herself sobbing with rage on to the sofa, with her face buried in the cushions.*

AMANDA [*wailing*]:   Oh, oh, oh—

ELYOT: I'm sorry, I didn't mean it—I'm sorry, darling, I swear I didn't mean it.

AMANDA: Go away, go away, I hate you.

[ELYOT *kneels on the sofa and tries to pull her round to look at him.*

ELYOT: Amanda—listen—listen—

AMANDA [*turning suddenly, and fetching him a welt across the face*]:   Listen indeed; I'm sick and tired of listening to you, you damned sadistic bully.

ELYOT [*with great grandeur*]:   Thank you. [*He stalks towards the door, in stately silence.* AMANDA *throws a cushion at him, which misses him and knocks down a lamp and a vase on the side table.* ELYOT *laughs falsely*] A pretty display I must say.

AMANDA [*wildly*]:   Stop laughing like that.

ELYOT [*continuing*]:   Very amusing indeed.

AMANDA [*losing control*]:   Stop—stop—stop— [*She rushes at him, he grabs her hands and they sway about the room, until he manages to twist her round by the arms so that she faces him, closely, quivering with fury*]—I hate you—do you hear? You're conceited, and overbearing, and utterly impossible!

ELYOT [*shouting her down*]:   You're a vile-tempered, loose-living, wicked little beast, and I never want to see you again so long as I live.

[*He flings her away from him, she staggers, and falls against a chair. They stand gasping at one another in silence for a moment.*

AMANDA [*very quietly*]:   This is the end, do you understand? The end, finally and forever.

[*She goes to the door, which opens on to the landing, and wrenches it open. He rushes after her and clutches her wrist.*

ELYOT: You're not going like this.

AMANDA: Oh, yes I am.

ELYOT: You're not.

AMANDA: I am; let go of me—[*He pulls her away from the door, and once more they struggle. This time a standard lamp crashes to the ground.* AMANDA, *breathlessly, as they fight*] You're a cruel fiend, and I hate and loathe you; thank God I've realized in time what you're really like; marry you again, never, never, never . . . I'd rather die in torment—

ELYOT [*at the same time*]: Shut up; shut up. I wouldn't marry you again if you came crawling to me on your bended knees, you're a mean, evil-minded, little vampire—I hope to God I never set eyes on you again as long as I live—

[*At this point in the proceedings they trip over a piece of carpet, and fall on to the floor, rolling over and over in paroxysms of rage.* VICTOR *and* SIBYL *enter quietly, through the open door, and stand staring at them in horror. Finally* AMANDA *breaks free and half gets up,* ELYOT *grabs her leg, and she falls against a table, knocking it completely over.*

AMANDA [*screaming*]: Beast; brute; swine; cad; beast; beast; brute; devil—

[*She rushes back at* ELYOT *who is just rising to his feet, and gives him a stinging blow, which knocks him over again. She rushes blindly off Left, and slams the door, at the same moment that he jumps up and rushes off Right, also slamming the door.* VICTOR *and* SIBYL *advance apprehensively into the room, and sink on to the sofa—*

CURTAIN

ACT THREE

The scene is the same as Act II. It is the next morning. The time is about eight-thirty. VICTOR *and* SIBYL *have drawn the two sofas across the doors Right, and Left, and are stretched on them, asleep.* VICTOR *is in front of* AMANDA'S *door, and* SIBYL *in front of* ELYOT'S.

The room is in chaos, as it was left the night before.

As the curtain rises, there is the rattling of a key in the lock of the front door, and LOUISE *enters. She is rather a frowsy-looking girl, and carries a string bag with various bundles of eatables crammed into it, notably a long roll of bread, and a lettuce. She closes the door after her, and in the half light trips over the standard lamp lying on the floor. She puts her string bag down, and gropes her way over to the window. She draws the curtains, letting sunlight stream into the room. When she looks round, she gives a little cry of horror. Then she sees* VICTOR *and* SIBYL *sleeping peacefully, and comes over and scrutinizes each of them with care, then she shakes* SIBYL *by the shoulder.*

SIBYL [*waking*]: Oh dear.

LOUISE: Bon jour, Madame.

SIBYL [*bewildered*]: What?—Oh—bon jour.

LOUISE: Qu'est-ce que vous faites ici, Madame?

SIBYL: What—what?—Wait a moment, attendez un instant—oh dear—

VICTOR [*sleepily*]: What's happening? [*Jumping up*] Of course, I remember now. [*He sees* LOUISE] Oh!

LOUISE [*firmly*]: Bon jour, Monsieur.

VICTOR: Er—bon jour—What time is it?

LOUISE [*rather dully*]: Eh, Monsieur?

SIBYL [*sitting up on the sofa*]: Quelle heure est-il, s'il vous plaît?

LOUISE: C'est neuf heures moins dix, Madame.

VICTOR: What did she say?

SIBYL: I think she said nearly ten o'clock.

VICTOR [*taking situation in hand*]: Er—voulez—er—wake—reveillez Monsieur et Madame—er—toute suite?

LOUISE [*shaking her head*]: Non, Monsieur. Il m'est absolument defendu de les appeler jusqu'à ce qu'ils sonnent.

[*She takes her bag and goes off into the kitchen.* VICTOR *and* SIBYL *look at each other helplessly.*

SIBYL: What are we to do?

VICTOR [*with determination*]: Wake them ourselves.

[*He goes towards* AMANDA's *door.*

SIBYL: No, no, wait a minute.

VICTOR: What's the matter?

SIBYL [*plaintively*]: I couldn't face them yet, really, I couldn't; I feel dreadful.

VICTOR: So do I. [*He wanders gloomily over to the window*] It's a lovely morning.

SIBYL: Lovely.

[*She bursts into tears.*

VICTOR [*coming to her*]: I say, don't cry.

SIBYL: I can't help it.

VICTOR: Please don't, please—

SIBYL: It's all so squalid; I wish we hadn't stayed; what's the use?

VICTOR: We've got to see them before we go back to England, we must get things straightened out.

SIBYL [*sinking down on to the sofa*]: Oh dear, oh dear, oh dear, I wish I were dead.

VICTOR: Hush, now, hush. Remember your promise. We've got to see this through together and get it settled one way or another.

SIBYL [*sniffling*]: I'll try to control myself, only I'm so . . . so tired, I haven't slept properly for ages.

VICTOR: Neither have I.

SIBYL: If we hadn't arrived when we did, they'd have killed one another.

VICTOR: They must have been drunk.

SIBYL: She hit him.

VICTOR: He'd probably hit her, too, earlier on.

SIBYL: I'd no idea anyone ever behaved like that; it's so disgusting, so degrading, Elli of all people—oh dear—

[*She almost breaks down again, but controls herself.*

VICTOR: What an escape you've had.

SIBYL: What an escape we've both had.

[AMANDA *opens her door and looks out. She is wearing travelling clothes, and is carrying a small suitcase. She jumps, upon seeing* SIBYL *and* VICTOR.

AMANDA: Oh!—good morning.

VICTOR [*with infinite reproach in his voice*]: Oh, Amanda.

AMANDA: Will you please move this sofa, I can't get out.

[VICTOR *moves the sofa, and she advances into the room and goes towards the door.*

VICTOR: Where are you going?

AMANDA: Away.

VICTOR: You can't.

AMANDA: Why not?

VICTOR: I want to talk to you.

AMANDA [*wearily*]: What on earth is the use of that?

VICTOR: I must talk to you.

AMANDA: Well, all I can say is, it's very inconsiderate.

[*She plumps the bag down by the door and comes down to* VICTOR.

VICTOR: Mandy, I—

AMANDA [*gracefully determined to rise above the situation*]: I suppose you're Sibyl; how do you do? [SIBYL *turns her back on her*] Well, if you're going to take up that attitude, I fail to see the point of your coming here at all.

SIBYL: I came to see Elyot.

AMANDA: I've no wish to prevent you; he's in there, probably wallowing in an alcoholic stupor.

VICTOR: This is all very unpleasant, Amanda.

AMANDA: I quite agree, that's why I want to go away.

VICTOR: That would be shirking; this must be discussed at length.

AMANDA: Very well, if you insist, but not just now, I don't feel up to it. Has Louise come yet?

VICTOR: If Louise is the maid, she's in the kitchen.

AMANDA: Thank you. You'd probably like some coffee, excuse me a moment.

[*She goes off into the kitchen.*

SIBYLS Well! How dare she?

VICTOR [*irritably*]: How dare she what?

SIBYL: Behave so calmly, as though nothing had happened.

VICTOR: I don't see what else she could have done.

SIBYL: Insufferable I call it.

[ELYOT *opens his door and looks out.*

ELYOT [*seeing them*]: Oh God.

[*He shuts the door again quickly.*

SIBYL: Elyot—Elyot—[*She rushes over to the door and bangs on it*] Elyot—Elyot—Elyot—

ELYOT [*inside*]: Go away.

SIBYL [*falling on to the sofa*]: Oh, oh, oh.

[*She bursts into tears again.*

VICTOR: Do pull yourself together for heaven's sake.

SIBYL: I can't, I can't—oh, oh, oh—

[AMANDA *re-enters.*

AMANDA: I've ordered some coffee and rolls, they'll be here soon. I must apologize for the room being so untidy.

[*She picks up a cushion, and pats it into place on the sofa. There is a silence except for* SIBYL's *sobs.* AMANDA *looks at her, and then at* VICTOR; *then she goes off into her room again, and shuts the door.*

VICTOR: It's no use crying like that, it doesn't do any good.

[*After a moment, during which* SIBYL *makes renewed efforts to control her tears,* ELYOT *opens the door immediately behind her, pushes the sofa, with her on it, out of the way, and walks towards the front door. He is in travelling clothes, and carrying a small suitcase.*

SIBYL [*rushing after him*]: Elyot, where are you going?

ELYOT: Canada.

SIBYL: You can't go like this, you can't.

ELYOT: I see no point in staying.

VICTOR: You owe it to Sibyl to stay.

ELYOT: How do you do, I don't think we've met before.

SIBYL: You must stay, you've got to stay.

ELYOT: Very well, if you insist. [*He plumps his bag down*] I'm afraid the room is in rather a mess. Have you seen the maid Louise?

VICTOR: She's in the kitchen.

ELYOT: Good. I'll order some coffee.

[*He makes a movement towards the kitchen.*

VICTOR [*stopping him*]:   No, your—er—my—er—Amanda has already ordered it.

ELYOT: Oh, I'm glad the old girl's up and about.

VICTOR: We've got to get things straightened out, you know.

ELYOT [*looking around the room*]:   Yes, it's pretty awful. We'll get the concierge up from downstairs.

VICTOR: You're being purposely flippant, but it's no good.

ELYOT: Sorry.

[*He lapses into silence.*

VICTOR [*after a pause*]:   What's to be done?

ELYOT: I don't know.

SIBYL [*with spirit*]:   It's all perfectly horrible. I feel smirched and unclean as though slimy things had been crawling all over me.

ELYOT: Maybe they have; that's a very old sofa.

VICTOR: If you don't stop your damned flippancy, I'll knock your head off.

ELYOT [*raising his eyebrows*]:   Has it ever struck you that flippancy might cover a very real embarrassment?

VICTOR: In a situation such as this, it's in extremely bad taste.

ELYOT: No worse than bluster and invective. As a matter of fact, as far as I know, this situation is entirely without precedent. We have no prescribed etiquette to fall back upon. I shall continue to be flippant.

SIBYL: Oh Elyot, how can you—how can you.

ELYOT: I'm awfully sorry, Sibyl.

VICTOR: It's easy enough to be sorry.

ELYOT: On the contrary. I find it exceedingly difficult. I seldom regret anything. This is a very rare and notable exception, a sort of red letter day. We must all make the most of it.

SIBYL: I'll never forgive you, never. I wouldn't have believed anyone could be so callous and cruel.

ELYOT: I absolutely see your point, and as I said before, I'm sorry.

[*There is silence for a moment. Then* AMANDA *comes in again. She has obviously decided to carry everything off in a high handed manner.*

AMANDA [*in social tones*]: What! Breakfast not ready yet? Really, these French servants are too slow for words. [*She smiles gaily*] What a glorious morning. [*She goes to the window*] I do love Paris, it's so genuinely gay. Those lovely trees in the Champs Elysées, and the little roundabouts for the children to play on, and those shiny red taxis. You can see Sacre Cœur quite clearly today; sometimes it's a bit misty, particularly in August, all the heat rising up from the pavements you know.

ELYOT [*drily*]: Yes, dear, we know.

AMANDA [*ignoring him*]: And it's heavenly being so high up. I found this flat three years ago, quite by merest chance. I happened to be staying at the Plaza Athenée, just down the road—

ELYOT [*enthusiastically*]: Such a nice hotel, with the most enchanting courtyard with a fountain that goes plopplopplop-plopplopplopplopplopplop—

VICTOR: This is ridiculous, Amanda.

ELYOT [*continuing*]: Plop plop plop plop plop plop plop plop plop plop—

AMANDA [*overriding him*]: Now, Victor, I refuse to discuss anything in the least important until after breakfast. I couldn't concentrate now, I know I couldn't.

ELYOT [*sarcastically*]: What manner. What poise. How I envy it. To be able to carry off the most embarrassing situation with such tact, and delicacy, and above all—such subtlety. Go on Amanda, you're making everything so much easier. We shall all be playing Hunt the Slipper in a minute.

AMANDA: Please don't address me, I don't wish to speak to you.

ELYOT: Splendid.

AMANDA: And what's more, I never shall again as long as I live.

ELYOT: I shall endeavor to rise above it.

AMANDA: I've been brought up to believe that it's beyond the pale for a man to strike a woman.

ELYOT: A very poor tradition. Certain women should be struck regularly, like gongs.

AMANDA: You're an unmitigated cad, and a bully.

ELYOT: And you're an ill-mannered, bad-tempered slattern.

AMANDA [*loudly*]: Slattern indeed.

ELYOT: Yes, slattern, slattern, slattern, and fishwife.

VICTOR: Keep your mouth shut, you swine.

ELYOT: Mind your own damned business.

[*They are about to fight, when* SIBYL *rushes between them.*

SIBYL: Stop, stop, it's no use going on like this. Stop, please. [*To* AMANDA] Help me, do, do, do, help me—

AMANDA: I'm not going to interfere. Let them fight if they want to; it will probably clear the air anyhow.

SIBYL: Yes but—

AMANDA: Come into my room; perhaps you'd like to wash or something.

SIBYL: No, but—

AMANDA [*firmly*]: Come along.

SIBYL: Very well.

[*She tosses her head at* ELYOT, *and* AMANDA *drags her off.*

VICTOR [*belligerently*]: Now then!

ELYOT: Now then what?

VICTOR: Are you going to take back those things you said to Amanda?

ELYOT: Certainly. I'll take back anything, if only you'll stop bellowing at me.

VICTOR [*contemptuously*]: You're a coward too.

ELYOT: They want us to fight, don't you see?

VICTOR: No, I don't, why should they?

ELYOT: Primitive feminine instincts—warring males—very enjoyable.

VICTOR: You think you're very clever, don't you?

ELYOT: I think I'm a bit cleverer than you, but apparently that's not saying much.

VICTOR [*violently*]: What?

ELYOT: Oh, do sit down.

VICTOR: I will not.

ELYOT: Well, if you'll excuse me, I will; I'm extremely tired.
[*He sits down.*

VICTOR: Oh, for God's sake, behave like a man.

ELYOT [*patiently*]: Listen a minute, all this belligerency is very right and proper and highly traditional, but if only you'll think for a moment, you'll see that it won't get us very far.

VICTOR: To hell with all that.

ELYOT: I should like to explain that if you hit me, I shall certainly hit you, probably equally hard, if not harder. I'm just as strong as you, I should imagine. Then you'd hit me again, and I'd hit you again, and we'd go on until one or the other was knocked out. Now if you'll explain to me satisfactorily how all that can possibly improve the situation, I'll tear off my coat, and we'll go at one another hammer and tongs, immediately.

VICTOR: It would ease my mind.

ELYOT: Only if you won.

VICTOR: I should win all right.

ELYOT: Want to try?

VICTOR: Yes.

ELYOT [*jumping up*]: Here goes then—
[*He tears off his coat.*

VICTOR: Just a moment.

ELYOT: Well?

VICTOR: What did you mean about them wanting us to fight?

ELYOT: It would be balm to their vanity.

VICTOR: Do you love Amanda?

ELYOT: Is this a battle or a discussion? If it's the latter I shall put on my coat again; I don't want to catch a chill.

VICTOR: Answer my question, please.

ELYOT: Have a cigarette?

VICTOR [*stormily*]: Answer my question.

ELYOT: If you analyze it, it's rather a silly question.

VICTOR: Do you love Amanda?

ELYOT [*confidentially*]:   Not very much this morning, to be
perfectly frank; I'd like to wring her neck. Do you love her?

VICTOR: That's beside the point.

ELYOT: On the contrary, it's the crux of the whole affair. If
you do love her still, you can forgive her, and live with her
in peace and harmony until you're ninety-eight.

VICTOR: You're apparently even more of a cad than I thought
you were.

ELYOT: You are completely in the right over the whole business, don't imagine I'm not perfectly conscious of that.

VICTOR: I'm glad.

ELYOT: It's all very unfortunate.

VICTOR: Unfortunate: My God!

ELYOT: It might have been worse.

VICTOR: I'm glad you think so.

ELYOT: I do wish you'd stop about being so glad about everything.

VICTOR: What do you intend to do? That's what I want to
know. What do you intend to do?

ELYOT [*suddenly serious*]:   I don't know, I don't care.

VICTOR: I suppose you realize that you've broken that poor
little woman's heart?

ELYOT: Which poor little woman?

VICTOR: Sibyl, of course.

ELYOT: Oh, come now, not as bad as that. She'll get over it,
and forget all about me.

VICTOR: I sincerely hope so . . . for her sake.

ELYOT: Amanda will forget all about me too. Everybody will
forget all about me. I might just as well lie down and die in
fearful pain and suffering, nobody would care.

VICTOR: Don't talk such rot.

ELYOT: You must forgive me for taking rather a gloomy view
of everything but the fact is, I suddenly feel slightly depressed.

VICTOR: I intend to divorce Amanda, naming you as co-re-
spondent.

ELYOT: Very well.

VICTOR: And Sibyl will divorce you for Amanda. It would be foolish of either of you to attempt any defence.

ELYOT: Quite.

VICTOR: And the sooner you marry Amanda again, the better.

ELYOT: I'm not going to marry Amanda.

VICTOR: What?

ELYOT: She's a vile-tempered, wicked woman.

VICTOR: You should have thought of that before.

ELYOT: I did think of it before.

VICTOR [*firmly*]: You've got to marry her.

ELYOT: I'd rather marry a ravening leopard.

VICTOR [*angrily*]: Now look here. I'm sick of all this shilly-shallying. You're getting off a good deal more lightly than you deserve; you can consider yourself damned lucky I didn't shoot you.

ELYOT [*with sudden vehemence*]: Well, if you'd had a spark of manliness in you, you would have shot me. You're all fuss and fume, one of these cotton wool Englishmen. I despise you.

VICTOR [*through clenched teeth*]: You despise me?

ELYOT: Yes, utterly. You're nothing but a rampaging gas bag! [*He goes off into his room and slams the door, leaving* VICTOR *speechless with fury,* AMANDA *and* SIBYL *re-enter.*

AMANDA [*brightly*]: Well, what's happened?

VICTOR [*sullenly*]: Nothing's happened.

AMANDA: You ought to be ashamed to admit it.

SIBYL: Where's Elyot?

VICTOR: In there.

AMANDA: What's he doing?

VICTOR [*turning angrily away*]: How do I know what he's doing?

AMANDA: If you were half the man I thought you were, he'd be bandaging himself.

SIBYL [*with defiance*]: Elyot's just as strong as Victor.

AMANDA [*savagely*]: I should like it proved.

SIBYL: There's no need to be so vindictive.

AMANDA: You were abusing Elyot like a pickpocket to me a little while ago, now you are standing up for him.

SIBYL: I'm beginning to suspect that he wasn't quite so much to blame as I thought.

AMANDA: Oh, really?

SIBYL: You certainly have a very unpleasant temper.

AMANDA: It's a little difficult to keep up with your rapid changes of front, but you're young and inexperienced, so I forgive you freely.

SIBYL [*heatedly*]:   Seeing the depths of degradation to which age and experience have brought you, I'm glad I'm as I am!

AMANDA [*with great grandeur*]:   That was exceedingly rude. I think you'd better go away somewhere.

[*She waves her hand vaguely.*

SIBYL: After all, Elyot is my husband.

AMANDA: Take him with you, by all means.

SIBYL: If you're not very careful, I will! [*She goes over to* ELYOT's *door and bangs on it*] Elyot—Elyot—

ELYOT [*inside*]:   What is it?

SIBYL: Let me in. Please, please let me in; I want to speak to you!

AMANDA: Heaven preserve me from nice women!

SIBYL: Your own reputation ought to do that.

AMANDA [*irritably*]:   Oh, go to hell!

[ELYOT *opens the door, and* SIBYL *disappears inside,* AMANDA *looks at* VICTOR, *who is standing with his back turned, staring out of the window, then she wanders about the room, making rather inadequate little attempts to tidy up. She glances at* VICTOR *again.*

AMANDA: Victor.

VICTOR [*without turning*]:   What?

AMANDA [*sadly*]:   Nothing.

[*She begins to wrestle with one of the sofas in an effort to get it in place.* VICTOR *turns, sees her, and comes down and helps her, in silence.*

VICTOR: Where does it go?

AMANDA: Over there. [*After they have placed it,* AMANDA *sits on the edge of it and gasps a little*] Thank you, Victor.

VICTOR: Don't mention it.

AMANDA [*after a pause*]: What did you say to Elyot?

VICTOR: I told him he was beneath contempt.

AMANDA: Good.

VICTOR: I think you must be mad, Amanda.

AMANDA: I've often thought that myself.

VICTOR: I feel completely lost, completely bewildered.

AMANDA: I don't blame you. I don't feel any too cosy.

VICTOR: Had you been drinking last night?

AMANDA: Certainly not!

VICTOR: Had Elyot been drinking?

AMANDA: Yes—gallons.

VICTOR: Used he to drink before? When you were married to him?

AMANDA: Yes, terribly. Night after night he'd come home roaring and hiccoughing.

VICTOR: Disgusting!

AMANDA: Yes, wasn't it?

VICTOR: Did he really strike you last night?

AMANDA: Repeatedly, I'm bruised beyond recognition.

VICTOR [*suspecting slight exaggeration*]: Amanda!

AMANDA [*putting her hand on his arm*]: Oh, Victor, I'm most awfully sorry to have given you so much trouble, really I am! I've behaved badly, I know, but something strange happened to me. I can't explain it, there's no excuse, but I am ashamed of having made you unhappy.

VICTOR: I can't understand it at all. I've tried to, but I can't. It all seems so unlike you.

AMANDA: It isn't really unlike me, that's the trouble. I ought never to have married you; I'm a bad lot.

VICTOR: Amanda!

AMANDA: Don't contradict me. I know I'm a bad lot.

VICTOR: I wasn't going to contradict you.

AMANDA: Victor!

VICTOR: You appal me—absolutely!

AMANDA: Go on, go on, I deserve it.

VICTOR: I didn't come here to accuse you; there's no sense in that!

AMANDA: Why did you come?

VICTOR: To find out what you want me to do.

AMANDA: Divorce me, I suppose, as soon as possible. I won't make any difficulties. I'll go away, far away, Morocco, or Tunis, or somewhere. I shall probably catch some dreadful disease, and die out there, all alone—oh dear!

VICTOR: It's no use pitying yourself.

AMANDA: I seem to be the only one who does. I might just as well enjoy it. [*She sniffs*] I'm thoroughly unprincipled; Sibyl was right!

VICTOR [*irritably*]: Sibyl's an ass.

AMANDA [*brightening slightly*]: Yes, she is rather, isn't she? I can't think why Elyot ever married her.

VICTOR: Do you love him?

AMANDA: She seems so insipid, somehow—

VICTOR: Do you love him?

AMANDA: Of course she's very pretty, I suppose, in rather a shallow way, but still—

VICTOR: Amanda!

AMANDA: Yes, Victor?

VICTOR: You haven't answered my question.

AMANDA: I've forgotten what it was.

VICTOR [*turning away*]: You're hopeless—hopeless.

AMANDA: Don't be angry, it's all much too serious to be angry about.

VICTOR: You're talking utter nonsense!

AMANDA: No, I'm not, I mean it. It's ridiculous for us all to stand round arguing with one another. You'd much better go back to England and let your lawyers deal with the whole thing.

VICTOR: But what about you?

AMANDA: I'll be all right.

VICTOR: I only want to know one thing, and you won't tell me.

AMANDA: What is it?

VICTOR: Do you love Elyot?

AMANDA: No, I hate him. When I saw him again suddenly at Deauville, it was an odd sort of shock. It swept me away completely. He attracted me; he always has attracted me, but only the worst part of me. I see that now.

VICTOR: I can't understand why? He's so terribly trivial and superficial.

AMANDA: That sort of attraction can't be explained, it's sort of a chemical what d'you call 'em.

VICTOR: Yes; it must be!

AMANDA: I don't expect you to understand, and I'm not going to try to excuse myself in any way. Elyot was the first love affair of my life, and in spite of all the suffering he caused me before, there must have been a little spark left smouldering, which burst into flame when I came face to face with him again. I completely lost grip of myself and behaved like a fool, for which I shall pay all right, you needn't worry about that. But perhaps one day, when all this is dead and done with, you and I might meet and be friends. That's something to hope for, anyhow. Good-bye, Victor dear.

[*She holds out her hand.*

VICTOR [*shaking her hand mechanically*]: Do you want to marry him?

AMANDA: I'd rather marry a boa constrictor.

VICTOR: I can't go away and leave you with a man who drinks, and knocks you about.

AMANDA: You needn't worry about leaving me, as though I were a sort of parcel. I can look after myself.

VICTOR: You said just now you were going away to Tunis, to die.

AMANDA: I've changed my mind, it's the wrong time of the year for Tunis. I shall go somewhere quite different. I believe Brioni is very nice in the summer.

VICTOR: Why won't you be serious for just one moment?

AMANDA: I've told you, it's no use.

VICTOR: If it will make things any easier for you, I won't divorce you.

AMANDA: Victor!

VICTOR: We can live apart until Sibyl has got her decree against Elyot, then, some time after that, I'll let you divorce me.

AMANDA [*turning away*]:   I see you're determined to make me serious, whether I like it or not.

VICTOR: I married you because I loved you.

AMANDA: Stop it, Victor! Stop it! I won't listen!

VICTOR: I expect I love you still; one doesn't change all in a minute. You never loved me. I see that now, of course, so perhaps everything has turned out for the best really.

AMANDA: I thought I loved you, honestly I did.

VICTOR: Yes, I know, that's all right.

AMANDA: What an escape you've had.

VICTOR: I've said that to myself often during the last few days.

AMANDA: There's no need to rub it in.

VICTOR: Do you agree about the divorce business?

AMANDA: Yes. It's very, very generous of you.

VICTOR: It will save you some of the mud-slinging. We might persuade Sibyl not to name you.

AMANDA [*ruefully*]:   Yes, we might.

VICTOR: Perhaps she'll change her mind about divorcing him.

AMANDA: Perhaps. She certainly went into the bedroom with a predatory look in her eye.

VICTOR: Would you be pleased if that happened?

AMANDA: Delighted.

[*She laughs suddenly.* VICTOR *looks at her, curiously.* SIBYL *and* ELYOT *come out of the bedroom. There is an awkward silence for a moment.*

SIBYL [*looking at* AMANDA *triumphantly*]:   Elyot and I have come to a decision.

AMANDA: How very nice!

VICTOR: What is it?

AMANDA: Don't be silly, Victor. Look at their faces.

ELYOT: Feminine intuition, very difficult.

AMANDA [*looking at* SIBYL]:   Feminine determination, very praiseworthy.

SIBYL: I am not going to divorce Elyot for a year.

AMANDA: I congratulate you.

ELYOT [*defiantly*]:   Sibyl has behaved like an angel.

AMANDA: Well, it was certainly her big moment.

[LOUISE *comes staggering in with a large tray of coffee and rolls,*

*etc., she stands peering over the edge of it, not knowing where
to put it.*

ELYOT: Il faut le mettre sur la petite table là bas.

LOUISE: Oui, monsieur.

[ELYOT *and* VICTOR *hurriedly clear the things off the side table,
and* LOUISE *puts the tray down, and goes back into the kitchen.*
AMANDA *and* SIBYL *eye one another.*

AMANDA: It all seems very amicable.

SIBYL: It is, thank you.

AMANDA: I don't wish to depress you, but Victor isn't going
to divorce me either.

ELYOT [*looking up sharply*]: What!

AMANDA: I believe I asked you once before this morning, never
to speak to me again.

ELYOT: I only said "What." It was a general exclamation de-
noting extreme satisfaction.

AMANDA [*politely to* SIBYL]: Do sit down, won't you?

SIBYL: I'm afraid I must be going now. I'm catching the
Golden Arrow; it leaves at twelve.

ELYOT [*coaxingly*]: You have time for a little coffee surely?

SIBYL: No, I really must go!

ELYOT: I shan't be seeing you again for such a long time.

AMANDA [*brightly*]: Living apart? How wise!

ELYOT [*ignoring her*]: Please, Sibyl, do stay!

SIBYL [*looking at* AMANDA *with a glint in her eye*]: Very well,
just for a little.

AMANDA: Sit down, Victor, darling. [*They all sit down in silence.* AMANDA *smiles sweetly at* SIBYL *and holds up the coffee
pot and milk jug*] Half and half?

SIBYL: Yes, please.

AMANDA [*sociably*]: What would one do without one's morning coffee? That's what I often ask myself.

ELYOT: Is it?

AMANDA [*withering him with a look*]: Victor, sugar for Sibyl.
[*To* SIBYL] It should be absurd for me to call you anything
but Sibyl, wouldn't it?

SIBYL [*not to be outdone*]: Of course; I shall call you Mandy.
[AMANDA *represses a shudder.*

ELYOT: Oh God! We're off again. What weather!

[AMANDA *hands* SIBYL *her coffee.*

SIBYL: Thank you.

VICTOR: What's the time?

ELYOT: If the clock's still going after last night, it's ten-fifteen.

AMANDA [*handing* VICTOR *cup of coffee*]:   Here, Victor dear.

VICTOR: Thanks.

AMANDA: Sibyl, sugar for Victor.

ELYOT: I should like some coffee, please.

[AMANDA *pours some out for him, and hands it to him in silence.*

AMANDA [*to* VICTOR]:   Brioche?

VICTOR [*jumping*]:   What?

AMANDA: Would you like a brioche?

VICTOR: No, thank you.

ELYOT: I would. And some butter, and some jam.

[*He helps himself.*

AMANDA [*to* SIBYL]:   Have you ever been to Brioni?

SIBYL: No. It's in the Adriatic, isn't it?

VICTOR: The Baltic, I think.

SIBYL: I made sure it was in the Adriatic.

AMANDA: I had an aunt who went there once.

ELYOT [*with his mouth full*]:   I once had an aunt who went to
    Tasmania.

[AMANDA *looks at him stonily. He winks at her, and she looks
away hurriedly.*

VICTOR: Funny how the South of France has become so fa-
    shionable in the summer, isn't it?

SIBYL: Yes, awfully funny.

ELYOT: I've been laughing about it for months.

AMANDA: Personally, I think it's a bit too hot, although of
    course one can lie in the water all day.

SIBYL: Yes, the bathing is really divine!

VICTOR: A friend of mine has a house right on the edge of
    Cape Ferrat.

SIBYL: Really?

VICTOR: Yes, right on the edge.

AMANDA: That must be marvellous!

VICTOR: Yes, he seems to like it very much.

[*The conversation languishes slightly.*

AMANDA [*with great vivacity*]:   Do you know, I really think I
love travelling more than anything else in the world! It always
gives me such a tremendous feeling of adventure. First of all,
the excitement of packing, and getting your passport visa'd
and everything, then the thrill of actually starting, and
trundling along on trains and ships, and then the most
thrilling thing of all, arriving at strange places, and seeing
strange people, and eating strange foods—

ELYOT: And making strange noises afterwards.

[AMANDA *chokes violently.* VICTOR *jumps up and tries to offer
assistance, but she waves him away, and continues to choke.*

VICTOR [*to* ELYOT]:   That was a damned fool thing to do.

ELYOT: How did I know she was going to choke?

VICTOR [*to* AMANDA]:   Here, drink some coffee.

AMANDA [*breathlessly gasping*]:   Leave me alone. I'll be all right
in a minute.

VICTOR [*to* ELYOT]:   You waste too much time trying to be
funny.

SIBYL [*up in arms*]:   It's no use talking to Elyot like that; it
wasn't his fault.

VICTOR: Of course it was his fault entirely, making rotten
stupid jokes—

SIBYL: I thought what Elyot said was funny.

VICTOR: Well, all I can say is, you must have a very warped
sense of humor.

SIBYL: That's better than having none at all.

VICTOR: I fail to see what humor there is in incessant trivial
flippancy.

SIBYL: You couldn't be flippant if you tried until you were
blue in the face.

VICTOR: I shouldn't dream of trying.

SIBYL: It must be very sad not to be able to see any fun in
anything.

[AMANDA *stops choking, and looks at* ELYOT. *He winks at her
again, and she smiles.*

VICTOR: Fun! I should like you to tell me what fun there is in—

SIBYL: I pity you, I really do. I've been pitying you ever since we left Deauville.

VICTOR: I'm sure it's very nice of you, but quite unnecessary.

SIBYL: And I pity you more than ever now.

VICTOR: *Why* now particularly?

SIBYL: If you don't see why, I'm certainly not going to tell you.

VICTOR: I see no reason for you to try to pick a quarrel with me. I've tried my best to be pleasant to you, and comfort you.

SIBYL: You weren't very comforting when I lost my trunk.

VICTOR: I have little patience with people who go about losing luggage.

SIBYL: I don't go about losing luggage. It's the first time I've lost anything in my life.

VICTOR: I find that hard to believe.

SIBYL: Anyhow, if you'd tipped the porter enough, everything would have been all right. Small economies never pay; it's absolutely no use—

VICTOR: Oh, for God's sake be quiet!

[AMANDA *lifts her hand as though she were going to interfere, but* ELYOT *grabs her wrist. They look at each other for a moment, she lets her hand rest in his.*

SIBYL [*rising from the table*]: How dare you speak to me like that!

VICTOR [*also rising*]: Because you've been irritating me for days.

SIBYL [*outraged*]: Oh!

VICTOR [*coming down to her*]: You're one of the most completely idiotic women I've ever met.

SIBYL: And you're certainly the rudest man I've ever met!

VICTOR: Well then, we're quits, aren't we?

SIBYL [*shrilly*]: One thing, you'll get your deserts all right.

VICTOR: What do you mean by that?

SIBYL: You know perfectly well what I mean. And it'll serve you right for being weak-minded enough to allow that woman to get round you so easily.

VICTOR: What about you? Letting that unprincipled roué persuade you to take him back again!

[AMANDA *and* ELYOT *are laughing silently.* ELYOT *blows her a lingering kiss across the table.*

SIBYL: He's nothing of the sort, he's just been victimized, as you were victimized.

VICTOR: Victimized! What damned nonsense!

SIBYL [*furiously*]: It isn't damned nonsense! You're very fond of swearing and blustering and threatening, but when it comes to the point you're as weak as water. Why, a blind cat could see what you've let yourself in for.

VICTOR [*equally furious*]: Stop making those insinuations.

SIBYL: I'm not insinuating anything. When I think of all the things you said about her, it makes me laugh, it does really; to see how completely she's got you again.

VICTOR: You can obviously speak with great authority, having had the intelligence to marry a drunkard.

SIBYL: So that's what she's been telling you. I might have known it! I suppose she said he struck her, too!

VICTOR: Yes, she did, and I'm quite sure it's perfectly true.

SIBYL: I expect she omitted to tell you that she drank fourteen glasses of brandy last night straight off; and that the reason their first marriage was broken up was that she used to come home at all hours of the night, screaming and hiccoughing.

VICTOR: If he told you that, he's a filthy liar.

SIBYL: He isn't—he isn't!

VICTOR: And if you believe it, you're a silly scatterbrained little fool.

SIBYL [*screaming*]: How dare you speak to me like that! How dare you! I've never been so insulted in my life! How dare you!

[AMANDA *and* ELYOT *rise quietly, and go, hand in hand, towards the front door.*

VICTOR [*completely giving way*]: It's a tremendous relief to me to have an excuse to insult you. I've had to listen to your weeping and wailings for days. You've clacked at me, and snivelled at me until you've nearly driven me insane, and I controlled my nerves and continued to try to help you and

look after you, because I was sorry for you. I always thought
you were stupid from the first, but I must say I never realized
that you were a malicious little vixen as well!

SIBYL [*shrieking*]:   Stop it! Stop it! You insufferable great brute!
[*She slaps his face hard, and he takes her by the shoulders and
shakes her like a rat, as* AMANDA *and* ELYOT *go smilingly out of
the door, with their suitcases, and—*

CURTAIN